Iowa
Legal Research

CAROLINA ACADEMIC PRESS
LEGAL RESEARCH SERIES

Suzanne E. Rowe, Series Editor
❧

Arizona, Second Edition — Tamara S. Herrera

Arkansas, Second Edition — Coleen M. Barger, Cheryl L. Reinhart &
Cathy L. Underwood

California, Third Edition — Aimee Dudovitz, Hether C. Macfarlane
& Suzanne E. Rowe

Colorado — Robert Michael Linz

Connecticut — Jessica G. Hynes

Federal, Second Edition— Mary Garvey Algero, Spencer L. Simons,
Suzanne E. Rowe, Scott Childs & Sarah E. Ricks

Florida, Fourth Edition — Barbara J. Busharis, Jennifer LaVia & Suzanne E. Rowe

Georgia — Nancy P. Johnson, Elizabeth G. Adelman & Nancy J. Adams

Idaho, Second Edition — Tenielle Fordyce-Ruff & Kristina J. Running

Illinois, Second Edition — Mark E. Wojcik

Iowa, Second Edition — John D. Edwards, Karen L. Wallace & Melissa H. Weresh

Kansas — Joseph A. Custer & Christopher L. Steadham

Kentucky — William A. Hilyerd, Kurt X. Metzmeier & David J. Ensign

Louisiana, Second Edition — Mary Garvey Algero

Massachusetts, Second Edition — E. Joan Blum & Shaun B. Spencer

Michigan, Third Edition — Cristina D. Lockwood & Pamela Lysaght

Minnesota — Suzanne Thorpe

Mississippi — Kristy L. Gilliland

Missouri, Third Edition — Wanda M. Temm & Julie M. Cheslik

New York, Third Edition — Elizabeth G. Adelman, Theodora Belniak
Courtney L. Selby & Brian Detweiler

North Carolina, Second Edition — Scott Childs & Sara Sampson

North Dakota — Anne Mullins & Tammy Pettinato

Ohio, Second Edition — Sara Sampson, Katherine L. Hall
& Carolyn Broering-Jacobs

Oklahoma — Darin K. Fox, Darla W. Jackson & Courtney L. Selby

Oregon, Third Edition Revised Printing — Suzanne E. Rowe

Pennsylvania — Barbara J. Busharis & Bonny L. Tavares

Tennessee, Second Edition — Scott Childs, Sibyl Marshall & Carol McCrehan Parker

Texas, Second Edition — Spencer L. Simons

Washington, Second Edition — Julie Heintz-Cho, Tom Cobb
& Mary A. Hotchkiss

West Virginia — Hollee Schwartz Temple

Wisconsin — Patricia Cervenka & Leslie Behroozi

Wyoming, Second Edition — Debora A. Person & Tawnya K. Plumb
❧

Iowa
Legal Research

Second Edition

John D. Edwards
Karen L. Wallace
Melissa H. Weresh

Suzanne E. Rowe, Series Editor

CAROLINA ACADEMIC PRESS

Durham, North Carolina

Library of Congress Cataloging-in-Publication Data

Names: Edwards, John (John Duncan), 1953- author. | Wallace, Karen L.,
author. | Weresh, Melissa H., author.
Title: Iowa legal research / John D. Edwards, Karen L. Wallace, and Melissa
H. Weresh.
Description: Second Edition. | Durham, NC : Carolina Academic Press,
[2016] |
Series: Legal Research Series | Includes bibliographical references and
index.
Identifiers: LCCN 2016027274 | ISBN 9781611638837 (alk. paper)
Subjects: LCSH: Legal research--Iowa.
Classification: LCC KFI4275 .I587 2016 | DDC 340.072/0777--dc23
LC record available at https://lccn.loc.gov/2016027274

Carolina Academic Press, LLC
700 Kent Street
Durham, North Carolina 27701
Telephone (919) 489-7486
Fax (919) 493-5668
www.cap-press.com

Summary of Contents

Contents

List of Tables and Figures

Tables

Figures

Series Note

The Legal Research Series published by Carolina Academic Press includes titles from states around the country as well as a separate text on federal legal research. The goal of each book is to provide law students, practitioners, paralegals, college students, laypeople, and librarians with the essential elements of legal research in each jurisdiction. Unlike more bibliographic texts, the Legal Research Series books seek to explain concisely both the sources of state law research and the process for conducting legal research effectively.

Foreword

Chief Justice Mark S. Cady
Iowa Supreme Court

Lawyers and law students endure years of formal education in a wide variety of subjects and are institutionally trained in the art of critical analysis and precise communication. These tools are refined for years following graduation, and they are tested outside the classroom with issues affecting citizens of our state every day. Of course, these trials in research can be motivated to excellence by the desire to more efficiently serve clients in order to make a living, and every lawyer in Iowa has an obligation to the client, the courts, and the profession to uphold the established standards of service to society. But Iowa lawyers have long been committed to providing legal service above and beyond the call of duty. When the rule of law is critically examined in each new factual circumstance, well-trained servants of the law can also be agents of change in our laws because they have a new understanding of the world in which we live. This ability to provide legal counsel that constantly challenges established principles is our strength as a community. It is only through a spirited commitment to resolving the legal issues presented in each case that our law develops over time. As advocates for this standard of practicing law, it is essential that the most effective method of performing legal research be the cornerstone of our practice.

Because effective legal research is so fundamental, a lawyer's education is not complete without it. For over one hundred years, the Iowa legal community has had the benefit of the Drake University Law School's legal research program, which has been at the forefront of both technological and methodological innovations. True to their reputations as dedicated legal research educators, Dean John Edwards and Professors Karen Wallace and Melissa Weresh have tirelessly worked to produce this invaluable guide for law students and Iowa lawyers. *Iowa Legal Research* was the first comprehensive research book that synthesized various sources of Iowa law with the process necessary to isolate a research path among those sources and follow it confidently to its conclusion. The second edition follows that foundation and highlights the expanded electronic options researchers have today in addition to print. I am honored to have the opportunity to introduce such an exemplary piece of the work done to advance Iowa legal research.

The book begins where all legal practice should: by keeping the client's problem central to the research process. As a result, the researcher's understanding of the issue will sharpen as the research evolves. Effective research does not always unveil a definitive answer to the problem that is presented like a treasure at the end of a rainbow; instead, effective research typically creates more need for research. This book identifies that the sustainable practice of legal research starts with the recognition that research and analysis are intertwined and their development is codependent. As the authors point out, "[l]egal research cannot be divorced from legal analysis." Yet, under the direction of this Iowa-specific guide, researchers in Iowa can begin the intricate process of research and analysis without first having to spend countless hours acquainting or reacquainting themselves with methods for finding the applicable sources of law.

The authors have left no practical stone unturned. Consistent with the practice in most other industries today, much of Iowans' legal work is done electronically. Researchers unfamiliar with local web hosts need not spend time attempting to assess the credibility of these sources on their own; this book includes reputable Iowa-specific online databases and websites for lawyers and law students looking for Iowa-specific practice aides at little or no charge. Additionally, this book presents information about researching legal ethics opinions and disciplinary actions in Iowa. Sources of law related to professional regulation can be particularly difficult to locate as a new attorney, but this thorough guide lightens the burden of the search considerably.

The legal community is enriched by the publication of this book, which gives law students, practitioners, and anyone seeking the sources of Iowa law a firm foundational tool for any research task that lies before them.

Preface and Acknowledgments

Much has changed in the field of legal research since the publication of the first edition of *Iowa Legal Research* in 2011. This edition incorporates those changes to help the reader better understand the nature of legal research today. Perhaps the most significant trend has been the expansion of online resources. In particular, governmental websites increasingly provide a wealth of digital information. These sites, as well as subscription research services, constantly evolve. Keeping up with this evolution can be a challenge, and this edition reflects several changes that occurred as this book was in final production.

The U.S. Government Publishing Office (GPO) released the beta version of govinfo.gov with an indication that it would be replacing FDsys.gov. In the text you may see references to FDsys, but we have also provided select references to govinfo.gov where information was available about the new site. Westlaw eliminated Westlaw Classic and released WestlawNext. During production of the current edition Westlaw announced that WestlawNext was being renamed Thomson Reuters Westlaw. This edition therefore refers to the Thomson Reuters product as Westlaw, the name with which most users are familiar. Lexis announced that it was discontinuing Lexis.com, leaving Lexis Advance as its premier product. This text calls that product Lexis, consistent with its well-known moniker. Lexis, Lexis Advance, and Shepard's are now part of RELX Inc., formerly known as Reed Elsevier Inc. The transition from Thomas.gov to Congress.gov continues, and this edition reflects that process; at some point the few remaining Thomas references in this book may lead to a site no longer available.

The screen shots and descriptions of governmental and other websites are current as of the manuscript completion date. Based on the number of upgrades in just the past few years, you can expect that sites may differ somewhat from what is described or illustrated here. Should that occur, the authors are confident that you will be able to adapt, successfully navigating the updated site and applying the general research techniques and processes suggested throughout the book.

This edition would not have been possible without the support from the exceptional personnel at Drake University Law School. Thanks to the assistance from research assistants, librarians, library staff, and law school support personnel, our job was made easier. Special thanks goes to administrative assistant Kristi Longtin for her meticulous review of the page proofs, to research assistant Kelli Orton for her keen eye in reviewing the draft and her assistance with the compilation of the index, and to administrative assistant Amy Cutler for her work on copyright permissions. We also wish to thank series editor Suzanne Rowe, who has been extraordinarily helpful throughout the work on both editions.

Iowa
Legal Research

Chapter 1

The Research Process and Legal Analysis[1]

I. Introduction to Iowa Legal Research

The process of legal research — finding the law — is essentially the same in every American jurisdiction. Locating applicable law requires that the researcher understand certain basic components, including the legal issue, potential sources of law that may be applicable to the resolution of that issue, the resources that may contain that law, and knowledge of how those resources are organized. Beyond these basic components, there may be variations between jurisdictions in terms of the substantive law; the law-making processes; and the type, variety, and organization of the sources. While some of these variations are minor, others require specialized knowledge of the resources available and the analytical framework in which those resources are used. This book focuses on sources of Iowa law and the techniques for locating relevant Iowa authority. It supplements this focus with brief explanations of federal research and research into the law of other states, both to introduce and to highlight some of the variations.

II. The Intersection of Legal Research and Legal Analysis

While all researchers understand that legal analysis is difficult, some falsely assume that legal research is a distinct, mechanical task. Researchers may form this impression because many of the basic *techniques* of legal research are relatively simple. For most print resources, you will begin with an index, find entries that appear relevant, and read those sections of the text. You will

---

1. Portions of this chapter are based on Suzanne E. Rowe, *Oregon Legal Research* (3d ed. 2014).

then locate additional sources identified within the text and update your research to determine whether more recent material is available. For online research, you will search particular databases or websites using words likely to appear in the text of relevant documents, or you will construct searches that seek to find information on a particular topic. Chapter 2 describes basic print and online search techniques in detail.

The simplicity of those techniques, however, can be misleading. Legal analysis is implicated in all steps of the research process, raising challenging questions. In print research, which words will you look up in the index? How will you decide whether an entry looks promising? With regard to online research, how will you choose relevant words and construct a search most likely to produce the documents you need? When you read the text of a document, how will you determine whether it is relevant to your client's situation? How will you learn whether more recent material changed the law or merely applied it in a new situation? In order to answer these questions, a researcher must engage in legal analysis. This interdependency of research and analysis can make legal research complex, especially for the novice.

As someone just starting out — either in law school or as a new lawyer in Iowa — take this opportunity to carefully consider what the process of legal research entails. Legal research cannot be divorced from legal analysis and entails far more than simply understanding the available resources. For the research to be useful and effective, the legal researcher must consistently and recursively analyze the client's problem and the resources discovered during the research process. This takes time, creativity, and patience. As Peter Friedman observed:

> The answers to difficult legal questions don't lie around waiting to be found as if they are treasure chests left lying on forest floors. They are constructed and created by elements buried within our universe of databases. Thus, research that is genuine research not only requires Sisyphean patience in combing through the sources, it requires also consideration, observation, and study of what one finds within those sources so that one can, first, *identify the elements that matter*, and, second, *put those important, buried, and isolated elements together in some useful and novel way.*

* * *

In short, research, analysis, and theorizing are all a single activity—finding things, making sure they are the right things, and putting them together in the right ways.[2]

This book is not designed to be a blueprint for every resource in the law library or search engine on the Internet; many resources contain their own detailed explanations in a preface or a "Help" section. This book is more like a manual or field guide, introducing the various resources available and explaining when and how to use them.

III. Types and Sources of Legal Authority

In finding the law that is applicable to your client's problem, you need to distinguish between resources that control the client's situation—primary, mandatory authority—and those that may be merely applicable to the situation—persuasive authority. *Primary authority* is law produced by governmental bodies with law-making power. Sources of primary authority include constitutional provisions, statutes, and administrative regulations. These sources are known as *enacted law*. The other source of primary authority comes from the judiciary. Judicial opinions are primary authority whether they interpret statutes or develop the *common law*, the legal principles established through court decisions. Primary authority is distinguished from *secondary authority*, which includes all other legal sources such as treatises, law review articles, and legal encyclopedias. Secondary authority is typically written by individuals who do not have law-making authority, or who are not writing in their law-making authority capacity.[3] These secondary sources summarize, clarify, and comment on primary authorities and are therefore designed to aid in understanding the law and locating primary authority. Secondary sources often cite extensively to primary authority, making these sources valuable research tools.

---

2. Peter Friedman, *Research Only Begins with Information: Patience, Insight, and Imagination Are the Most Important Parts of It*, Learning to be a Lawyer (Mar. 26, 2010), http://peterbenfriedman.blogspot.com/2010/03/research-only-begins-with-information.html.

3. Note that judges and legislators may author law review articles and other secondary authority. Notwithstanding, judges only have law-making authority when they author primary authority in the form of a judicial opinion, and legislators only have law-making authority when they author primary authority in the form of enacted law (statutes and regulations).

In terms of beginning a research project, your principal objective is typically to locate primary authority, which is the law that controls the client problem. For any legal problem, you need to determine the applicable sources of law. Thus, in every situation, you will need to ascertain whether the client matter is controlled by a constitutional provision, a statute, or an administrative regulation. In any of these instances, there are also likely to be relevant judicial opinions that interpret the enacted law and are therefore applicable to the client problem. For some client problems, the only source of authority is judicial opinions that develop the common law. In short, you are searching for the controlling authority — primary, mandatory authority, as opposed to authority that is merely persuasive.

Mandatory authority is binding on the court that would decide a conflict if the situation were litigated. In a question of Iowa law, mandatory or binding authority includes the Iowa Constitution, statutes enacted by the Iowa legislature, Iowa administrative regulations, and opinions of the Supreme Court of Iowa.[4] *Persuasive authority* is not binding, but may be followed if relevant and well reasoned. Authority is merely persuasive if it is from a different jurisdiction or if it is a resource that has not been produced by a law-making body. In a question of Iowa law, examples of persuasive authority include primary authorities from outside Iowa, such as a similar Nebraska statute or an analogous opinion of an Illinois state court.

Secondary materials, such as a law review article or a treatise written by a legal scholar, are also considered persuasive authority.[5] The impact or influence of different sources of persuasive authority varies by source. For example, the Restatements of Law, a secondary resource produced by the American Law Institute as discussed in Chapter 3, may have more persuasive weight in a particular jurisdiction than the primary authority from a different jurisdiction.[6] See Chapter 3 for a further discussion of secondary sources.

Table 1-1 provides a list of the most frequently encountered sources of law. Each source is explained later in this book. Notice in Table 1-1 that persuasive

---

4. An opinion from the Iowa Court of Appeals is binding on the trial courts if the Supreme Court of Iowa has not addressed a particular topic.

5. This should make sense because secondary authority is generally written by individuals who do not have law-making authority.

6. Indeed, courts routinely adopt restatement rules, although they are not obligated to do so. According to the 2014–15 Annual Report of ALI, as of June 2015, there were nearly 200,000 case citations to the restatements and another ALI series, Principles of the Law.

Table 1-1. Examples of Authority in Iowa Research

	Mandatory Authority	Persuasive Authority
Primary Authority	The Iowa Constitution Iowa statutes Iowa regulations Iowa Supreme Court cases	The Nebraska Constitution Illinois statutes Missouri regulations South Dakota cases
Secondary Resources		Treatises and other books Restatements Uniform Laws and Model Codes Commentary Law journal articles Looseleafs and portfolios Legal dictionaries

authority may be either primary or secondary authority, while mandatory authority is always primary.

For sources of mandatory authority, there is a hierarchy of law involving constitutions, statutes, administrative rules, and judicial opinions. The constitution of each state is the supreme law of the state. If a statute is on point, that statute comes next in the hierarchy, followed by administrative rules. Judicial opinions may interpret the statute or rule, but they cannot disregard them. A judicial opinion may, however, decide that a statute violates the constitution or that an administrative regulation is overbroad. In that instance, the judicial opinion that invalidates the statute controls. Finally, if there is no constitutional provision, statute, or administrative regulation applicable to the client matter, the issue will be controlled by the common law (judicial opinions).

IV. Court Systems

Legal research often includes reading judicial opinions, so researchers need to understand the court system. The basic court structure includes a trial court, an intermediate court of appeals, and an ultimate appellate court, often called the "supreme" court. These courts exist at both the state and federal levels. In Iowa, trial courts are known as district courts. Iowa has two appellate courts: the Court of Appeals and the Supreme Court. All appeals from Iowa trial courts proceed directly to the Supreme Court. The Supreme

Court then transfers a majority of those appeals to the Court of Appeals. For a more detailed discussion of the Iowa court system, see Chapter 5.

In the federal judicial system, the trial courts are called United States District Courts. There are ninety-four district courts in the federal system, with each district drawn from a particular state.[7] The state of Iowa has been divided into two geographic regions for federal district court jurisdiction. The United States District Court for the Northern District of Iowa is headquartered in Cedar Rapids, and the United States District Court for the Southern District of Iowa is headquartered in Des Moines.

Intermediate appellate courts in the federal system are called United States Courts of Appeals. There are courts of appeals for each of the thirteen federal circuits. Twelve of these circuits are based on geographic jurisdiction. In addition to eleven numbered circuits covering all the states, there is the District of Columbia Circuit. The thirteenth federal circuit, called the Federal Circuit, hears appeals from certain specialized courts and agencies as well as appeals on issues related to patent law from district courts in all circuits. Iowa is in the Eighth Circuit. This means that cases from the United States District Court for both the Northern and Southern Districts of Iowa are appealed to the United States Court of Appeals for the Eighth Circuit. This circuit encompasses Arkansas, Iowa, Minnesota, Missouri, Nebraska, North Dakota, and South Dakota.

The highest court in the federal system is the United States Supreme Court. It decides cases concerning the United States Constitution and federal statutes. This court does not have the final say on matters of purely state law; that authority rests with the highest court of each state. Parties who wish to have the U.S. Supreme Court hear their case must file a petition for *certiorari*, as the court has discretion over which cases it hears.

Not all states have the three-tier court system of Iowa and the federal judiciary. A number of states do not have an intermediate appellate court; Iowa did not have one until 1977. Another difference in some court systems is that the "supreme" court is not always the highest court. In New York, the trial courts are called supreme courts and the highest court is the Court of Appeals. Two states, Massachusetts and Maine, call their highest court the Supreme Judicial Court.

Most jurisdictions provide information about their court structure online. For example, the website of the Iowa Judicial Branch is http://www.iowacourts.gov.

---

7. An illustrative map of the federal districts can be accessed at the website for the federal courts: http://www.uscourts.gov/uscourts/images/CircuitMap.pdf.

In addition, citation manuals are good references for learning the names and hierarchy of the courts, as well as for learning proper citation to legal authorities. The two most popular are the *ALWD Guide to Legal Citation,* written by Coleen M. Barger and the Association of Legal Writing Directors,[8] and *The Bluebook: A Uniform System of Citation,* written by students from several law schools.[9] Both manuals provide information on federal and state courts and are covered in more detail in the appendix of this book.

V. Overview of the Research Process

A. Ethical and Professional Considerations

Conducting effective research is more than an important part of an attorney's role in assisting clients; it is an ethical obligation of the attorney. The Iowa Rules of Professional Conduct[10] govern the conduct of lawyers who are admitted to practice in Iowa. The rules require that an attorney be competent in all aspects of legal practice, including the research and analysis of client issues. Section 2 of the preamble notes that lawyers engage in a variety of functions:

> As advisor, a lawyer provides a client with an informed understanding of the client's legal rights and obligations and explains their practical implications. As advocate, a lawyer zealously asserts the client's position under the rules of the adversary system. As negotiator, a lawyer seeks a result advantageous to the client but consistent with requirements of honest dealings with others. As an evaluator, a lawyer

---

8. ALWD & Coleen M. Barger, *ALWD Guide to Legal Citation* (5th ed. 2014) ("*ALWD Guide*"). Most citations in this book conform to the *ALWD Guide* unless there is a clear preference in Iowa for a different form.

9. *The Bluebook: A Uniform System of Citation* (The Columbia Law Review et al. eds., 20th ed. 2015).

10. The Iowa Rules of Professional Conduct are codified in Chapter 32 of the Iowa Court Rules and can be accessed electronically through the Iowa Legislative Branch website at https://www.legis.iowa.gov/law/courtRules/courtRulesListings. The rules are modeled after the Model Rules of Professional Conduct. As such, they mimic the numbering system of the Model Rules, but are prefaced with their designation in Chapter 32 of the Iowa Court Rules. So, for example, the Model Rule on competence is Rule 1 in the Model Rules, and is referenced in the Iowa Court Rules as Iowa R. Prof. Conduct 32:1.1.

acts by examining a client's legal affairs and reporting about them to the client or to others.[11]

In terms of research and analysis, the rules require that lawyers provide competent representation and, in Rule One, note that "[c]ompetent representation requires the legal knowledge, skill, thoroughness, and preparation reasonably necessary for the representation."[12]

Comments to the rule on competence clarify that "[c]ompetent handling of a particular matter includes inquiry into and analysis of the factual and legal elements of the problem, and use of methods and procedures meeting the standards of competent practitioners."[13] The obligation of competence is continuing, requiring that lawyers "keep abreast of changes in the law and its practice."[14]

In terms of a lawyer's ethical obligation as an officer of the court, there is a prohibition against asserting claims that are not supported by law.[15] Further, lawyers must provide the court with all relevant authority, including authority that may be adverse to the client's position.[16] These prohibitions and responsibilities require that the competent, ethical lawyer be capable of locating and analyzing applicable authority.

B. Getting Started on a Research Project

Conducting efficient, effective, ethical legal research means following a process. This process leads to the authority that controls a legal issue as well as to commentary that may help you analyze new and complex matters. All too often the novice researcher embarks on a research project without an appropriate plan, which can result in lost opportunities and wasted time. The

---

11. Iowa R. Prof. Conduct Preamble 2.

12. Iowa R. Prof. Conduct 32:1.1.

13. *Id*. at cmt. 5.

14. *Id*. at cmt. 6.

15. Iowa R. Prof. Conduct 32:3.1 provides, "A lawyer shall not bring or defend a proceeding, or assert or controvert an issue therein, unless there is a basis in law and fact for doing so that is not frivolous, which includes a good faith argument for an extension, modification, or reversal of existing law."

16. Iowa R. Prof. Conduct 32:3.3 notes that a "lawyer shall not knowingly ... fail to disclose to the tribunal legal authority in the controlling jurisdiction known to the lawyer to be directly adverse to the position of the client and not disclosed by opposing counsel." Comment 4 further explains that "[t]he underlying concept is that legal argument is a discussion seeking to determine the legal premises properly applicable to the case."

following brief description of the research process is outlined in Table 1-2 and further explored in Chapter 12.

Table 1-2. Basic Research Process

1.	Identify the issues, jurisdiction, and scope of the project.
2.	Gather facts and identify preliminary search terms.
3.	Identify, prioritize, and consult relevant sources.
4.	Expand and update your research.
5.	Make sure your research is responsive to the question(s) presented.
6.	Determine when to stop.

1. Identify the Issues, Jurisdiction, and Scope of the Project

The first step in developing a research plan is to have a firm understanding of the project. This will require that you evaluate the client's problem to determine, at least initially, what legal issues arise. A good preliminary step is to determine the relevant area of law. Is this a criminal or civil matter? Is this an issue of property, or does the client problem involve personal injury? Note that you will further develop the issue(s) as you conduct research.

You should also determine the jurisdiction. If you practice in Davenport, Iowa, which sits on the Iowa-Illinois border, for example, you should carefully consider whether the client's issue will be governed by the law of Iowa or if the facts indicate the law of Illinois could apply. If you have a client who has received correspondence regarding, for example, an environmental matter, you must determine whether the issue is likely to be governed by state or federal law.

Finally, you need to determine the scope of the project. You should ascertain what the form of the final work product should be and approximately how much time the client expects you to spend on the matter. To that end, you should inquire as to whether there are any limitations on research including how much expensive electronic research is appropriate. In terms of evaluating the scope of the project, you should also consider whether there are resources available to you, such as reference librarians or other associates in a law firm, whose assistance might be beneficial to the project.[17]

---

17. By the same token, you should consider whether there are limitations on using such outside resources, as is likely to be the case in a law school project.

2. Gather Facts and Identify Preliminary Search Terms

Getting started on a research project will require you to familiarize your-self with the facts and, in many cases, to learn additional facts. The facts should suggest preliminary search terms so you can begin your research.

Many legal resources in print use lengthy indexes as the starting point for finding legal authority. Electronic sources often require the researcher to enter words that are likely to appear in a synopsis or in the full text of relevant documents. Alternatively, the researcher might begin research by focusing on a particular topic. The terms used to search topically might appear in the topic heading, but not in the resulting documents (or vice versa), even though the resulting documents are on point. To ensure you are thorough in beginning a research project, you will need a comprehensive list of words, terms, and phrases that may lead to law on point. These may be legal terms or common words that describe the client's situation. The items on this list are *search terms*.

Organized brainstorming is the best way to compile a comprehensive list of search terms. Some researchers ask the journalistic questions Who? What? When? Where? Why? How? Others use a mnemonic device like TARPP, which stands for Things, Actions, Remedies, People, and Places.[18] Whether you use one of these suggestions or develop your own method, you should attempt to generate a broad range of terms describing your client's situation. Include in the list both specific and general words. Try to think of synonyms and antonyms for each term since at this point you are uncertain which terms an index may include. Using a legal dictionary or thesaurus may generate additional terms.

As an example, assume you are working for a defense attorney who was recently assigned to a burglary case. Around midnight, your client used a credit card to spring the lock to a stereo store, where she stole $2,000 worth of equipment. She was charged with first-degree burglary and possession of burglary tools. You have been asked to determine whether there is a good argument for challenging the charge of possession of burglary tools based on the fact that she used a credit card and not professional burglary tools. Moreover, you have been asked to consider whether a successful defense of the possession of burglary tools charge will impact the first-degree burglary charge. Table 1-3 provides examples of research terms you might use to begin work on this project.

---

18. *See* Steven M. Barkan, Barbara A. Bintliff & Mary Whisner, *Fundamentals of Legal Research* 20 (10th ed. 2015) (explaining "TARPP," a similar mnemonic device).

Table 1-3. Generating Research Terms

Journalistic Approach

Who:	Thief, robber, burglar, business owner, property owner
What:	Burglary, first degree, second degree, crime
How:	Breaking and entering, burglary tools, trespassing
Why:	Theft, stealing, stolen goods
When:	Midnight
Where:	Store, building, commercial establishment, business, shop

TARPP Approach

Things:	Burglary tools, stolen goods
Actions:	Burglary, breaking and entering, trespassing, damages, crime
Remedies:	First degree, second degree, incarceration
People:	Thief, robber, burglar, business owner, property owner
Places:	Store, building, commercial establishment, business, shop

As your research progresses, you will learn new research terms to include in the list and decide to take others off. For example, you may read cases that give you insights into the key words judges tend to use in discussing the topic. Or you may learn a *term of art*, a word or phrase that has special meaning in a particular area of law. Add these to your list.

3. Identify, Prioritize, and Consult Relevant Sources

Determining where you will start your research depends on what you need to know, what you already know, what sources you can access, and how much that access will cost in terms of both time and money. For instance, assume you know you need a specific Iowa code section and you also want to look at related case law. If your law firm pays to subscribe to Westlaw or Lexis, your most efficient starting point might be the annotated version of the Iowa code on one of these platforms. That source would provide both the code section itself and references to cases interpreting it. On the other hand, if you were simply quoting a particular Iowa statute and wanted to verify the wording, you might choose to look at the Code of Iowa available through the Iowa General Assembly website. This source, available without charge, provides an official, up-to-date version of the code.

When you want a broader perspective on an area of law, particularly a topic unfamiliar to you, secondary sources and practice aids, discussed more fully in Chapters 3 and 10, respectively, are excellent starting points for legal research. These sources contain useful commentary and analysis, and can help you broaden both the legal theories and search terms relevant to the client. For most secondary sources, you should be able to use the search terms you created to examine the index for entries in the secondary source that are relevant to the client's issue. You can then use the narrative, analytical material in the secondary sources to find primary legal authorities.

Even if you start in secondary sources, your ultimate goal will be to find relevant primary sources. You will need to read these carefully to evaluate their applicability to your client's problem. Resist the urge to skim; print or download and thoroughly review the source to determine whether it is relevant and helpful. Be aware that this step is likely to be the most time-consuming. Secondary authority may lead you to some primary authority, but be prepared to invest considerable time and energy searching for primary authority. Chapters 4 through 6 and 8 discuss how to locate primary authority in print and online resources. Moreover, consider whether the primary authority itself can lead to additional relevant materials. The information on updating in Chapter 9 should be helpful in this regard.

4. Expand and Update Your Research

You cannot rely on a legal authority until you determine that it is still good law, or that it has not been overruled or modified by a subsequent authority. A specialized research tool called a *citator* helps you to ensure your authorities are still good law. In addition, citators can be used to expand your research, pointing to other research sources relevant to your issue. Chapter 9 identifies several available citators and explains how to use them.

5. Make Sure Your Research Is Responsive to the Question(s) Presented

As the research process unfolds, you might encounter dead-ends, unanticipated leads, or both. As you use your preliminary results to adjust your research strategy, make sure you do not lose sight of your objective and get off track by researching related, but irrelevant issues. Throughout the process, remind yourself of the work you did in the first step, making sure you thoroughly understood your project. As you begin to synthesize the authorities you have found, make sure you are answering the particular question(s) presented and that your sources address your specific issues.

6. Determine When to Stop

Novice legal researchers tend to stay on the research wheel longer than necessary. For most legal problems, there is no "smoking gun." In instances when there is a dispositive authority, one that definitively conveys the rule of law, you should be able to find it efficiently if you have employed appropriate search terms and looked in the relevant resources. However, for some research projects there will not be a dispositive authority. Instead, you may have to gather information from a variety of legal sources to synthesize the law and predict a result. A good rule of thumb is to stop researching when the same authorities keep coming up.

This basic process should be customized for each research project. Consider whether you need to follow all six steps, and if so, in what order. If you are unfamiliar with an area of law, beginning your research in a secondary resource may be quite helpful. In contrast, if you know that a situation is controlled by a statute, you may choose to begin with the statute rather than reviewing a secondary resource.

C. Keeping an Efficient Research Trail

One of the most important components of a good research plan is an effective strategy for tracking research. In most situations, a failure to keep track of research will result in lost sources and the frustrating feeling that you have read an applicable source, but no longer know where to locate it. Keeping track of where you have searched, and brief notes about the sources you have reviewed, will save considerable time and make your research more efficient. Some lawyers choose to keep index cards with brief notes about the source including, at a minimum, the citation and the relevant information contained in the source. Other lawyers keep research charts, in either handwritten or electronic format. Different strategies are further explored in Chapter 12, but the importance of a system for tracking research cannot be overstated.

D. The Most Overlooked Research Resource in the Law Library

One of the most effective and overlooked resources in the law library is the librarian. Reference librarians have specialized training and education in legal resources. The efficient lawyer knows this and benefits from the expertise offered by these individuals. Librarians can direct you to relevant resources and help you navigate them. When asking for assistance outside your organization, be careful that you not divulge confidential or privileged information.

VI. Researching the Law — Organization of This Text

The remainder of this book explains how to use your research terms to conduct legal research in a variety of sources. Chapter 2 provides an overview of types of legal research sources and describes basic techniques for their use. Subsequent chapters expand on this introduction in discussing specific sources, both print and electronic, and explaining unique caveats in their use. Because the research process often begins with secondary sources, the book begins its examination of legal sources in Chapter 3 with secondary sources. We then turn to primary legal authority. Chapter 4 addresses the Iowa Constitution, which is the highest legal authority in the state. Chapter 5 contains an overview of the Iowa and federal court systems and explains how to use reporters and digests to research judicial decisions. Chapter 6 addresses statutes and local ordinances, and Chapter 7 explores legislative history. Chapter 8 covers Iowa administrative law resources. After this focus on primary authority, Chapter 9 explains how to update legal authority using citators (e.g., *Shepard's Citations* or Westlaw's *KeyCite*). Chapter 10 introduces the reader to practice aids, and Chapter 11 illustrates Iowa legal ethics research. Finally, Chapter 12 delves into a more detailed explanation of legal research strategy. You may prefer to skim that chapter now and refer to it frequently, even though a number of references in it may not become clear until you have read the intervening chapters. The Appendix provides an overview of the conventions lawyers follow in citing legal authority in their documents.

VII. Legal Research in Context

In order to understand the relationship between legal analysis and legal research, you must examine legal sources in context. To that end, consider the following client problem, the Welch matter, shown in the text box below. Later chapters will explore this hypothetical situation further, suggesting ways you can use certain legal research sources to analyze this problem.

The Welch Matter

Your client, Mary Welch, has come to see you regarding a family matter. Welch would like your advice concerning her granddaughter, Claire Lewis.

Welch's daughter, Jessica Lewis, had one daughter, Claire, from her marriage to James Lewis. James died when Claire was two years old. He was a chronic drug user and died of an overdose. Jessica has sole, full custody of Claire.

Jessica has also struggled with substance abuse and has attended inpatient substance abuse treatment on three occasions. Welch paid the medical fees associated with those treatment programs and cared for Claire while Jessica underwent treatment. Jessica relapsed after the first two treatments, but has been substance-free for eight months.

Unfortunately, Jessica and Welch have argued recently, and Jessica told Welch that she no longer wants to have a relationship with her. Moreover, Jessica has said that Welch may no longer see Claire. Welch would like to investigate her rights to have visitation with Claire.

Chapter 2

Legal Research Sources and Techniques

I. Introduction

An effective legal researcher knows the available research sources and how to select and use them. This chapter introduces some essential research tools and techniques that will help you proficiently use a wide variety of research sources. Some of these sources and research methods may be familiar from your prior experience, while others are unique to legal research. Later chapters will build on this foundation, introducing more specific research tools and sophisticated search techniques applicable to particular sources.

II. Key Resources

A. Librarians and Library Catalogs

One of the first places to start researching is the law library. The law library has a wealth of resources and trained personnel to help you find materials to address your research needs. Librarians can be particularly helpful at the initial stages of your research and when you encounter an obstacle. Researchers sometimes search fruitlessly for an item that a librarian could have helped them find in a matter of minutes. The type of assistance a law librarian can provide includes (1) identifying authoritative secondary sources for your project, (2) suggesting databases likely to contain relevant materials, (3) explaining search techniques particular to each research question, (4) providing guidance on navigating the online catalog or a specialized database, and (5) obtaining materials from other libraries through interlibrary loan. Consulting a law librarian provides personalized, expert advice. If you are unable to visit a law library in person, some assistance may be available online or via the phone; check the library's website for headings like "Public services" or "Reference." Note that law librarians will not typically actually conduct research on behalf of researchers, as indicated in that library's policy, but will provide research guidance.

Librarians and other informed researchers often consult the online *catalog* to find library materials. It includes *records* for the books, e-books, print periodicals, and non-book materials, e.g., DVDs, held at the library. Catalog records briefly describe each item in the collection and indicate where the item can be found in the library.

Many library catalogs can be freely accessed on the web, and Table 2-1 provides addresses for the main Iowa law library catalogs. Iowa's two law schools — Drake University Law School and the University of Iowa College of Law — both offer no-charge catalog access to the vast holdings of all libraries at their institutions. The State Library of Iowa's catalog includes the materials at the State Law Library, located in Des Moines. Although smaller than an academic law library collection, the State Law Library's collection includes some unique materials. One of the primary clients of the State Law Library is the state government, including the courts, legislature, and many state agencies. The collection includes treatises, statutes, regulatory law, judicial decisions, materials from the legislature, periodicals, and other resources available to the general public.[1]

Another catalog of note, WorldCat, offers access to materials from thousands of libraries around the world. After finding books of interest in WorldCat, you can determine which libraries contain these resources. If the library is conveniently located, you can obtain the materials there. Otherwise, you can request that the materials be sent to you through your home library's *interlibrary loan* service.

After accessing a library catalog, you can search it in a variety of ways including keyword, subject, author, title, or a combination thereof.[2] The search results will provide information to help you begin to determine which books or other resources will be the most useful. In addition to print resources, the results may include ebooks and some titles in electronic databases. When you access the full record for one of your search results, you will find basic information about the book, such as the author, title, publisher, number of pages, and publication date. Some catalogs also offer additional information, such as

---

1. For additional information go to http://www.statelibraryofiowa.org/services /collections/law-library.

2. In a keyword search, you enter any word or phrase that might appear anywhere in the online record for the item, ranging from the title of a book to the listing of the contents, if available. A subject search enables you to find all the materials cataloged under a particular topic, such as "Visitation rights" to find materials on grandparent visitation rights. Other options to enhance searching include applying date restrictions and searching for titles in a series, such as the Nutshell series of study aids.

Table 2-1. Iowa Law Library Catalogs

Drake University Law School	http://library.drake.edu/go-to/lawsupersearch
University of Iowa College of Law	http://infohawk.uiowa.edu
State Library of Iowa	https://koha.silo.lib.ia.us
WorldCat OCLC	http://worldcat.org

synopses, tables of contents, and reviews, to help you begin to narrow and focus your results.

Library catalogs offer helpful cross-references, making your research more efficient. By viewing the full catalog record and reviewing the subject headings that describe a book's contents, one useful result in the catalog may lead to others. In most catalogs, you can click directly on a subject heading to search for all other materials in the catalog that have that subject.

For instance, if you were asked to do research on a federal securities issue of insider trading, you might search the catalog to see what was available. Figure 2-1 shows the first few results of a search of the Drake Law Library catalog for the terms *insider trading* as title words. The display gives you basic information about the work, such as author, title, date, and location. In scanning the list, you can see that, among others, the first title, "Insider Trading Law and Policy," might be relevant. By clicking on "Details" you can see the subject headings as shown in Figure 2-2. The subject terms for the item indicate that other useful materials may be found under the heading "Insider trading in securities — Law and legislation — United States." When you click on that link, you will see a list of the entries under that general subject heading and the number of titles the library has for each one.

The catalog search results will also show the location of each item within the library. Location information generally includes a *call number* that reflects the subject of the book and leads the researcher to its exact location. In the example, the call number is KF 1073 .I5 B345 2014. Because other books shelved at KF 1073 will be on the same subject, you may be able to find other relevant items by browsing that call number in the catalog or by perusing that area in the stacks.[3]

---

3. The stacks are the area of a library in which most of the books are shelved. For example, see the location information in Figures 2-1 and 2-2.

Figure 2-1. Screenshot of Drake Law Library Catalog: Results List

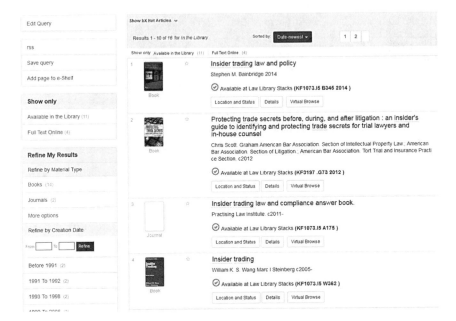

Source: Drake Law Library Catalog, library.drake.edu/go-to/lawsupersearch..

However, browsing the stacks is not a definitive way to find all relevant books; some might be in use and some might be shelved in a different location, such as on reserve. You can determine where to find a particular call number in the library by asking library personnel or consulting library guides, such as maps and location lists.

B. Government, Organization, and Educational Websites

The web offers an abundance of legal information, some of it extraordinarily useful. However, the open nature of the web — allowing almost anyone to post almost anything — means you must exercise particular caution when using the web for legal research. The Digital Access to Legal Information Committee of the American Association of Law Libraries has developed spe-

Figure 2-2. Screenshot of Drake Law Library Catalog Record

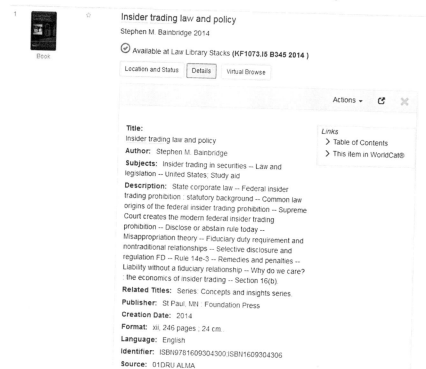

Source: Drake Law Library Catalog, library.drake.edu/go-to/lawsupersearch.

cific guidelines for evaluating government information on the web.[4] These guidelines offer multiple questions to ask in reviewing each aspect of the website. Those general areas include:

- Jurisdiction (What law applies?)
- Authorship (What person or organization is the source of the information?)
- Content (How comprehensive is it?)
- Currency (How up-to-date is the site's information?)
- Quality (Is the text on the site well written? Do other sites link to it?)

Although you will still want to evaluate a website yourself before relying on it, you can increase your odds of accessing high-quality sites by locating

---

4. *See* http://www.aallnet.org/mm/Advocacy/access/websiteguidelines.html.

sites through research guides and directories provided by libraries, reputable associations, and official government agencies. The Iowa government sites for the judicial, legislative, and executive branches provide information that can be essential to researchers.[5] County and city sites also can be invaluable, especially for municipal codes.[6] *Research guides,* such as Drake Law Library's guide to Iowa Legal Research,[7] provide tips on researching a particular area and note sources of interest. *Directories* provide organized links of lists. For instance, sites like Cornell's Legal Information Institute, the Public Library of Law, and FindLaw all provide an abundance of legal information arranged by topic and jurisdiction.[8]

Specific websites will be discussed throughout this book, but one site bears mention now: The Iowa State Bar Association (ISBA) page at iowabar.org. On the publicly accessible part of the site, you can find ethics opinions, bar publications such as *The Iowa Lawyer,* and links to many other items. Of particular interest to lawyers and law students is the "Practice Tools" tab that provides member access to Fastcase online legal research,[9] civil and criminal jury instructions, title standards, and other materials often needed by Iowa attorneys.

C. Commercial Databases

Law libraries and law offices purchase a vast array of databases to facilitate research. Westlaw, Lexis, and Bloomberg Law are the dominant providers of computer-assisted legal research (CALR) services in the United States and are recognized by lawyers for their value-added features that facilitate research. Each of these platforms provides access to a range of individual and combined resources, such as compilations of case law from different jurisdictions, statutory codes, and specific secondary sources. You can search across all the re-

---

5. The Iowa Legislature site is https://www.legis.iowa.gov, the Judicial Branch site is http://www.iowacourts.gov, and the Executive Branch site is https://governor.iowa.gov. The state government homepage, Iowa Government Online, is http://www.iowa.gov.

6. *See Iowa Municipal and County Law Research Guide* at http://libguides.law .drake.edu/IowaLocalCodes for links to those sites.

7. *Iowa Legal Research: Sources of Iowa Law* is at http://libguides.law.drake.edu /IowaBasic.

8. Cornell's LII can be accessed at https://www.law.cornell.edu, the Public Library of Law is at http://www.plol.org, and FindLaw is at http://lp.findlaw.com.

9. Full-time law students at Drake or Iowa, or Iowa residents attending another ABA-accredited law school, can access those materials by becoming a student member of the ISBA by completing a form on its website. No fee is charged for student membership.

sources available in the platform or limit your search to a smaller subset of available resources. For instance, you could choose to search all case law, cases from a specific jurisdiction (e.g., Iowa), or cases from a specific court (e.g., Supreme Court of Iowa). Other limits include searching just a specific title or searching a set of sources all related to a particular topic.

Although these platforms may share some of the same underlying resources, each also provides unique content. This variety may be most apparent among secondary sources. Frequently, a secondary source is only available on the platform that corresponds to its publisher. That is, West (or Thomson Reuters) secondary sources, such as the Iowa Practice series, are only available on Westlaw. Bloomberg Law has exclusive access to Bloomberg BNA titles, and only Lexis has many Lexis and Matthew Bender titles. Throughout the book, you will find descriptions of which platforms offer access to specific Iowa law resources.

The costs for using these services in a law firm or office can be quite high. Understanding the billing plan for the firm subscription and formulating efficient searches are imperative. Vendors such as Loislaw, VersusLaw, and Fastcase provide access to a more finite set of resources at costs that are generally lower than either Lexis or Westlaw. As noted, Fastcase is a member benefit for ISBA members. Many other state bar associations also offer Fastcase, or an alternative source, such as Casemaker, making these services cost-effective CALR choices for bar members.

Academic law libraries subscribe to hundreds of commercial databases that offer comprehensive information on almost every area of law.[10] The databases are often arranged by subject, such as bankruptcy, and also by database title, such as HeinOnline.[11] In these databases, you will be able to find in-depth information on your area of research. Access to these databases is normally limited to the primary clients of a library who have passwords, e.g., currently enrolled students at an academic library. Other researchers may be able to ac-

---

10. Go to "Databases" from the Drake page at http://www.law.drake.edu/library, and go to "Electronic Resources" under the Research tab from the Iowa page at http://library.law.uiowa.edu.

11. HeinOnline is an image-based legal research database with more than 130 million pages and 60 collections composed of law and law-related materials, including an extensive collection of law journals, U.S. government documents, and other materials. All law journals date back to inception and most continue to the current issue. The database is fully searchable with new content, features, and collections are added regularly. More details are at http://home.wshein.com/about; to see a complete listing of current content go to http://heinonline.org.

cess the databases if they come into the library in person; however, when you try to access these research sources outside of the library, you will likely be prompted for login credentials.

As you use CALR services and other databases, be sure to focus on developing the skills of an efficient researcher. It is easy to lose sight of how much time is being spent online and how much that time costs. Some new researchers in law firms make the mistake of accumulating thousands of dollars in search charges because they did not understand the firm's pricing plan and were used to unlimited searching in law school. In a law office setting, make sure you understand the costs and when CALR can be used. Starting with basic research on a lower cost or free service, such as Public Library of Law at plol.org, may help you refine your search strategy so you can see what terms are most effective.

III. Efficient and Effective Searching

Today's researcher has access to a vast array of online resources to assist in conducting legal research. The dominant commercial vendors offer unique features and resources that may not be found elsewhere. However, government and other sites offer free access to primary materials that can be very useful. You may find that a combination of more than one online or print resource may be needed to help you answer your research questions.

In practice, when conducting legal research, the two main costs are time and the price of the materials being accessed, so both must be kept in mind. If a free resource is difficult and time consuming to use, it may not be much of a bargain. The key is to ensure that your research is thorough, regardless of how it is conducted. The starting point in your process is to consider what you need and what source would be best to use. Keep in mind that starting with a secondary authority, such as a treatise, may be helpful initially to enable you to better understand your legal issues and what terms may help inform your search strategy formulation. Diving directly into case research can often lead to frustrations. Be sure to know what search options are available, whether free or fee-based. If you are asked to find a federal regulation, for example, the free government databases at FDsys[12] may be a better starting point than a commercial database.

---

12. The Advanced Search function from the FDsys homepage at https://www .gpo.gov/fdsys allows you to narrow to a particular source and search with terms and connectors. GPO's new govinfo.gov will eventually replace FDsys. The beta version of govinfo.gov was released as this book was being finalized. Govinfo.gov will include everything in FDsys but with a new interface and features to facilitate use.

Academic law libraries typically have helpful treatises and other secondary materials that can be reviewed in print to gain background information on your issues. Once you have that background and know your key terms and concepts, you might consider searching in a free database, such as the Public Library of Law at plol.org.

A. Cost-Effective Searching

Because you are balancing time and monetary expenditures, such as resource access fees, because different organizations have CALR contracts with different pricing plans, and because different research needs have unique considerations, there is no single path to conducting research in the most cost-effective manner. The wise researcher will consider factors related to cost before diving into a research project. A typical list of cost-effective searching techniques includes many of the following:[13]

Use government and free sites. State and federal government sites typically offer ready access to primary materials, such as statutes, regulations, and judicial opinions.

Consider reading offline. Rather than reading or accessing a case or document online on a commercial database, consider whether a free online source could provide that same document for you to download or print. Some vendors don't charge for accessing the cite list but do charge if you access the full document.

Develop your strategy before signing on. Make sure you understand what the issues are in your problem, including identification of key terms. That may require some background research in a secondary authority. When you sign on, you should already have your search query drafted, including the connectors, quotes, and other refinements. When you enter your search terms, take a moment before hitting send to make sure there are no obvious errors in your search.

Carefully consider how much content to search within a platform. If you only want cases from one state or one circuit, filter to what you need from the outset. By doing so, you have fewer cases to filter once you retrieve results. This is particularly important on Westlaw, where your search results might omit relevant cases from your jurisdiction if you only limit content after you search

---

13. Adapted from Mary Garvey Algero et al., *Federal Legal Research* 44–45 (2d ed. 2015).

by applying post-search filters to your results.[14] If, on the other hand, you are not sure what source or type of source would be most useful for your research need, searching across a wider array of content can reveal helpful sources you might not have known about. However, the broader your initial search, the more important it will be to filter your results, as described below.

Filter your results. Once you have your results, it is likely there will be more results than what you can or should review. Take advantage of the filters that allow you to narrow the results by date, court, topic, search term, or other category.

Review your history. Most platforms will provide a way to save your searches to a history or research trail for a period of time; in many cases, this is automatic. You may be able to review results without incurring further charges. Being familiar with these systems and looking back at what you have done will be invaluable as you continue research on a project.

Strategically download, email, or file results. Take advantage of the ability to download or email documents, so you can file them for later review. Avoid the temptation to print everything, or you may be overwhelmed by the volume of printed material.

B. Commercial Database Considerations

When you are using a commercial database, be sure you are as efficient and cost-effective as possible, especially if your employer is paying for the service. If you need help, each of the major vendors has research assistance via phone, chat, or other means, typically from a "Help" link. Whenever you are using a commercial database for an employer, be sure you understand the parameters of the billing plan. You don't want to accidentally access a database that is outside the normal billing plan and incur additional charges for the firm.

Vendors often provide cost-effective tips for searching, and it may be helpful to review those before you sign on.[15] Some of their common tips, in addition to using filters and history, include the following:

Review Citator Features. Using Shepard's on Lexis, KeyCite on Westlaw, or BCite on Bloomberg Law not only will tell you if the authority you have found remains good law but also can lead you to additional authorities which have cited it.

---

14. See the explanation in Chapter 5, Section IV.C. for more details.

15. Lexis provides a top 10 list at http://www.lexisnexis.com/documents/pdf /20120308094017_large.pdf. Westlaw tips are at http://static.legalsolutions.thomson reuters.com/product_files/westlaw/wlawdoc/web/wlncost.pdf.

Browse a Table of Contents. Treatises, statutes, and a few other documents will include a table of contents. If one is available, take a few minutes to determine whether the topic you need is listed. In most billing plans, you can view that at no charge.

Organize using Folders. Documents or portions of them can normally be saved to folders for later review. Not only will using these help keep your research organized but it will also enable you to share your research with others. Most plans allow you to review them later at no additional cost for up to a year.

Set up Alerts. If you want to track a topic or case, or have regular updates on a search you have performed, you can create an alert to update your research on a regular basis and notify you of the results.

Access Custom Features. Each system will have some special features designed to facilitate your work. For example, Lexis has a Legal Issue Trail that traces the development of the rule of law in a case. Westlaw offers key number searching, so you can quickly find cases on a particular point of law. Both provide headnotes for cases and allow you to search for other cases with the same headnote classifications.

IV. Overview of Commercial Database Searches

A. Introduction

As noted earlier in this chapter under Section II.C. Commercial Databases, legal researchers today have access to a wealth of information from various vendors in addition to what is freely available on the web. Westlaw, Lexis, and Bloomberg Law dominate the market for CALR service. Because of their prevalence in law offices, these services will be the focus of the discussions on CALR. The basic techniques for forming search queries for Westlaw, Lexis, and Bloomberg Law are generally applicable to other services, such as Fastcase. Note, however, the specific manner in which you create a search query may vary. Before searching, read the help screens or other introductory material or take advantage of each vendor's online training materials, such as tutorials and videos.[16] Investing this time should make your searches more effective.

The world of electronic research is constantly evolving as vendors develop products to meet the needs of researchers. Thanks to the success of Google,

---

16. Lexis materials are at http://www.lexisnexis.com/en-us/support/lexis-advance /default.page; Westlaw's are at http://legalsolutions.thomsonreuters.com/law-pro ducts/westlaw-legal-research. Bloomberg Law provides resources from the "Help" link once you log on at https://www.bloomberglaw.com.

new platforms for legal research function more like Google than prior versions.[17] The explanations that follow will cover some of the search functions that are basic to Westlaw, Lexis, and Bloomberg Law but that may also be common on other systems. It is beyond the scope of this book to teach the intricacies of using each of these systems;[18] however, the following sections cover some of the most basic functions.

B. Developing a Search Strategy

Formulating a search that will retrieve the most relevant documents for your problem requires thoughtful preparation. As discussed in Chapter 1, after analyzing your research problem, you need to identify the key words or phrases a court, legislature, or author may have used in discussing a situation similar to yours. Those key words should then be formulated into a search strategy to find documents relevant to your issue. The research process is often one of trial and error as you determine the best approach to searching. For instance, you may need to narrow your original search to retrieve a manageable number of results without excluding relevant items. In the context of the Welch example presented in Chapter 1, you might do a broad natural-language search (described further in Section IV.B.1) for *grandparent visitation* and find hundreds of cases. If you narrowed the results by filtering by topic or with more specific terms, you might reduce the list of documents to a more manageable number that focus more directly on the facts of your problem.[19] The paragraphs that follow provide more details on this process.

1. Searching with Natural Language

Search boxes on Lexis and Westlaw accommodate users familiar with Google searching and default to a natural-language search. Little training is

---

17. For example, WestlawNext (the name of Westlaw prior to 2016) was described as Googlizing legal research. *See, e.g.,* http://outofthejungle.blogspot.com/2010/01/westlaw-next.html.

18. If you are a law student, your school will likely provide separate training sessions on each system. Attorneys who subscribe to these products can arrange training sessions with the vendors, or, if they have a librarian at their firm or organization, that person can be an invaluable resource. In addition, you can take advantage of each platform's specific online training.

19. For example, in the Welch matter in Chapter 1, a parent with a history of drug abuse was preventing her mother from visiting her grandchild. Terms and synonyms for drug abuse could be used in the filter to narrow the results found in the grandparent visitation search.

required to use this function because all you need to do is type in a question, sentence, or fragment that includes all of your key words. The computer then develops a search query based on the terms you have included and provides results ranked by relevance based on the database's search algorithm. An example of a natural language search would be, "Must a manufacturer warn about the side effects of a drug?" The computer would focus on the key words — manufacturer, warn, side effects, drug — and display the number of results the user designates as the default in order of relevancy, as determined by the system. Bloomberg Law does not support natural-language searching. If you entered the sample search into Bloomberg, it would translate it into a terms-and-connectors search (discussed in the next section) by joining keywords with an "and" connector.

Researchers who use natural language must understand its limitations. In particular, the computer's manner of determining relevancy may not be clear. Natural-language searches tend to be most helpful early in the process. Relatively easy to compose, these searches can quickly identify a sample of relevant results. Reviewing these results may suggest additional search terms, sources, or important citations that can help you focus your search to find other relevant materials. Natural-language searches might also be used after a terms-and-connectors search to be sure you haven't missed anything.

2. Searching with Terms and Connectors (Boolean)

Although the impact of Google has resulted in vendors creating simplified natural-language searching, using terms and connectors, often referred to as *Boolean* searching, enables the researcher to exercise more precision than a natural-language approach.[20] When you construct a Boolean search, you specify the way you want the terms to connect to each other, rather than relying on unknown algorithms. For instance, you might input the following search: *(grandparent or grandmother or grandfather) /s visit!* This will bring up results in which one of the following words — grandparent, grandmother, or grandfather — appears in the same sentence as any word that begins with the letters visit, such as visit or visitation. Boolean searches can be relatively simple or more complex. This manner of constructing a search inquiry gives you greater control over the search and can lead to more precise results than natural language but may also require a bit more thought to construct.

---

20. The Boolean name comes from the late English mathematician George Boole. Boolean connectors establish a logical relationship between search terms.

Table 2-2 outlines the most frequently used connectors, which also may be included in library research guides.[21]

The most common connectors are: OR (results will include at least one of the search terms), AND (results will include all of the search terms), NOT or BUT NOT (results will include the first search term but not the second search term), and " " (results will include the terms in the exact order they appear within the quotation marks). Sophisticated databases employ a wider range of operators and special characters to increase search precision. For example, Westlaw, Lexis, and Bloomberg Law also allow the connectors /p (in same paragraph), /s (in same sentence), and /n (within *n* words). Using connectors enables you to request that the documents retrieved have terms within a certain proximity or relationship to other terms. Doing so effectively increases the likelihood that the results of your search will yield relevant results. If you searched for *design /s defect* you would retrieve documents which have both words anywhere in the same sentence, such as when a court mentioned a design defect or a defect in the design. Using *design /p defect* would expand the results where the words were in the same paragraph and using *design /4 defect* would only retrieve results where the terms were within four words of each other.

The systems also use some of the same special characters. An asterisk (*) is used as a universal character representing any letter in a word or number except the first. To find cases that mention blood or bleed you could enter *bl**d*. The exclamation point (!) is used as a root expander so that if you typed *negligen!* you would find words with that root, such as negligence, negligent, or negligently. In the design defect example, you could use *design! /s defect!* to expand your results to include documents that mention defective design, designed defectively, or similar phrases. Not all databases use the same characters and connectors, so it is important to be familiar with the search function of the database you are using. Westlaw, Lexis, and Bloomberg Law provide easy help links from the search screens to the list of connectors and explanations on how to use them.

3. Field and Segment Searches

You can also increase search precision by specifying the part of the document where you want your search terms to appear. To accomplish this, you can use fields in Westlaw and Bloomberg Law and segments in Lexis. For instance, in

---

21. See chart in *Bloomberg Law, Lexis, and Westlaw Search Techniques: Connectors & Wildcards* at http://libguides.law.drake.edu/LexisWest.

Table 2-2. Commonly Used Terms and Connectors[22]

Goal	Bloomberg Law	Lexis	Westlaw*
Exact phrase	Terms in quotation marks	Terms in quotation marks	Terms in quotation marks
Find alternate terms anywhere in document	OR	OR	OR or blank space
Find both terms anywhere in document	AND or blank space	AND or &	& or AND
Find terms within a specified distance from each other	n/n or w/n or /n = within n words s/ or /s or /sent = within the same sentence p/ or /p or /para = within the same paragraph	w/n or /n = within n words w/s or /s = within the same sentence w/p or /p = within the same paragraph	/n = within n words /s = within the same sentence /p = within the same paragraph
Control the search order/hierarchy	Parentheses	Parentheses	Parentheses
Expand a term	!	!	!
Hold place of letters in a term	*	*	*
Exclude terms in parentheses	NOT or AND NOT or BUT NOT	AND NOT	% or BUT NOT
At least n occurrences of term in parentheses	ATLn or ATLEASTn	ATLEASTn or ATLn	ATLEASTn

* Check your preferences on Westlaw to ensure that Boolean terms and connectors are recognized by selecting "Preferences" at the bottom of any page. In the pop-up window, select the "Search" tab and make sure that the box under the heading "Always run these searches as Boolean Terms & Connectors" is checked before clicking on "Save."

Used with permission from *New York Legal Research* by Elizabeth G. Adelman, Theodora Belniak, Courtney L. Selby, and Brian Detweiler, published by Carolina Academic Press.

---

22. Adapted from the table in Elizabeth G. Adelman et al., *New York Legal Research* 15 (3d ed. 2015).

Lexis you could find U.S. Supreme Court opinions authored by Justice Sandra Day O'Connor by selecting the jurisdiction "United States Supreme Court" and the category "Cases" and then entering *writtenby(o'connor)* in the red search box. Available segments can be found through the "Advanced Search" link above the search box on the homepage and will vary depending on the category of documents searched. For example, the category of cases permits searching by the following segments: party name, court, date, number, citation, summary, attorney name, judges, and written by.

The Advanced Search function on Westlaw operates in a similar manner. From the home page, you first choose a category, such as cases, and click on the "advanced" link to the right of the "Search" button. An array of field boxes allows you to refine your search by party name, date, judge, attorney, etc. Note that when you input search terms into one of these advanced search form boxes, the large search box at the top is automatically filled in with your search terms and the limiter (such as *writtenby* in Lexis) that restricts the search to the specified field or segment. As you learn these limiters, you can enter them directly into the search box without having to access the search form. They can also be combined with terms and connectors.

In Bloomberg Law, when you "Search & Browse" court opinions, dockets, and a few other databases where field searching is helpful, you are automatically provided with a search form to enter field limits. Those search forms also are available when those database choices are made directly on the home page under "Research."

4. Working with Search Results

After retrieving a list of results, review the documents to see if they are relevant. For most categories of documents, you can select how you want the results to display using the options listed under the "Sort" or "Sort by" menu. Common display options include reverse chronological order with the most recent result first and relevancy with those results the system deems the best match for your query listed first. If your search retrieves an excessive number of results, narrow those results. From an efficiency perspective, narrowing normally involves applying filters to your initial results. After retrieving results, all three systems provide options in the left column to filter your results by category (e.g., cases or secondary sources/materials). Once you select a category, you will see additional filters, as well as limits like jurisdiction, date, and topic, specific to the content type selected. On Westlaw and Lexis these filters all appear on the same page. On Bloomberg Law, a new screen opens once the content type is selected. Westlaw and Lexis also provide options to

"Search within results," adding more search terms to the original query. In Bloomberg Law, you can add terms to the keywords search box to modify your original search. Once you have narrowed your search results, review the documents to answer your research issue. Keep in mind that even the best search query may retrieve only a fraction of the documents relevant to the issue and that many of the documents you retrieve may not be relevant at all.

For example, if you used *"grandparent visitation"* as your search query you would find all documents containing those two words together. However, your results might include documents in which those terms were mentioned but perhaps weren't relevant. You might retrieve an attorney discipline case that mentioned a mishandled grandparent visitation case or a law review article in which the terms only appear once, perhaps in a parenthetical citing a case, but not in any way helpful to your research. It is very important to carefully review the results you retrieve to see if they are applicable.

Your search strategy also could be eliminating relevant results. Changing your search from *"grandparent visitation"* to *grandparent /s visitation* might double the number of documents retrieved and find cases including the phrase "grandparents were given visitation" or "visitation with grandparents," providing relevant items that were excluded by the original search. Continuing to refine your search strategy is typically a necessary process.

C. Starting with a Citation

In addition to keyword searching, there are other approaches to formulating a query. As noted earlier in this chapter, if you have a citation to begin your research, you have a good start to your research. The search boxes on Westlaw, Lexis, and Bloomberg Law recognize when you enter the citation for the case, statute, article, or other document you want to retrieve. If the format you use is not what the system accepts, you will be guided to the correct one. For example, if you wanted to locate the case *State v. Jordan*, 409 N.W.2d 184 (Iowa 1997), you would enter the citation, 409 N.W.2d 184, into the search box to retrieve the case. If you have a party name, docket number, date, or other information on a case, you can use the advanced search function to enter that information to retrieve the case on Westlaw or Lexis. Bloomberg Law automatically provides name, judge, attorney, and date boxes for searching those fields.

D. Topic Searches

A variety of options allow you to limit your searches to particular areas of law. For example, Westlaw offers a tab for Practice Areas. The "Browse" feature in Lexis provides an option to view content by Topics, and through the Lexis Practice Advisor you can also access pages with sources related to a number of practice areas. Bloomberg Law offers Practice Centers. From these lists of topics, select the one most relevant to your research and then select narrower topics from more specific subject lists or search within a select subset of materials. You might start on the practice area of Bankruptcy, for example, and then decide to first review a bankruptcy treatise to better understand the issues. All three services will have several treatises in each subject area you can review.

Another approach to topic searching on Westlaw is found through the "Key Numbers" link allowing you to browse or search the more than 400 topics in the West key number system.[23] Over 100 years ago, West developed the key number system to organize legal issues using a topic and a key number that represents a more specific aspect of that topic. The system was designed to help lawyers find cases addressing specific legal issues, and its chief use is still for case law. However, key numbers are also used in other West print and electronic publications to identify legal issues. Chapter 5, which covers case law, will describe the key number system in greater depth. The important thing to understand now is that the key number system is essentially an index; each topic and number identifies a legal issue and helps the researcher find materials that address that issue.

Most decisions in Westlaw will include headnotes at the beginning of the opinion summarizing the key points of law or holdings in the case. The heading for each headnote includes a key number based on the established topic and key number system. By using that key number you can find other cases on that exact point of law. Bloomberg Law and Lexis also have their own headnote and classification systems that enable you to find similar cases on the topic covered in the headnote, but they have no connection to the West system.

V. Bloomberg Law

The entry of Bloomberg Law into the market opened up resources not available on Lexis and Westlaw. Easy access to federal docket information on PACER (Public Access to Court Electronic Records)[24] and publications from BNA are two notable offerings. To begin searching, you can use the <GO> bar

---

23. The key number system and its use, introduced in this chapter at Section III, are explained more thoroughly in Chapter 5.

24. PACER information is at https://www.pacer.gov.

Figure 2-3. Screenshot of Bloomberg Law Search & Browse

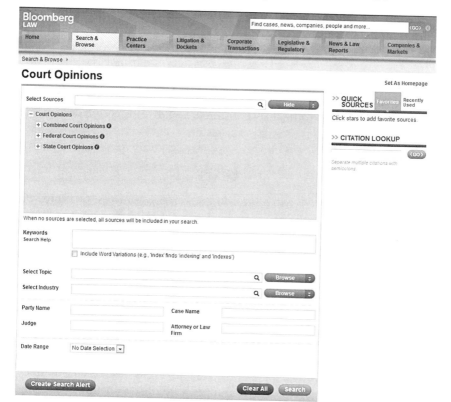

at the top of the page, which serves as a quick way to pull up a citation or enter a simple search. As you type in the search bar, the auto-complete function enables you to see sources, legal phrases, and documents that begin with the letters you are typing and can be selected below the search box.[25] Tabs across the top enable you narrow your search to particular content. Under "Search & Browse," for example, you could choose "Court Opinions" and then narrow your search by jurisdiction and court as shown in Figure 2-3. Boxes are provided for you to enter your keywords, including a checkbox to

---

25. For example, as you type *mir* the screen is populated with choices such as Miranda Rule, Miranda v. Arizona, etc.

accept word variations such as -ing. "Search Help" offers a list of Boolean connectors. Other boxes enable you to restrict your search further, such as by name, date, judge, or attorney.

When viewing your search results you have the ability from a drop-down to sort them to meet your needs, such as by relevance or date. Filters on the left enable you to narrow your results depending on the content searched. In court opinions, for example, you might be able to narrow by date, court, topic, or judge. Hot links from the display list take you directly to the document. You can print, download, or email your results.

VI. Lexis

The Lexis search box enables you to enter terms, sources, citations, or Shepardize a citation.[26] As you type in the box, Lexis offers legal phrases, sources, and documents that begin with the letters you are typing and can be selected below the search box. To narrow your search to particular content there are three options. A drop-down to the right of the search box labeled "Search: Everything" enables you to choose a jurisdiction, category (such as cases, statutes, etc.), practice area or topic, or recent or favorite search. The "Explore Content" tool just below the search box enables you to drill down to find the content you need as shown on the lower half of Figure 2-4. By using the "Browse" option at the top, you can limit to specific content as shown in Figure 2-4. Within "Browse," you can click "Sources" to "Search for a Source" or "Topics" and "Search for a Topic," and Lexis will display options matching the letters you are typing. From "Browse," you also can drill down to find a specific database. For example, if you wanted to find what was available in Iowa you could go to Browse > Sources > By Jurisdiction > Iowa and see a list of Iowa content. From the list, you can find the library you want, such as "IA Supreme Court Cases," and use a drop-down to add it as a search filter.

Once you have selected your content to search, you are ready to enter your search strategy. Words entered into the search box are assumed to be a natural language search unless Boolean connectors or operators are used. The landing page provides an "Advanced Search" function above the search bar that opens a page with boxes for you to search by document fields, such as date or by terms and connectors if you are searching for cases. After you run your search, you can narrow your results with filters, which for cases might include

---

26. Using citators such as Shepard's to make sure your authority is still good law and to find additional citing references is described in Chapter 9.

Figure 2-4. Screenshot of Lexis Advance® Browse

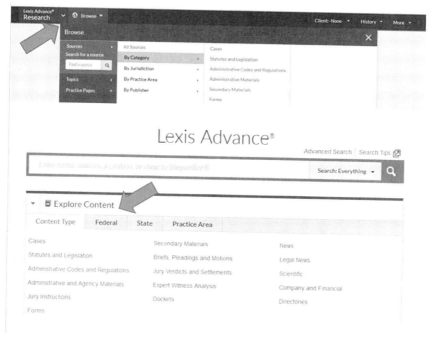

searching additional terms or restricting by segments such as court, date, topic, attorney, or judge. Documents can be sorted in several ways; case options include relevance, document title, jurisdiction, court, and date. Clicking on the document title takes you to the full text of the item. Delivery options include print, email, download, and DropBox.

VII. Westlaw

A search box on the top of the Westlaw screen enables you to enter search terms, citations, case names, etc. Much like Bloomberg Law and Lexis, Westlaw offers options for sources, documents, and dockets that begin with the letters you are typing and are displayed under the search box for selection. Narrowing your search to particular content can be done using the dropdown jurisdiction selector on the right of the search box or by using "Browse" below the search box to choose a database from the thousands possible. For example, from "Browse," you could choose State Materials > Iowa to see what Iowa databases are available and select the one you need, such as "Iowa Court of Appeals." Figure 2-5 shows the Browse selections on the home page.

Figure 2-5. Screenshot of Westlaw Browse

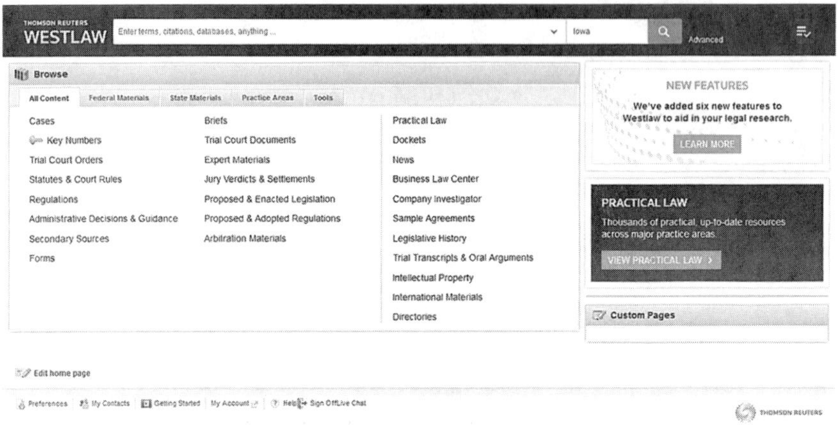

Source: Westlaw screenshot. Published with permission of West, a Thomson Reuters business.

After you identify the content you are going to search, you can enter your search query. Westlaw assumes you are performing a natural language search unless you enter connectors or Boolean operators to indicate a terms and connectors search. A link to the right of the search box offers an "Advanced Search" link which provides boxes for building a Boolean terms-and-connectors query, including searches by various fields found in a particular database, such as date, party name, citation, and judge. When a search is initiated from the homepage, an overview page will present the results.[27] From there, the content type you want to review can be selected from the list, such as cases, and then narrowed further if necessary from various choices, such as by date, judge, attorney, or topic. From the list of documents, you can click on the document title to see the full text. Delivery options include email, print, download, Dropbox, and Kindle.

---

27. When you "Browse" and choose a specific database, the overview of content choices does not appear because you have already selected one database. From those results, you can narrow by date, judge, or other parameter.

VIII. Using Special Features and Techniques

The previous parts of this chapter show that vendors offer many of the same resources in terms of federal and state cases, statutes, and regulations. However, as noted earlier, some unique content may be available on one that will not be found on another. In addition, each platform offers some unique features. For instance, West key numbers and the Iowa Practice series can only be searched on Westlaw. Only Lexis provides Shepard's Citations, Iowa jury instructions, and Lexis Topic Summaries (reports which include background and key authorities for select legal topics). For the researcher looking for federal court docket information found on PACER (Public Access to Court Electronic Records)[28] or transactional clauses,[29] Bloomberg Law is a helpful source. Vendors take advantage of the depth of resources publishers have created and make some available online. A list of major U.S. legal publishers normally includes West/Thomson Reuters, LexisNexis (including Matthew Bender), Bloomberg BNA, Wolters Kluwer (including CCH and Aspen), and Hein. Publishers may use some of the same organizational schemes or finding aids in many of their resources, which is one reason it can be useful to know who published a particular source.

Each system provides differing levels of access and databases to the law school community. For example, although both Westlaw and Lexis have a subject organization of law, the West key number system has broad applicability in secondary sources as well as cases. Special features have been added to each system to facilitate your research. Below are a few that can be especially helpful to you.

Margin Features. On the screen where you view your search results after selecting the content you want to see, such as cases, Westlaw displays additional resources that may be helpful. These features found at the right margin are called "Related Documents" on initial search results and "Selected Topics" for a particular document. In Lexis, you will find "Topic Summaries" with information about the legal topic(s) addressed in the case you are viewing. If you were searching for cases on sex discrimination, for example, those features would provide you with links to secondary sources, briefs, and other

---

28. PACER provides attorneys and the public with access to records and briefs from federal cases. For more information, see https://www.pacer.gov.

29. In addition to an extensive collection of real SEC filings, Bloomberg Law has a special tool, the Draft Analyzer, that allows you to compare your draft language to these filings.

materials related to that topic. Bloomberg Law provides general information on the right margin, such as citation analysis, and a note pad.

Case Enhancements. Several features make reading and citing relevant cases easier. *Headnotes* that summarize and sometimes simplify the key legal holdings of cases are included with most opinions on Lexis and Westlaw and some opinions on Bloomberg Law. Most opinions also include *star pagination* that alerts you to where the page breaks are located in the print volume. Star pagination appears on Westlaw as an asterisk and a number in bold italics, such as **475* shown in Figure 2-6, and on Lexis and Bloomberg Law as an asterisk and a number in bold with brackets, such as [*475]. If a case has parallel citations, you may be able to select the pagination you wish to see displayed. Some services display all pages for parallel citations; the page numbers for each reporter will be preceded by a different number of asterisks, as shown in Figure 2-6. This allows you to provide page numbers indicating the exact location of material you cite in any of the reporters.

In the case of *McCarty v. Jeffers*, 261 Iowa 470, 154 N.W.2d 718 (1967), shown in Figure 2-6, **475* shows where the page breaks in the official printed copy of the *Iowa Reports*, so you could give a pinpoint citation if you needed to cite the official report. The ***722* refers to the page break in the *North Western 2d* reporter, so you could provide a pinpoint citation for it without having to consult the bound volume of the reporter.

Copied Citations. Another helpful tool allows you to highlight relevant text and paste it directly into a document together with the pinpoint citation to that material. On Westlaw, when you highlight text you want to copy a pop-up appears that allows you to "Copy with Reference"; on Lexis, the pop-up box offers "Copy (Advanced)"; and on Bloomberg Law, the small pop-up is "Copy with Citation." When using these tools, be sure to check citations you use in work product to make sure they adhere to the citation system preferred by your court, office, or supervisor, even if you were able to select that system as a preference for the copy function. Also, remember that excessive quotations and citations sometimes indicate weak analysis.

Folders/Workspace. Organizing your materials is one of the keys to effective legal research, and online folders or a workspace can facilitate that process. Documents retrieved from Lexis and Westlaw can be saved into a folder so that all of your materials on a topic are located in one place. From there, you can easily retrieve them and share them with others at no additional cost for a year. You also can annotate documents. In Lexis and Westlaw, when you highlight text to save it, the pop-up allows you to add a note or use color high-

Figure 2-6. Westlaw Screenshot Showing Star Pagination

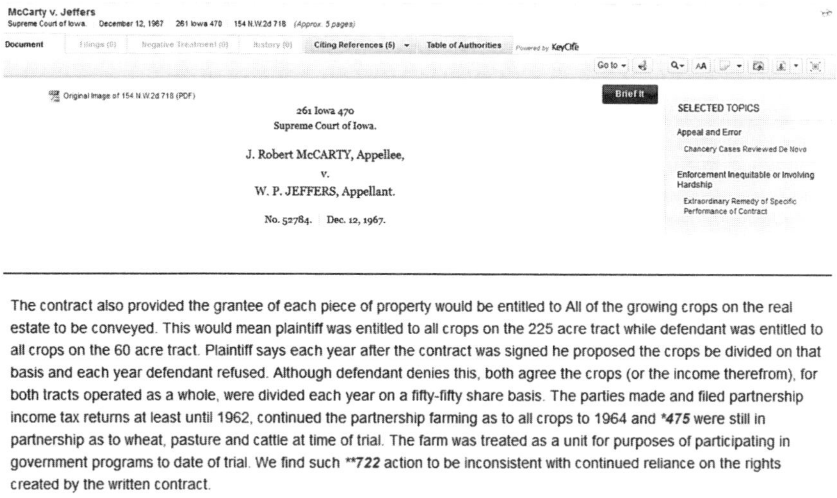

McCarty v. Jeffers
Supreme Court of Iowa.   December 12, 1967   261 Iowa 470   154 N.W.2d 718   *(Approx. 5 pages)*

Document | Filings (0) | Negative Treatment (0) | History (8) | **Citing References (5)** ▾ | **Table of Authorities** | *Powered by* KeyCite

Go to ▾ | Q▾ AA | ... | Brief It

▨ Original Image of 154 N.W.2d 718 (PDF)

261 Iowa 470
Supreme Court of Iowa.

J. Robert McCARTY, Appellee,
v.
W. P. JEFFERS, Appellant.

No. 52784.   Dec. 12, 1967.

SELECTED TOPICS

Appeal and Error

Chancery Cases Reviewed De Novo

Enforcement Inequitable or Involving Hardship

Extraordinary Remedy of Specific Performance of Contract

The contract also provided the grantee of each piece of property would be entitled to All of the growing crops on the real estate to be conveyed. This would mean plaintiff was entitled to all crops on the 225 acre tract while defendant was entitled to all crops on the 60 acre tract. Plaintiff says each year after the contract was signed he proposed the crops be divided on that basis and each year defendant refused. Although defendant denies this, both agree the crops (or the income therefrom), for both tracts operated as a whole, were divided each year on a fifty-fifty share basis. The parties made and filed partnership income tax returns at least until 1962, continued the partnership farming as to all crops to 1964 and ***475** were still in partnership as to wheat, pasture and cattle at time of trial. The farm was treated as a unit for purposes of participating in government programs to date of trial. We find such ****722** action to be inconsistent with continued reliance on the rights created by the written contract.

Source: Westlaw screenshot. Published with permission of West, a Thomson Reuters business.

lighting before saving it to a folder. Both also have a folder icon that enables you to save documents to a folder. In Bloomberg Law, you can save items to your "Workspace" and also have the ability to add notes using a "Notepad" on the right of the documents.

Download/Delivery. You can save materials for later use or send them to another device. Westlaw options from the download icon include email, print, download, Dropbox, and Kindle. The delivery drop-down on Lexis enables you to print, email, download, send to Dropbox, or create a printer-friendly view. On Bloomberg Law, you can choose to quick print, print/download, or email. In addition to capturing individual documents you can save a citation list of all the documents retrieved. You can also select only certain documents to print or download.

History and Alerts. Past searches can be saved, which allows you to review an earlier search: Lexis retains your History for three months, Bloomberg Law's Research Trail is saved for six months, and Westlaw's History is available for one year. If you need to run the same search periodically, retrieving only new additions to your original result list, you can set up an Alert to do so on all three services.

Support. A "Help" link is available on the home page if you should need assistance. This link will direct you to phone support as well as other options, such as email and live chat.[30] Training materials and tutorials are provided from the vendor's webpages.[31]

Citators. As explained in Chapter 9, citators are an indispensable tool in legal research and must be used to verify that each authority on which you plan to rely remains good law. An authority is good law if no later legal authority has reversed, overruled, or otherwise diminished its value. Each system has its own citator that lists negative subsequent treatment of authorities: KeyCite on Westlaw, Shepard's on Lexis, and BCite on Bloomberg Law. Additionally, these citators enable you to find every source that has cited your authority neutrally or positively, providing a powerful research tool. For court decisions you can also retrieve a list of all authorities a case relied on, a feature called *Table of Authorities.* It allows you to determine the current weight of authority for the cases cited within the opinion.

Table of Contents. Most books begin with a table of contents that provides the reader with a quick overview of what is covered in the volume. Electronic sources normally also include the table of contents, and that can be very helpful in understanding the scope and coverage of a work and helping you focus on the materials you need. In addition to enabling you to consider your topic in a broader context it also may help you find related topics that you might miss from just relying on the results of keyword searching. This is not only helpful with secondary sources, but can provide critical perspective with code sections, clarifying the overall statutory scheme.

IX. Print Search Techniques

A. Why Use Print?

One misconception novice legal researchers often have is that everything, including unlimited legal resources, is online. Although numerous materials are available in electronic form, many helpful resources are still available only in print or other formats. Studies have found that only a small percentage of an academic law library collection is duplicated online, especially treatises

---

30. Phone support is available for Bloomberg Law at 1-888-560-2529; Lexis at 1-800-45-LEXIS; and Westlaw at 1-800-REF-ATTY. In addition, Bloomberg Law and Westlaw offer email and live chat help. Lexis offers live chat.

31. Bloomberg Law provides resources from the "Help" link once you log on at https://www.bloomberglaw.com. Lexis materials are at http://www.lexisnexis.com /en-us/support/lexis-advance/default.page; Westlaw's are at http://legalsolutions .thomsonreuters.com/law-products/westlaw-legal-research.

and monographs.[32] Some questions can be more easily and efficiently answered in a print resource, while others are better suited for an online resource. The following sections provide tips on using print materials.

B. Indexes

The starting point for most print resources is an *index*. An index provides an alphabetical listing of key concepts and notes the pages, chapters, or sections that address these subjects. For a single-volume book, the index will be at the back of the book. For multi-volume sets, the index is often a separate volume or multiple volumes, typically shelved at the end of the set. Indexes in some multi-volume sets appear at the end of each book or in the back of the final volume in the set. For any title with pocket parts or supplements, also check these updates to see if they include a revised index or table of contents listings.

An initial step in conducting research is identifying key words that describe what you plan to research. The same technique applies when using any index. Identify your key words and look for those words. If you don't find them listed, consider synonyms or other terms. For example, if one of your key words is "Automobiles" and that word is not listed, you may need to look under "Motor Vehicles." A good index will help you identify the proper term by providing references. In the example above, the index entry after "Automobiles" might instruct "See Motor Vehicles."

An index normally includes an alphabetical listing of major subject headings, such as "Evidence," with more detailed subheadings, such as "Suppression of Evidence." Some listings will continue for several pages, requiring careful attention as to whether you are still looking under the initial heading or are now seeing entries under a subheading. Subheadings are normally indented and main headings should appear at the top of the page to guide you. If you were looking for treatise information on grandparent visitation, for example, you might turn to the *Iowa Practice General Index*, excerpted in Figure 2-7.[33] The main heading "Children and Minors" extends for pages and is repeated at the top of each page with an indication that it continues from the

---

32. *See, e.g.,* Elizabeth R. Breakstone, *Now How Much of Your Print Collection is Really Online? An Analysis of the Overlap of Print and Digital Holdings at the University of Oregon Law Library*, 29 Leg. Ref. Servs. Q. 255 (2010); Erik Eckholm, *Sacrificing a Legal Trove for the Digital Age*, N.Y. Times, Oct. 29, 2015, at A15 (noting that Harvard's entire collection of U.S. case law will be digitized and freely available on Ravellaw.com by 2017).

33. This work is described more thoroughly in Chapter 10.

Figure 2-7. Excerpt from *Iowa Practice General Index*

CHILDREN AND MINORS — Cont'd

Endangerment of child

    Generally, Crimlaw § 7:7-7:20

    * * *

    Parental authority, Crimlaw § 7:16

    Penalties, Crimlaw § 7:18, 7:20

    * * *

    Willful deprivation, Crimlaw § 7:11

Estate planning, minor distributees, Probate § 29:8

Filing minor's actions, Civillit § 10:2, 10:4

Grandparents' visitation rights, Methprac § 31:34

Habeas corpus writ, child custody provision, Civpracfm § 9:22

Illegitimate Children, this index

Incest, this index

Source: Iowa Practice General Index. Published with permission of West, a Thomson Reuters business.

prior page, as seen in Figure 2-7. Under this heading, you find scores of sub-headings, many with additional subentries, such as "Endangerment of child," as also seen in Figure 2-7. Looking down the alphabetized list,[34] you find the subheading "Grandparents' visitation rights," followed by the reference "**Methprac** § 31:34."

A table of abbreviations at the front of the index tells you that Methprac means the Methods of Practice volume. The § symbolizes section, so by locating the Methods of Practice volume and turning to section 31:34, you find a discussion on grandparent visitation rights.

Note that the index entry in Figure 2-7 also includes cross-references. If you were researching information on illegitimate children, under the heading "Children and Minors" you would see an entry for "Illegitimate Children, this index," telling you to look for entries under that heading under the letter "I" rather than as a subheading under "Children and Minors." Other indexes may use the terminology "Generally this index" to indicate the term should be searched as a main heading rather than as a subheading.

---

34. An exception to the alphabetization of subheads may be the initial subhead "Generally." This indicates places in the source that broadly discuss the topic.

C. Tables of Contents

Most research books begin with a table of contents. The table of contents provides an outline of the chapters and coverage of the book. Reviewing the table of contents may provide a quick way to find your topic of interest. Some books first provide a summary of contents that list all of the chapter topics, followed by a more detailed outline of the contents of each chapter. In multi-volume sets, the table of contents may be fully printed in each volume or only appear in the first volume.

So, for example, if you were asked to research the criminal law question of when shoplifting becomes robbery, you might start with a book on the topic, such as the treatise *Iowa Practice: Criminal Law*.[35] Examining the beginning pages of the book, you find a Summary of Contents listing all the chapters. At a glance, you can see that robbery is covered in Chapter 8. You can then go to the more detailed Table of Contents and examine the listing for Chapter 8 on Robbery, shown in Figure 2-8.

As you scan the Table of Contents, note that § 8:5 covers "Shoplifting elevated to robbery." You can turn to § 8:5 in the treatise and the answer to your research question appears in the first paragraph. This paragraph also reveals the key Iowa Supreme Court decision on the issue.[36]

The table of contents is especially useful because it provides an outline of the topics covered in the book, giving context to the research task. While the index is also an option to find the appropriate section, it does not provide the same context. Continuing with the robbery example, Figure 2-9 shows both robbery and shoplifting are listed as index headings and either will guide you to § 8:5.

---

35. Robert R. Rigg, 4 *Iowa Practice: Criminal Law* (2015). The Iowa Practice series of treatises is also available on Westlaw.

36. The treatise explains:

When the legislature enacted the new criminal code, it expanded the time frame of the assault that created the crime of robbery. At common law, robbery occurred if fear or force was used before or concurrently with the theft. The Iowa Supreme court interpreted the statute in State v. Jordan.

In Jordan, a shoplifting incident was converted into a robbery when the defendant, after having left the store with stolen articles, was accosted by security guards who had followed him into another store. A scuffle followed, resulting in defendant's arrest. The court upheld the robbery conviction, finding the assault assisted the defendant's escape.

Id. at § 8:5 (internal citations omitted).

Figure 2-8. Excerpt from *Iowa Practice: Criminal Law*

Chapter 8 table of contents

§ 8:1.	Robbery
§ 8:2.	—Robbery in the second degree
§ 8:3.	——Specific intent to commit a theft
§ 8:4.	——Lesser-included offenses
§ 8:5.	——Shoplifting elevated to robbery
§ 8:6.	——Penalty
§ 8:7.	—Robbery in the first degree
§ 8:8.	——Serious injury
§ 8:9.	——Dangerous weapon
§ 8:10.	——Penalty

Source: Iowa Practice: Criminal Law. Published with permission of West, a Thomson Reuters business.

D. Understanding and Using Legal Citations

A *citation* is the marker used by legal researchers to indicate where an authority can be located. Frequently, citations will provide information based on print resources, even when the information is accessed electronically. Most legal citations will include three parts: volume or title number, publication abbreviation, and page or section (§) number.[37] For example, in the citation *State v. Jordan*, 409 N.W.2d 184 (Iowa 1997), the case can be found in volume 409 of the *North Western Reporter, Second Series*, at page 184. Some citations omit the volume/title number. For instance, Iowa Code § 232.102 refers to the *Code of Iowa* volume that contains section 232.102; the spines of the books indicate the range of code sections they contain.

Some cases or statutes may be found in more than one source. Court rules or statutes designate one source as the *official* version of the law. When preparing court documents, you should cite to the source(s) required by court rules, which may include official or unofficial sources. *Unofficial* sources may be easier to access, be updated more frequently, provide additional content, or offer other advantages over official sources.

Legal sources frequently provide *parallel citations*, two or more citations in a row indicating multiple places where the same case or statute can be found.

37. *See, e.g.*, *Legal Abbreviations* at http://libguides.law.drake.edu/abbreviations.

Figure 2-9. Excerpt from *Iowa Practice: Criminal Law* Index

ROBBERY

Generally, §§ 8:1–8:10

Dangerous weapon, first degree robbery, § 8:9

* * *

Serious injury, first degree robbery, § 8:8

Shoplifting elevated to robbery, § 8:5

* * *

SHOPLIFTING

Robbery, elevation to, § 8:5

Source: Iowa Practice: Criminal Law. Published with permission of West, a Thomson Reuters business.

Consider this citation: *Lysinger v. Hayer*, 87 Iowa 335, 54 N.W. 145 (1893). The official citation, 87 Iowa 335, is to the *Iowa Reports* and the unofficial, 54 N.W. 145, is to the *North Western Reporter*.[38] Researchers can retrieve the case using either citation. In the appendix to this book, you will find examples of citations to other types of resources, such as statutes, regulations, and treatises. For most citations, it will be clear where you need to look to find the authority. If you encounter a citation that is unfamiliar, such as Misc. 3d,[39] consult a dictionary of legal abbreviations[40] or a librarian.

Sometimes you will have a citation that is no longer accurate. An area of the law may have had considerable growth, and, in a new edition or printing, the publisher may have renumbered all of the old sections to make room for new ones. If you have a citation to the old volume, you can still typically locate the relevant information. Most publishers provide a *correlation* or *conversion table* that takes you from the old numbering system to the new one. If

---

38. Note that the official *Iowa Reports* ceased publication in 1968, so you will not have an *Iowa Reports* citation for cases after that date. An official *Iowa Reports* citation is required when a *North Western Reporter* citation is not available, according to Iowa R. App. P. 6.904. However, the long-standing practice of the Iowa appellate courts is to include both when citing Iowa Supreme Court decisions, so seeing both in Iowa legal documents is very common. Both were required by court rule until 2009 when the rules changed to permit citation only to the *North Western Reporter*.

39. This abbreviation refers to *New York Miscellaneous Reports, Third Series.*

40. *See, e.g.*, Mary Miles Prince, *Prince's Bieber Dictionary of Legal Abbreviations* (6th ed. 2009).

you are not able to find the cited section you need, be sure to check the front or back for a correlation table, especially if you are looking in a newer book.

X. Updating

The law changes as new statutes are passed, regulations promulgated, and court cases decided. To obtain the most current information, you must understand how the source you are using is updated. Many legal books are updated with a separately issued supplement that complements the main text. One of the most common mistakes a novice researcher makes is to look in the main text of the volume and base the answer on that information without also checking the supplementation. The supplement often will contain later cases, statutes, or other updates that may affect the validity and weight of what is in the original text.

The main forms of print supplementation are *pocket parts*, inserts placed in the back of the book, and supplemental pamphlets or volumes, shelved next to the main volume.[41] Be sure to check the date of the latest print supplementation; particularly if it is more than a year old, ask the librarian whether more recent information may be available elsewhere. Many law libraries have cancelled select print subscriptions in favor of electronic access but retained many older print volumes on the shelves for historical reference. In electronic databases, the most recent information will often be integrated into the text and notes. Although most online sources integrate updates, some do not. If you were looking in the Code of Federal Regulations (CFR), for example, neither the print nor online version issued by the government may note recent changes in regulations. You would have to consult another resource, the List of Sections Affected (LSA), to update your research.[42] You should be sure to check the scope information to determine the currency of the source.

In addition to thoroughly checking the source to make sure you are using the most current information it provides, you will also learn to update your research to ensure that the law, as stated, is still in effect. This form of updating using citators will be discussed in Chapter 9.

---

41. Print products may also be updated as *looseleafs*. These are essentially ringed binders where individual pages are replaced to incorporate changes. Unless there are additional supplements, looseleaf page replacements allow a researcher to look in a single place to get the most up-to-date information.

42. The official CFR and LSA are available at http://www.gpo.gov/fdsys or https://govinfo.gov.

XI. Recording Legal Citations

As you research, you need to accurately record where you find information. In formulating your legal argument, you will have to review and present many authorities.[43] When the law is presented in a legal document, it must include attribution in an accepted citation format so that the judge, senior partner, opposing counsel, and anyone else can review the sources cited. For legal researchers, the two most well-known guides are *The Bluebook: A Uniform System of Citation*[44] and the *ALWD Guide to Legal Citation*.[45]

Most readers cannot distinguish the citation format for a document prepared using the *ALWD Guide* versus the *Bluebook* because the rules should be identical. However, each book focuses on a different primary citation purpose.[46] The *Bluebook* was written primarily as a guide for preparing citations that appear in law review articles. The majority of the text is devoted to that end, and the examples show how to cite authorities used in law review footnotes, including use of the unique typeface convention of large and small capitals.[47] The portion of the *Bluebook* most relevant to lawyers and law students is the Bluepages, which is a small grouping of pages at the beginning of the book that shows how to prepare citations for legal briefs and memoranda. The *ALWD Guide*, in contrast, provides primarily the typeface convention used for court documents and legal memoranda but also includes "Academic Footnoting" references throughout its pages. The appendix of this book discusses the use of these manuals and provides citation examples.

---

43. Thorough legal research seeks not only authorities that support your client's position, but also those authorities on which the opposing party's counsel may rely. This helps you anticipate the other party's arguments.

44. *The Bluebook: A Uniform System of Citation* (The Columbia Law Review et al. eds., 20th ed. 2015).

45. ALWD & Coleen M. Barger, *ALWD Guide to Legal Citation* (5th ed. 2014). Local citation rules must also be followed and the *ALWD Guide* includes links to those in Appendix 2. *See, e.g.,* Iowa R. App. P. 6.904, available at https://www.legis.iowa.gov/law/courtRules.

46. The 20th edition of the Bluebook in 2015 introduced a few rule changes that are not in the 5th edition of *ALWD Guide* since it was published in 2014.

47. For example, the *Bluebook* requires large and small caps for periodical abbreviations, e.g., DRAKE L. REV., and book citations, e.g., DEBORAH L. RHODE, JUSTICE AND GENDER.

Chapter 3

Secondary Sources

I. Introduction

People new to legal research sometimes mistakenly believe that you find the law in the same manner you would find the rules of a board game: by consulting one officially designated source that describes what is required or permitted. As explained earlier, however, there are multiple sources of law, broadly falling into the categories of constitutions, statutes, regulations, and court opinions. These sources are primary authority, and finding them is the goal of your research. However, if you start your research with any one of these sources, you may not understand how your source material interacts with other sources of law or how the area of law in question actually functions.

Secondary sources — written not to make law, but to summarize, clarify, and comment on it — offer one solution to this dilemma. Knowledgeable professionals conduct substantial research to write a secondary source, which provides a narrative description and explanation of an area of law. Secondary sources may also provide useful background information, explain key concepts and terminology, or otherwise point your research in the right direction. Secondary sources address a variety of different sources of law and cite important statutes, cases, regulations, and constitutional provisions in their discussion. These references can save you time when you begin to look at primary authorities. For all of these reasons, secondary sources can be an excellent place to begin many legal research projects, especially when the area of law is unfamiliar to you or is particularly complex.

Secondary sources commonly consulted by legal researchers include treatises and other books, restatements, uniform laws and model codes, legal periodicals, looseleafs and portfolios, *American Law Reports*, legal dictionaries, legal encyclopedias, and research guides. Another significant category of secondary sources, practice materials, is covered in Chapter 10. Choosing which secondary source to use to begin your research is not an exact science. Some secondary sources are better suited to certain research tasks, as described in Table 3-1. Other times several sources might work, and you may select a starting point based on availability, cost, and personal preference. By becoming familiar with how different resources are organized, you can greatly enhance your efficiency in using these sources.

Remember that secondary sources are not the law. Once you have used one or more secondary sources in your research, you will need to consult the relevant, current, and primary legal authorities. Assuming adequate primary authority exists to address your legal issues, you will likely not cite secondary sources at all. Moreover, the type of secondary source influences whether you would cite it. Some, like research guides, are strictly finding aids and should never be cited. Others, like encyclopedias, are introductory materials that would not be considered very authoritative by the court.

The four types of secondary sources most likely to be cited in a legal document are treatises, law review articles, restatements, and uniform laws and model codes. In addition to the quality of the content, the reputation of the title or author will be an important consideration in whether a treatise is cited. Similarly, law review articles are more likely to be cited when they are well reasoned and offer unique commentary on a topic. In addition, the status of the journal and the author affects their likelihood of being cited; student notes published in a law review are significantly less likely to be cited in a legal document than feature articles by established professionals. Restatements are prestigious and are cited fairly frequently. After a jurisdiction has adopted a uniform law or model code, the text and associated commentaries may be cited when the legislative intent of the adopted statute is at question. Even highly regarded secondary sources will often only be cited when relevant law cannot be found in your jurisdiction or as additional support for your argument.

II. Types of Secondary Sources

A. Treatises and Other Books

The wide range of available legal books means they can serve many purposes. Some legal books are small, single-volume works on a particular area of law, legal issue, or legal skill. Others, often called *treatises*, provide comprehensive treatment of a topic, often in multiple volumes of text. Treatises may be useful for experienced attorneys trying to answer a narrow question of law, understand a certain procedure, or otherwise gain more in-depth information on a legal topic. For instance, if you have a question on almost any

Table 3-1. Secondary Source Overview

Materials	Use
Treatises and Other Books	Obtain background information, overview, analysis, and practical tips. Treatises typically offer in-depth descriptions and analyses of the law. Other types of books may introduce an area of law or help sharpen legal skills.
Restatements	Obtain in-depth, analytical treatment of broad areas of law; use as a highly regarded persuasive authority. A restatement attempts to synthesize the common law, stating rules of law or principles that the courts have applied.
Uniform Law and Model Code Commentary	When the Iowa General Assembly adopts a uniform law or model code, related commentaries can help you find cases interpreting the statutes and understand their intent.
Law Journal Articles	Law reviews: Obtain a fairly in-depth treatment of a topic with extensive footnotes to primary law and other sources of interest. Other types of journals: Obtain practical tips and sharpen legal skills.
Looseleafs and Portfolios	Obtain thorough and up-to-date information related to different practice areas. These sources are often particularly good in areas that significantly rely on administrative law, such as tax, labor, and environmental law.
ALR and ALR Federal	Find key legal issues as well as citations to and descriptions of many interpretive court cases on a narrow topic.
Legal Dictionaries	Find definitions of unknown legal terms and phrases; discover related concepts and develop a list of search terms.
Legal Encyclopedias	Obtain a broad overview of an area of law; find references to key cases, laws, and secondary sources.
Legal Research Guides	A time-saving starting point when researching a new area of law or jurisdiction, use to learn specific research tips and techniques and obtain a compilation and description of specific research sources.

aspect of copyright law, you may well find an answer in the multi-volume title *Nimmer on Copyright*. As one former Iowa law librarian describes them, such reputable, in-depth treatises are "experts, just sitting on the shelves, waiting for you to ask them a question."[1]

Some legal books may be useful for novices who want to familiarize themselves with an area of law. The Nutshell series published by West is one well-known example. Each Nutshell is designed to provide a condensed overview of a particular legal topic; the series as a whole covers a vast array of subjects. *Hornbooks* are another type of introductory treatise. Usually written by law professors for students, hornbooks provide a narrative statement of the law in different areas with references to key cases. Other books written specifically for law students may help explain material presented in law school courses. For instance, the aptly named "Examples and Explanations" series published by Wolters Kluwer provides an overview of an area of law and then illustrates legal principles through examples and explanations.

1. Updating Treatises

As explained in Chapter 2, it is important to know how a source is updated to ensure you are consulting the most recent version. Legal books are updated in three ways, each with its own means of assessment. New pages might be issued to replace content in a looseleaf treatise. With this updating mechanism, look at the bottom of each page for a date and the front of the first volume for filing instructions with a date of the last release filed into the book. Pocket parts, supplements, and replacement volumes may update treatises, particularly in multi-volume sets. In this instance, look for a date on the cover of the pocket part or supplement. Other books may only be updated through release of a new bound edition, and the copyright date at the front of the volume will reflect its currency. For books available through a database, check the database scope note or information link to see what it includes and how current the contents are.

2. Finding Relevant Treatises

There are two steps to using a legal text: finding a relevant book and finding the material of interest in the book. As discussed in detail in Chapter 2, you might use a law library catalog to identify a book of interest. You might also get the title of a book suitable for your information need from a reference

---

1. Cheryl Gritton, former U.S. Court of Appeals Eighth Circuit branch librarian.

in another source or from a recommendation from a trusted professional, such as an attorney, professor, or librarian. For instance, you may check the Georgetown Law Library legal treatise finder, which lists reputable treatises in over sixty areas of law.[2] Each title list designates the books that are introductory or *study aids* — law student class supplements — and those that are widely regarded as the preeminent treatises in the field. Increasingly, books are available online, as well as in print. Electronic sources for books include subscription databases, such as Westlaw, Lexis, HeinOnline, Wolters Kluwer CCH, and Bloomberg Law, as well as some freely accessible sources on the Internet, such as Google Books. Librarians at state and academic law libraries can help you determine your options for accessing legal books.

Remember, like all books, some legal books provide higher quality information than others. When evaluating a legal book, consider not only the subject and depth of its coverage, but also the credentials of its author(s), the book's purpose, and the date of last update. When determining if a book is current, look at the book itself and do not limit yourself to the library catalog record. The publication date listed in a library catalog can be misleading, as it may either reflect the initial release of a treatise, but not the date of the last supplementation, or the date of the first book published in a series but not the last one. Once you have found a book of interest, you will need to find relevant sections within the book using one of the methods described in Chapter 2: searching by index, table of contents, or, for treatises available electronically, keyword.

B. Restatements of the Law

The American Law Institute (ALI) is a select group of highly regarded lawyers, judges, and law professors. Among its publications is a series called Restatements of the Law, which consist of two parts: text that attempts to clearly state what the common law is in a particular area of law and case citations which provide references to court cases that have cited the restatement.[3] The ALI does not approve, or adopt, a restatement until it has passed through a series of drafts; this process gives members opportunities to provide input and

---

2. The Georgetown Law Library legal treatise finder can be found at http://www .law.georgetown.edu/library/research/treatise-finders/index.cfm.

3. Another, newer, series is called Principles of the Law. While the restatements primarily state legal rules and their application in common law areas, the principles series suggests ways legislatures and regulatory agencies can reform areas of law.

improve the text. Restatements are somewhat like treatises in that they provide extensive commentary on a particular area of law. However, restatements are considered more authoritative than most treatises because they are authored by the leading authorities on the subject and are widely cited by courts.

In fact, courts may even adopt a restatement, or section of it, as law. For instance, in a 2009 Iowa Supreme Court opinion, Justice Hecht stated, "We find the drafters' clarification of the duty analysis in the Restatement (Third) compelling, and we now, therefore, adopt it."[4] Consulting the case citations part of a restatement as well as the textual part will help you identify such adoptions.

The textual part of the restatement begins with an introduction that explains the scope of the work. The bulk of the restatement consists of many sections, each addressing a particular legal issue. Each section begins with the rule of law, followed by the comment which explains the rule, and the reporter's notes, which includes information about the drafting of the restatement section and references to related laws and secondary sources.[5] Some sections also offer illustrations that provide examples of the application of the rule.

To use a restatement, the first step is to identify which one might cover your topic. To check for current restatement titles, consult the list of restatement topics on the ALI website, Westlaw, or Lexis.[6] Subjects covered include agency, conflict of laws, contracts, judgments, the law governing lawyers, property, torts, and more. Most titles include a series designator, i.e., second or third; the ALI issues a new restatement series to expand or update its coverage in that area of law. As new volumes are slowly released and individual chapters or sections of chapters approved, more than one series of an adopted restatement can be at least partially current at the same time. Generally, you will want to start with the most recent relevant restatement. Detailed information linked from the ALI list of restatements on its website will indicate if the newest restatement has completely replaced any older restatements or if you also need to consult an earlier series in whole or part. If the detailed information about the title indicates it is part of a current project, be sure to review the project

---

4. *Thompson v. Kaczinski*, 774 N.W.2d 829, 835 (Iowa 2009) (adopting Restatement (Third) of Torts).

5. The reporter is the person in charge of the restatement project and serves as the principal drafter.

6. The ALI website is at http://www.ali.org. Click on publications, then restatements of the law. On Westlaw, go to Secondary Sources > Restatements & Principles of the Law. On Lexis you can go to Browse > Source > By Category > Secondary Materials > R.

page to see which sections and chapters have been approved by the membership and may be cited.

Each restatement has its own index, often included at the end of the last volume with restatement text. Index entries point to the restatement section for a topic. They may also pinpoint the relevant discussion more precisely, referencing a specific part of the comment (Com), reporter's note (RN), or introductory note (Intro). In addition to the index, the table of contents may help you find a pertinent section.

After reading a relevant section, check to see which courts have cited it. In print, case citations are listed by restatement section in supplemental material. For a recently issued restatement, most case citations may be contained in the annual pocket part or separate softbound supplement. For older restatements, one or more bound appendix volumes may also include case citations for a particular range of years. When using the appendix volumes, carefully read the information on the spine to see what range of years and restatement sections each includes. In addition, a separate paperback supplement, *Interim Case Citations to the Restatements and Principles of the Law*, is released twice a year to add even more recent case citations.

Westlaw and Lexis also offer access to restatements. On both platforms, you can search a single restatement title or search across all restatements. Both services include the most recent case citations available. A Westlaw result gives the restatement text first, followed by a case citations section that provides all case citations. Westlaw also includes the index at the end of each title.[7] Lexis has separate, but linked, databases for restatement rules and case citations. The rule document provides a "Citators" link near the top right that provides the case citations. In addition, HeinOnline offers an American Law Institute library that includes access to the restatements. These searchable PDF files are arranged just like the books, with main textual volumes supplemented by appendix volumes and pocket parts with cases.

C. Uniform Laws and Model Codes

Sometimes organizations other than the government draft legislation that they encourage state legislatures to adopt. The Uniform Law Commission (ULC, formerly the National Conference of Commissioners on Uniform State Laws, or NCCUSL) has created hundreds of uniform laws in areas where it

---

7. When you click to open a particular restatement title, you will see the list of chapters, followed by tables, and finally the index.

believes standardization among state laws is most beneficial, typically private civil law. The best-known uniform law is the Uniform Commercial Code (UCC), drafted by the ULC and the American Law Institute (ALI).

Model acts or codes are also drafted for consideration by state legislatures, often in areas where uniformity is not as significant a concern. The Model Penal Code is one well-known example. Model legislation is somewhat more likely than uniform legislation to be changed by a state, although a legislature may modify either type of proposal before adoption. The ULC and the ALI both produce model acts, as do the American Bar Association and other organizations.

Some groups specialize in drafting legislation in a specific area. For instance, the National Association of Insurance Commissioners drafts model laws and regulations related to insurance. Similarly, the International Code Council (ICC) drafts building and safety codes. Although ICC titles do not include the word uniform or model, they have no authority unless adopted by a particular state or other jurisdiction, just like a uniform law or model code.

As you assess whether a uniform law, model code, or other draft legislation applies to your research, consider the following:

- Has Iowa, or another jurisdiction of interest, adopted this law?
- If so, did Iowa adopt the law in whole or make changes to it before adopting it?
- How can you find the text of the model or uniform law if it was *adopted by reference*, meaning the full text of the law is not reprinted in the local code? (As one example, 661-301.3 of the Iowa Administrative Code (IAC) adopts the International Building Code by reference.)
- What was the organization's intent when drafting this law?
- What court cases interpret this law?

Uniform Laws Annotated (ULA) is one of the best tools for answering all of these questions. This multi-volume work provides access to well over 100 acts and codes, categorized by area of law. The specific volume you need can be found using the annual Directory of Uniform Acts and Codes Tables-Index volume. This pamphlet provides an alphabetical listing of all acts and codes covered in the title, indicating the volume and page number on which coverage starts. (Hint: If you are looking for a uniform law, search for the first word after "uniform" in the name, but search under "model" for acts whose names begin with model.) The pamphlet also includes state tables that indicate which uniform legislation the state has adopted and provides the volume and page reference for the act's table of adoptions. Finally, the pamphlet includes a keyword index to help find relevant acts by subject.

For each piece of legislation, ULA coverage begins with very helpful preliminary matter: a table of jurisdictions where the act has been adopted, including the effective date and references to the state's code section and bill/session law number; historical notes; authorship; prefatory notes that explain the act's purpose; statutory notes that broadly discuss state derivations in adoption; and an outline of the act. Within each section of the act, ULA offers the text of the act, comments that further explain the text, specific notes on ways adopting jurisdictions have altered the original act, and references to interpreting court decisions and secondary sources, such as law review articles.

ULA is available as a Westlaw database. You can either search the full text of the title, using standard Westlaw search options, or navigate by the table of contents, which is the default view when selecting the ULA as a source.[8] Here you see a list of the acts and codes in the set. Click on one to open it and see the table of contents for that title. The "Refs & Annos" link at the top of each title provides access to the preliminary matter.

The organization that drafted the uniform law or model code might provide useful information about the legislation. For instance, the Uniform Law Commission site allows you to locate its acts by keyword, title, or category.[9] The site also has an option to select a state to see what ULC legislation it is currently considering or has recently enacted. Each act has its own page that may include the text of the final act, fact sheets and advocacy information about the legislation, a map of adoptions, legislative tracking information, and drafting history resources. Similarly, HeinOnline's American Law Institute Library offers a Uniform Commercial Code collection that includes an updated official text and comments as well as drafts and other historical information.

The *Code of Iowa* and *Iowa Code Annotated* both provide at least partial index access to the uniform and model acts that Iowa has adopted. Under the heading "Uniform Acts," the index volume of the *Code of Iowa* lists all the uniform laws in force in Iowa and the corresponding code sections. The General Index of the *Iowa Code Annotated* includes the heading "Uniform Laws" and, at the end of the last index volume, has a popular name table where you can look up legislation by its commonly known name and see where it has been codified. This table includes adopted model acts, such as the Business Corporation Act.

---

8. Open the ULA table of contents page in Westlaw by following this path: Home > Statutes & Court Rules > Uniform Laws Annotated.

9. The ULC website is available at http://uniformlaws.org/Default.aspx.

Table 3-2. Additional Sources for Uniform/Model Law Information

Source	Address
Uniform Law Commission Completed Acts	http://uniformlaws.org/Acts.aspx
American Law Institute (codifications and studies publications catalog)	https://www.ali.org. Click on "Publications."
Cornell Legal Information Institute, Uniform Laws	https://www.law.cornell.edu/uniform
Public.Resource.Org (bulk code collection)	https://law.resource.org/pub/us/code/

Other treatises and finding aids only focus on a particular uniform or model act. For instance, there are several well-known titles that explore the Uniform Commercial Code, including the *Uniform Commercial Code Reporting Service: Cases and Commentary*, the *Uniform Commercial Code Case Digest*, and *Anderson on the Uniform Commercial Code*. Such works can be found using a library catalog, as discussed in Chapter 2.[10]

A few additional options for finding information about uniform and model laws are listed in Table 3-2.

D. Legal Periodicals

1. Introduction

Legal periodicals are typically published more quickly than treatises, which makes them important for many research projects. Many legal periodicals are published several times a year, ensuring that the articles are current and topical when published. Often, periodical articles cover a developing area of the law before books on the subject are available. Furthermore, articles are useful tools for examining present trends and recent changes in the law. However, periodical articles are not updated, so the older the publication date, the more likely the content no longer reflects the current state of the law.

This section describes the different types of legal periodicals and their general use. It then explains how to find relevant articles by either subject or citation.

---

10. As mentioned in Section II.A, treatises may also be available online; the Anderson set also can be found on Westlaw under Secondary Sources.

Finally, it considers options for locating very recently published or forth-coming articles.

2. Types of Legal Periodicals and Their Use

Published periodically by law schools, bar associations, or commercial publishers, legal journals contain articles exploring legal issues, providing law-related news, and offering practical legal information. Law school periodicals, often generically called *law reviews*, and similar commercial publications typically contain analytical articles, many of which are quite lengthy and include extensive footnote references. Either "law review" or "journal" often appears in these titles, which can be general in scope, such as the *Iowa Law Review*, or focused on a specific subject, such as the *Drake Journal of Agricultural Law*. Bar association publications, often called *bar journals*, typically include shorter pieces that provide advice and information about current legal issues and events.

Law review articles can be an ideal starting place for legal research in a new area. They often begin with a brief summary of the evolution of the law and analyses of it, as well as a description of the current state of the law. The law review standard of heavy footnoting helps the researcher identify other primary and secondary sources on the topic.

3. Finding Articles by Topic: Indexes and Full-Text Databases

Library catalogs list the titles of journals, e.g., *Drake Law Review*, but do not list the individual articles within these journals. If you want to find articles on a particular subject or by a particular author, you will use an index or a full-text journal article database. Unlike library catalogs, which are usually freely available online, most journal indexes and databases are available only in-person in the library or online for the library's primary clientele, as described in Chapter 2.

Indexing and full text are two different dimensions. Sources can be indexed with or without having full-text availability. However, the kinds of searches that will be more successful in an index vary significantly from those that are better suited to searching the full text. This is primarily because an index labels articles by subject.

Indexes are compiled by people who actually read or review each article and then select the subjects covered by the article from a list of established subject descriptors, called a *controlled vocabulary*. For a simple illustration of the use and advantage of a controlled vocabulary, imagine you are searching for a restaurant using Yelp or the yellow pages of the phone book. In either case, you look under the heading Restaurants, and eateries of all types are found there. You do not have to also search for words like café, drive-through, bistro, pizzeria, buffet, or any other headings that are synonyms for restaurant or represent a specific type of restaurant. The use of a controlled vocabulary can make searching journal indexes more efficient than searching an un-indexed, full-text database where the searcher must try to think of the exact words that are used in the article in order to retrieve relevant results.

Further, a simple search in a full-text database will retrieve all articles that contain the keyword(s) or phrase(s), regardless of how often the terms appear or the context in which they are used.[11] Therefore, search results are likely to include many articles that are not relevant to your topic. In an index, the search can be limited to the subject headings, therefore yielding only results actually addressing the subject, not just mentioning the subject words. Moreover, once you find a relevant article, you can search for other articles with the same subject descriptors, which often produces other items of interest.

Full-text databases allow researchers a means of accessing articles beyond subject, title, and author searching. If you are looking for a specific article, finding it in a full-text database can save you time by combining the steps of locating citations and then locating the article text. Also, controlled vocabulary tends to change slowly. Some subjects, especially newer ones, may not have their own index terms yet. When the most relevant index term is still much broader than your research interest, using just that term to retrieve results will likely yield a significant number of irrelevant articles. In these situations, you may be more likely to find relevant articles if you can search the entire article text for your specific terms and concepts. Many successful researchers move back and forth between index and full-text searching. For example, if you find a highly relevant article in a full-text source, locate the same article in an indexed database to see if that yields any useful subject terms that can be used to find more articles.

Indexes may be available in print or electronically. Print indexes are generally arranged by topic, author, title, and cases and statutes mentioned in journal articles. These tools only provide citation information, e.g., journal title, volume, page number. Some electronic indexes provide either an *abstract* (a narrative description of the article) or the full text of an article in addition to

---

11. Some databases have advanced search techniques that let you specify that you want your terms to appear a certain number of times; most will also allow you to indicate that your search term should appear within a certain number of words of another term.

citation information. Examples of indexed databases of legal periodicals include *Index to Legal Periodicals & Books*, *LegalTrac*,[12] and *Index to Periodical Articles Related to Law*. Searching the electronic version of an index will almost always be more efficient than searching its print counterpart. In print, you will have to conduct the same search in multiple volumes to cover an extensive time period, while in an electronic index a single search can cover many years. Electronic indexes also provide more search options.

Full-text databases are only available electronically. Both Westlaw and Lexis offer databases containing the text of several hundred legal periodicals, some dating back to the 1980s, and others dating back to the 1990s. HeinOnline's law journal collections typically include full-text dating back to the inception of the journal. Another unique feature of HeinOnline is that it provides PDF images of the articles; this is particularly useful for articles with tables, charts or other graphics that might not display well in an html view. In all of these platforms, it is possible to search in one or more selected law journals at a time or to search a combined database of all the available law journals.

An increasing number of law reviews are also freely available in full-text format on the web. Many law reviews, particularly those affiliated with law schools, are making their content freely available on their websites. Schools may also have institutional repositories that provide full-text access to articles written by their faculty members and students. These articles can be found using a general search engine, or a more specialized site, such as Google Scholar, which focuses on scholarly works, or Law Review Commons, which offers the ability to search the contents of over 200 open access law reviews.[13]

Whether the database you are using is indexed or not, be aware of the coverage it provides by checking the scope note, as explained in Chapter 2. Many databases do not contain older articles. Although coverage varies from title to title, often it does not extend back further than 1980. Two notable exceptions are the *Index to Legal Periodicals Retrospective* database, which indexes articles published between 1908 and 1979, and the journals libraries in *Hein-Online*, which provide articles back to the first issue of each title included. The specific titles included in a database vary from source to source, which can mean you will get different results by searching different databases. Full-text databases usually cover fewer journals than indexes.

---

12. The database is called the Legal Resource Index on Westlaw and Lexis and the Current Law Index in print.

13. Google Scholar is available at https://scholar.google.com. The Law Review Commons site is http://lawreviewcommons.com/.

Because the practice of law is becoming increasingly interdisciplinary, you may also need to find information about subjects that are not necessarily included in traditional legal periodicals. There are many databases for finding multi-disciplinary or non-legal articles, such as EBSCO's Academic Search Complete, OCLC's ArticleFirst, and ScienceDirect.[14] Law school libraries will likely have access to a variety of legal and interdisciplinary indexes and full-text databases. Sometimes, these may be available through other libraries on campus. Public libraries also often offer cardholders access to one or more article databases that might be useful in legal research.

The Welch Matter

Here is an example of the research process for finding legal periodical articles by topic as it relates to the Welch matter, the hypothetical grandparents' visitation rights scenario described at the end of Chapter 1.

One approach to searching for law review articles is to search a full-text database of articles such as one available on Westlaw. You could search all available content and then narrow to law review articles, or you could limit your search just to that content. To limit the search, from the Westlaw home page, you would click on "Secondary Sources" and then "Law Reviews & Journals." Note the search box at the top now has light gray text that says "Search Law Reviews & Journals." One possible search to find articles that discuss grandparent visitation and include consideration of Iowa follows: *grandparent /3 visitation /10 iowa*. This search brings up articles that include the word *grandparent* within three terms of *visitation* within ten terms of *Iowa*. Figure 3-1 shows the first screen of results. The proximity operator in the first part of the search ensures that you retrieve not only articles that use the exact phrase "grandparent visitation," but also alternate constructions of that idea, such as one seen in the second result: "grandparents to petition for visitation." The default order of results is relevance, but that can be changed to sort by date or most cited.

Reviewing these results shows the power and pitfalls of full-text searching. The first result is focused on Florida law but mentions an Iowa case in passing. Some of the other articles more thoroughly discuss Iowa law, pointing to a relevant Iowa statute and case law. When you review search results, not only do you want to select articles that might be relevant, but you also want to determine whether you

---

14. For more information about these databases, see https://ebscohost.com/title-lists for Academic Search Complete, http://www.oclc.org/support/services/worldcat-org/documentation/dbdetails/details/ArticleFirst.en.html for ArticleFirst, and http://www.sciencedirect.com/ for ScienceDirect.

Figure 3-1. Screenshot of Westlaw Law Reviews & Journals Search Results

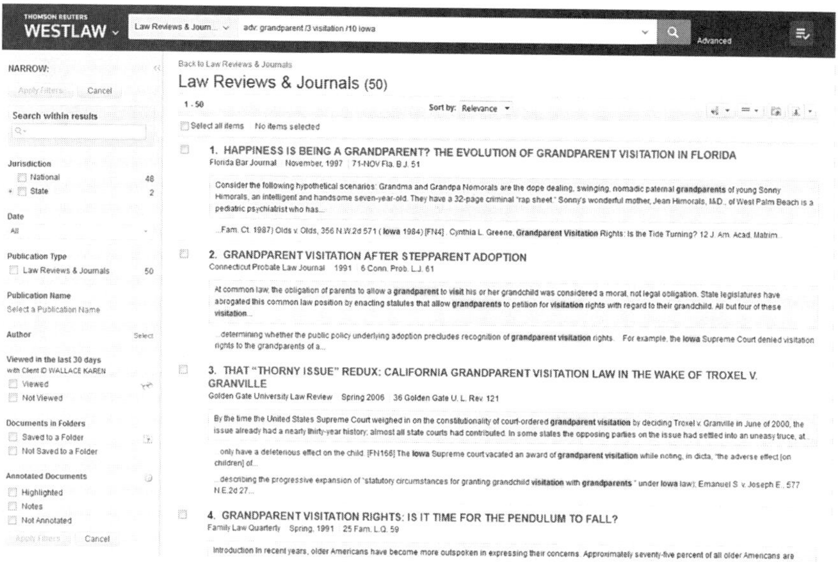

Source: Westlaw. Published with permission of West, a Thomson Reuters business.

might be able to refine your search to improve it. If there were many articles like the first one that only mentioned Iowa in passing, you could change from a proximity search operator (i.e., */10*) to one that specifies the number of times the term should appear, as shown with the ATLEAST operator in this search: *grandparent /3 visitation and ATLEAST6(Iowa)*. This specifies that the term *Iowa* should appear at least six times, helping reduce results that mention an Iowa case or two in passing but do not consider the jurisdiction in depth.

4. Finding an Article When You Already Have a Citation

If you already have a citation to a journal article or you find one in an index that does not offer full text, you will then need to determine where you can find the full text. (Tip: If you have a citation with a journal name you cannot decipher, look up the abbreviated name in *Bieber's Dictionary of Legal Abbreviations* or in the periodicals table of the *Bluebook* or the *ALWD Guide*.) Many libraries now offer journal finders that allow you to type in the name of the journal and see which library databases provide access to the full text of the

Figure 3-2. Screenshot of Drake Law Library Journal Finder Search Results

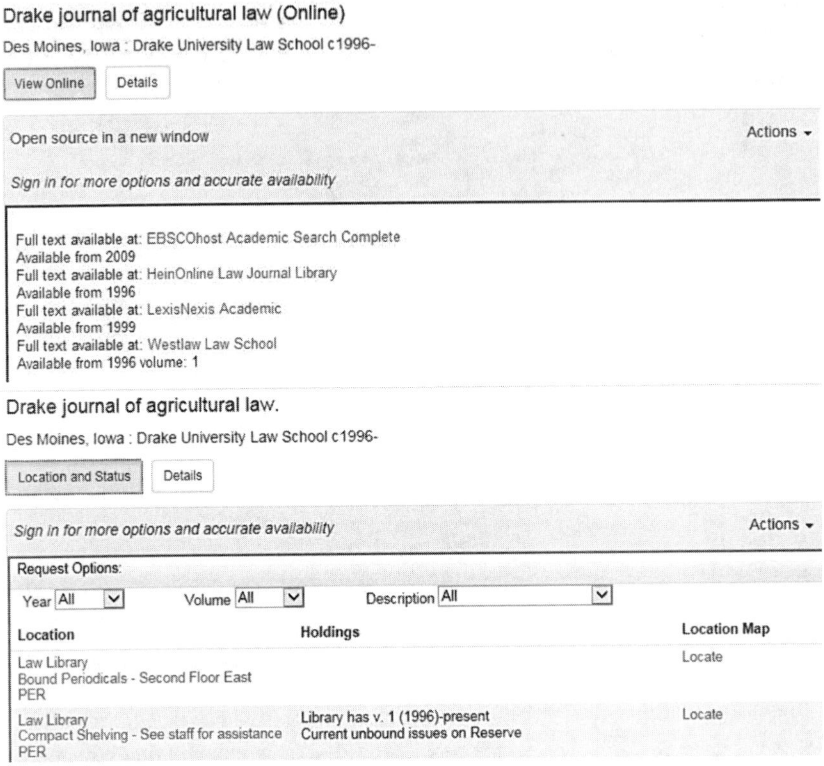

Drake journal of agricultural law (Online)

Des Moines, Iowa : Drake University Law School c1996-

| View Online | Details |

Open source in a new window   Actions ▾

Sign in for more options and accurate availability

Full text available at: EBSCOhost Academic Search Complete
Available from 2009
Full text available at: HeinOnline Law Journal Library
Available from 1996
Full text available at: LexisNexis Academic
Available from 1999
Full text available at: Westlaw Law School
Available from 1996 volume: 1

Drake journal of agricultural law.

Des Moines, Iowa : Drake University Law School c1996-

| Location and Status | Details |

Sign in for more options and accurate availability   Actions ▾

Request Options:

| Year | All ▾ | | Volume | All ▾ | | Description | All | ▾ |

Location	Holdings	Location Map
Law Library Bound Periodicals - Second Floor East PER		Locate
Law Library Compact Shelving - See staff for assistance PER	Library has v. 1 (1996)-present Current unbound issues on Reserve	Locate

Source: Drake Law Library.

articles in that journal. When using these tools, be sure you enter the title of the journal, not the title of the article. If your library does not have the full text of the article, you may still be able to obtain it through the interlibrary loan service, where libraries lend or provide copies of materials to each other on your behalf. It can take several days or longer to obtain material from interlibrary loan, so allow yourself some extra time if you pursue this option. Figure 3-2 depicts a search for the *Drake Journal of Agricultural Law* in the Drake Law Library's journal finder. Note that the results show which year ranges of the law review are available in each of the listed sources. Coverage dates back to 1996 for HeinOnline, Westlaw, and the library's print collection.

Table 3-3. Resources for Locating Recent and Forthcoming Articles

bepress Legal Repository

http://law.bepress.com

This database offers browsable and searchable access to many full-text, law-related research materials posted by law schools, research units, institutes, centers, think tanks, conferences, and other subject-appropriate groups (PDF format).

Current Index to Legal Periodicals (CILP)

http://lib.law.washington.edu/cilp/cilp.html

This weekly index of current articles from over 650 legal publications is organized by subject. The last eight issues are also available via Westlaw. It is compiled by the University of Washington School of Law.

Google Scholar

http://scholar.google.com

This specialized search engine provides access to a range of scholarly literature on the web, including working papers.

SSRN/Legal Scholarship Network

http://www.ssrn.com/en/index.cfm/lsn/

This database offers browsable and searchable access to abstracts and selected full-text preprints, articles, and studies. Use the "Search" command from the top menu line to retrieve papers by keyword search.

5. Locating Recent and Forthcoming Articles

Both indexes and full-text databases have some delay before adding new content. If you are searching for something very recent, special resources can help you find recently published articles, copies of working papers, preprints, articles accepted for publication, and the like. Some of these sources are listed in Table 3-3.

E. Looseleaf Services and Portfolios

Lawyers who specialize in an area of law will often subscribe to an electronic or print topical looseleaf service that reports and analyzes legal news, proposed statutes, and regulations and brings together cases, statutes, regulations, and other administrative law in the area. Such services are frequently updated, through issuing new pages to replace or add to the current pages, and/or by releasing newsletters that update coverage. Bloomberg BNA, Commerce Clearing House (CCH), and Research Institute of America (RIA) are three of the largest publishers of such services.

Portfolios are similar to looseleaf services in that they specialize in a particular area of law and the print versions are updated by replacing or inserting specific pages. Portfolio series are most often published in the areas of taxation, real estate, and corporate law; Bloomberg BNA series are among the most recognized. They consist of a number of individual portfolios, which present practitioner-oriented explanations and analysis on the application of a fairly narrow issue of law.

If you do not know what specific title you need, it may be easiest to check for a looseleaf service or portfolio series on your area of law by asking a librarian. The library may provide access either in print or electronically, and the library catalog may not specify whether the item is a looseleaf service or portfolio. Note again that publication dates listed in the catalog can be misleading, as they may reflect the initial release of a looseleaf, but not the date of the last update, or the date of the first book published in a series but not the last one. Table T15 in the *Bluebook* (20th ed.) lists some of the more commonly used looseleaf titles and their publishers. If your library subscribes to it, you can also check the annual *Legal Looseleafs in Print*, which includes both looseleaf services and looseleaf treatises.

Many attorneys now access looseleaf services and portfolios as subscription databases either available separately or through more comprehensive research tools, like Bloomberg Law, Lexis, and Westlaw.[15] Although the content and organization of the electronic versions is generally the same as the print source, online access is more up-to-date than print access, as there is no lag time while new material is mailed and filed. Electronic access also provides some user-friendly enhancements, such as automatic email delivery of news and search alerts.

1. Using Looseleaf Services

Whether in a print or electronic format, the key to using a looseleaf service successfully is making sure you know how it is organized. Print sources will typically have an explanation of how to use the service at the front of the first

---

15. Some looseleaf publishers only license their content for one of these three legal research platforms. Bloomberg BNA content is restricted to Bloomberg Law, Matthew Bender content to Lexis, and Wolters Kluwer CCH to Westlaw.

volume. Each looseleaf service is different, although some titles, especially those by the same publisher, may share similar features. The how-to-use section will show you the overall arrangement of the work. Looseleaf services often consist of a variety of parts. The main text may be subdivided by topic or organized by statutory code section. There may be separate sections for newsletters and for reported cases or statutes. Older cases may be transferred into other binders or bound volumes, and these might not even be shelved directly next to the rest of the looseleaf.

The how-to-use section will also introduce the different finding aids within the looseleaf service. There are often multiple indexes and tables, and the best one to use depends on what you need and what you already know. For instance, the decisions binder and case volumes of the *Environment Reporter* (BNA) offer a topical index to find cases by subject, a classification guide that categorizes environmental law topics and assigns each a number, an index digest that presents cases by their classification number, a table of cases to find a known case alphabetically by name, and a table of cases by jurisdiction to find cases decided in a particular jurisdiction.

Finally, you will benefit from reading the how-to-use section because it will explain other anomalies of the service. For instance, looseleaf services often have page numbers, but instead of using these as references, they use paragraph references or section numbers. These numbers on the page are typically preceded by the paragraph symbol (¶) or the section symbol (§). Note that a "paragraph" may consist of many paragraphs and even run many pages, and these references may be used electronically, as well as in print. When using a looseleaf index be sure to look for a note indicating whether references are to paragraph numbers, section numbers, or page numbers.

Online, you may have several options for familiarizing yourself with a looseleaf service. The database itself may offer help screens or other on-screen, step-by-step guidance, such as noting what search operators may be used. The publisher may provide online training sessions or training materials. Your librarian may also be able to provide training. Depending on the interface, you may find some sources easier to use in print and others easier to use electronically.

2. Using Portfolios

For print portfolios, such as Bloomberg BNA's *Tax Management Portfolios*, use the separate general index volume to locate relevant portfolios by subject; statutory or administrative code sections may also be search options for some portfolios. The index citation will provide the portfolio number and the section in which that subject is discussed. Electronically, you may have options to search an index, but you will also have options to search content by keyword. Note that as portfolios are replaced, they will keep their main number but add an edition signifier after it; e.g., 659 becomes 659-2nd. Each portfolio will also have a table of contents and may begin with a scope note describing what the portfolio covers.

F. *American Law Reports*

American Law Reports (ALR) provides *annotations*, which are essentially articles that focus on a narrow, often unsettled, legal topic. The annotation cites and describes relevant court cases. ALRs are published in different series, each consisting of many volumes. The earliest ALRs included federal issues, but this jurisdiction later split into a series of its own: *American Law Reports, Federal* (ALR Fed). ALR is now in its seventh series, and ALR Fed is in its third series.[16] Although the basic character of the annotations has remained largely the same over the years, specific features have changed, and the description that follows focuses on the newest series.

If you do not already have an ALR citation from another secondary source, you can look for one by using one of the index volumes found at the end of the set or the index on Westlaw.[17] Two separate, one-volume indexes include the third through sixth series of the ALRs (*ALR Quick Index*) or the first and second series of the ALR Feds (*ALR Fed Quick Index*). The multi-volume *ALR Complete Series Index* provides subject access to the annotations in all the ALR and ALR Fed series. Another multi-volume title, *West's ALR Digest*, allows you to find annotations from any of the ALR series using the West key number system.[18] You can also search for an annotation on Westlaw or Lexis.[19]

---

16. A related title, *ALR International*, first published in 2010, provides citations to U.S. and foreign court cases on topics of international importance.

17. On Westlaw, follow this path: Home > Secondary Sources > American Law Reports > American Law Reports Index (the index link is on the right side under the "Tools & Resources" menu).

18. The West key number system is introduced in Chapter 2 and described more fully in Chapter 5.

19. ALR International, however, is available online through Westlaw but not Lexis. It has a separate category page from the rest of the ALR materials: American Law Reports — International.

Each individual annotation begins by introducing the central issue and what the court found in a specific case. Other preliminary matter includes a table of contents showing the titles of the sections of the articles; research references to a variety of other secondary materials and West key numbers; an index to help find relevant sections within the article; and a table of cases, laws, and rules, which notes primary law cited in the annotation and the section where the law is discussed. This table is organized by jurisdiction, which makes it easy to determine whether any cases have been heard by the U.S. Supreme Court, the Eighth Circuit Court of Appeals, an Iowa court, or another jurisdiction of interest. Outside of court cases, the table only includes other types of laws that are discussed in the referenced court cases.

The text of each annotation begins with the same three sections: scope, indicating what the article includes; summary and comment, briefly describing the area of law; and practice pointers, offering guidance for attorneys representing clients on the legal topic. The annotations then continue with specific discussion of the legal issues involved in the topic and how courts have treated these. For volumes in the series prior to ALR 7th and ALR Fed 3d, a full reprint of a recent court decision involving the subject matter of the annotation is included. Those cases are reprinted at the end of each volume in a section called "Reported Cases," or, through ALR 4th and ALR Fed volume 110, directly before the annotation.

One of the most valuable features of the annotation is the presentation of authorities on both sides of an issue. Not only will you find cases supporting your client's position, but you also will be given cases that support the opposite position. This enables you to review authorities to strengthen your case as well as determine how contrary authorities, which opposing counsel may cite, can be distinguished from your client's case. Figure 3-3 provides a few lines from the outline in an annotation addressing grandparent visitation rights, showing sections where you can find supporting and opposing authorities.[20] Note that under [a] you find summaries of cases in which visitation was awarded and under [b] you find those in which visitation was denied.

Unlike law review articles, annotations are updated after publication. New cases decided on the issues, new developments in the area of law, and references to newer annotations are included in annual supplements to the ALR or released in paper as either a pocket part or a separate softbound supplement. West also offers a latest case hotline where you can learn whether any ad-

---

20. George L. Blum, Annotation, *Grandparents' Visitation Rights where Child's Parents are Living*, 71 A.L.R.5th 99 (1999).

Figure 3-3. ALR Outline Excerpt

§ 4[a] Where child's parents are living apart, generally — Visitation awarded or held permissible, or remand necessary

§ 4[b] Where child's parents are living apart, generally — Visitation denied or held impermissible

* * *

§ 7[a] — Where child is adopted after divorce — Visitation awarded or held permissible, or remand necessary

§ 7[b] — Where child is adopted after divorce — Visitation denied or held impermissible

§ 8[a] Where child's biological parents are living together — Visitation awarded or held permissible, or remand necessary

§ 8[b] Where child's biological parents are living together — Visitation denied or held impermissible

Source: 71 A.L.R.5th 99. Published with permission of West, a Thomson Reuters business.

ditional cases have been added to an annotation after the last supplement was issued.[21] Electronically, updates are merged into the text of the annotation on a weekly basis, so if you look at an annotation on Westlaw or Lexis, it will include any cases provided by the print supplements or the latest case hotline.

Sometimes a more recent annotation will replace an older one on the same topic. For instance, *Physician's or Other Healer's Conduct, or Conviction of Offense, Not Directly Related to Medical Practice, as Ground for Disciplinary Action*, 34 A.L.R.4th 609 (1984), replaced *Physician's Conviction of Offense Not Directly Related to Medical Practice as Ground of Disciplinary Action*, 12 A.L.R.3d 1213 (1967). On Westlaw and Lexis, the text of a superseded ALR is replaced by a link to the new annotation. In print, starting with the third series, the supplementation provides the citation to the replacement annotation.

G. Legal Dictionaries

Legal dictionaries provide an alphabetical list of legal terms and phrases with definitions for each. They may include additional features, such as a guide to pronunciation or notes on the term's history. In explaining the meaning of a term, legal dictionaries often provide valuable context about the broader

---

21. The latest case hotline phone number is (800) 225-7488.

area of law into which the term falls — introducing related concepts and suggesting alternative terms that can be used to search databases, indexes, and other research resources.

Legal dictionaries may also note other primary or secondary sources that further explain the term. For instance, *Ballentine's Law Dictionary* includes references to cases, statutes, and other secondary materials. Starting with the eighth edition, *Black's Law Dictionary* includes citations to the legal encyclopedia *Corpus Juris Secundum* and other legal sources that explain a term's meaning and history.

Legal dictionaries may offer broad coverage or specialize in a particular area of law, such as *West's Tax Law Dictionary*. Dictionaries may also be specifically written for a particular audience, whether attorneys, new law students, or members of the general public. Additional judicial definitions can be found in the multi-volume West title *Words and Phrases*, available in print and on Westlaw, and specific digests' Words and Phrases volumes, as described in Chapter 5. Table 3-4 lists a few well-known legal dictionaries.

Table 3-4. Selected Legal Dictionaries

Title	Audience	Electronic Access
Black's Law Dictionary	Law students; attorneys	Available on Westlaw; other digital versions include iOS and Android apps
Ballentine's Law Dictionary	Law students; attorneys	Available on Lexis
Merriam-Webster's Dictionary of Law	Public; law students	http://dictionary.findlaw.com
Oran's Dictionary of the Law	Paralegals; law students	E-book available for purchase
Research Guide: One-L Dictionary	New law students	http://law.wlu.edu/deptimages/Library/1Ldictionary.pdf

H. Legal Encyclopedias

Legal encyclopedias introduce different areas of law and refer to important primary law within each area. They may also reference other relevant secondary sources. Each area of law is discussed in its own topical article, which consists of separate sections. The topics are arranged alphabetically. Researchers primarily use legal encyclopedias to get an overview of a particular area of law.

Some encyclopedias have focused coverage. Some states have state-specific legal encyclopedias,[22] but Iowa does not. Examples of subject-specific encyclopedias include *Encyclopedia of Environmental Health Law and Practice* and *Encyclopedia of Information Technology Law.* You would search for these encyclopedias in the same way you would search for a treatise, described in this chapter in Section II.A.2.

The two major general legal encyclopedias in the United States are *Corpus Juris Secundum* (CJS) and *American Jurisprudence 2d* (AmJur). Historically, the two titles had different publishers and slightly different goals. West now publishes both titles, but their differing characteristics largely remain. CJS begins each section with *black letter law,* a succinct summary of the rule of law, and strives to provide an extensive list of citations to cases related to each area of law covered. AmJur sections do not begin with black letter law, they cite only the most important cases and ALR annotations, and the notes are more likely than those in CJS to provide a brief summary of the relevance of cited cases. Electronically, AmJur is available through both Westlaw and Lexis Advance, while CJS is only available through Westlaw. See Figure 3-4 for an excerpt from the AmJur topic Divorce and Separation.

In print, both titles are updated annually through a combination of replacement volumes, pocket parts, and supplements, so be sure to check the pocket part or separate supplement to see if there is additional information on your section. To find the database's currency electronically, click on the i-link, called source description in Lexis and found by browsing sources and scope information in Westlaw.

If you do not already have a specific CJS or AmJur reference, there are three ways to find a relevant topic, or section of a topic, in either encyclopedia. These methods, described in detail below, may differ depending on whether you are using the print or electronic version.

1. Use the Index to Find Encyclopedia Articles

This option is often the most efficient approach. In print, the general index, released annually in multiple volumes, is typically shelved after the main encyclopedia volumes. The AmJur and CJS indexes can also be accessed on West-

---

22. The Harvard Law School Library maintains a guide that lists state-specific legal encyclopedias and encyclopedia-like treatises. The main list of Harvard Library guides is at http://guides.library.harvard.edu/. Click on Harvard Law School Library to see its guide list. Select "Secondary Sources," and within the guide click on Legal Encyclopedias.

Figure 3-4. Excerpt from AmJur

DIVORCE AND SEPARATION   § 895

visitation has ended.[10]

b. Rights of Others

§ 895 Rights of grandparents and other relatives

Research References

West's Key Number Digest, Child Custody ⊶271, 282 to 289, 311 to 313
Grandparents' visitation rights where child's parents are living, 71 A.L.R.5th 99
Grandparents' visitation rights where child's parents are deceased, or where status of parents is unspecified, 69 A.L.R.5th 1
Grandparent Visitation and Custody Awards, 69 Am. Jur. Proof of Facts 3d 281
Am. Jur. Pleading and Practice Forms, Divorce and Separation §§ 48, 49 (Petition or application—By grandparent—For visitation rights), 50 (Affidavit—By grandparent—In support of petition for visitation rights), 330 (Judgment or decree—Provision—Visitation rights to grandparents)

The court's broad powers to determine all issues in a dissolution action have been recognized to include jurisdiction over issues of the rights of grandparents and other nonparents to visitation.[1] Grandparent visitation statutes provide a procedural mechanism for grandparents to acquire standing to seek visitation with minor grandchildren.[2] An award of visitation to grandparents ordinarily must arise out of a pending dissolution proceeding; the court normally has no jurisdiction to award visitation where there is an existing marriage.[3]

In some jurisdictions, grandparents and other relatives may have a legal right of visitation,[4] but other jurisdictions do not bestow a legal

---

[10]Breazeale v. Hayes, 489 So. 2d 1111 (Ala. Civ. App. 1986).

As to the requirement of bond, generally, see § 888.

[Section 895]

[1]Kanvick v. Reilly, 233 Mont. 324, 760 P.2d 743 (1988); In re Visitation of Z.E.R., 225 Wis. 2d 628, 593 N.W.2d 840 (Ct. App. 1999).

[2]E.S. v. P.D., 8 N.Y.3d 150, 831 N.Y.S.2d 96, 863 N.E.2d 100 (2007). Grandparent access statute gives only a biological or adoptive grandparent, and not a step-grandparent, standing to seek access to grandchildren. In re Derzapf, 219 S.W.3d 327 (Tex. 2007).

Grandparent visitation statute was unconstitutional as applied to parents in proceeding in which maternal grandparents sought visitation with grandchildren, where no threshold finding was made, regarding whether parents were unfit or whether exceptional circumstances existed demonstrating current or future detriment to the child absent visitation from grandparents, before proceeding to determine whether allowing visitation was in the children's best interests. Koshko v. Haining, 398 Md. 404, 921 A.2d 171 (2007).

[3]Sragowicz v. Sragowicz, 603 So. 2d 1323 (Fla. Dist. Ct. App. 3d Dist. 1992); Theodore R. v. Loretta J., 124 Misc. 2d 546, 476 N.Y.S.2d 720 (Fam. Ct. 1984).

[4]Santaniello v. Santaniello, 18 Kan. App. 2d 112, 850 P.2d 269 (1992); Olson v. Olson, 534 N.W.2d 547 (Minn. 1995).

Source: 24A Am. Jur. 2d Divorce and Separation § 895. Published with permission of West, a Thomson Reuters business.

Figure 3-5. Excerpts from AmJur General Index

**GRANDCHILDREN AND
GRANDPARENTS**
Adoption of Children (this index)
Advancements, **Advance § 23**
Custody of children, intervention, **Divorce
§ 213, 214**
Descent and distribution, **DescentDst § 74**
Estate and Inheritance Taxes (this index)
Funeral and burial, **DeadBodies § 22**
Homesteads (this index)
In loco parentis, **Parent § 13**
Insurance, **Insurance § 1702**
Railroad Retirement Act, **Pensions § 865**
Restitution and implied contracts, **Restitutn
§ 65**
Search and seizure, consent to, **Searches
§ 168**
Social Security, child's benefits, **SocialSec
§ 696, 697**
Visitation, **Divorce § 895**
Wills (this index)
Workers' compensation, death benefits,
Workers § 175
Wrongful death, **Death § 88**

. . . .

GRANDPARENTS
Grandchildren and Grandparents (this
index)

Source: American Jurisprudence 2d. 2015 General Index. Published with permission of West, a Thomson Reuters business.

law.[23] For detail on using indexes in general, see Chapter 2. Index entries in both titles provide the name, or abbreviation, of the topic and the section (§) number or numbers that discuss the specific indexed issue, such as Divorce § 895, shown in Figure 3-5 under the "Visitation" subheading. Both encyclopedias have a table at the front of each index volume that lists the topic abbreviations with the cor-

---

23. On Westlaw, follow this path: Home > Secondary Sources > Texts & Treatises. Then select either American Jurisprudence 2d or Corpus Juris Secundum and the corresponding index, linked on the right side under "Tools & Resources" menu.

Figure 3-6. Excerpt from AmJur Table of Abbreviations

Damages	Damages
DeadBodies	Dead Bodies
Death	Death
DeclJuds	Declaratory Judgments
Dedication	Dedication
Deeds	Deeds
Deposition	Depositions and Discovery
Deposits	Deposits In Court
DescentDst	Descent and Distribution
Desertion	Desertion and Nonsupport
Dismissal	Dismissal, Discontinuance, and Nonsuit
DistCol	District of Columbia
Disturb	Disturbing Meetings
Divorce	Divorce and Separation
Domestrel	Domestic Abuse and Violence
Domicil	Domicil
Dower	Dower and Curtesy
Drains	Drains and Drainage Districts
DrugsEtc	Drugs and Controlled Substances
Duress	Duress and Undue Influence

Source: *American Jurisprudence 2d.* 2015 General Index. Published with permission of West, a Thomson Reuters business.

responding full titles, e.g., "Divorce" abbreviates the full title "Divorce and Separation," shown in Figure 3-6.

With the reference to topic and section number, find the main volume(s) of the encyclopedia that includes that topic. Although volumes are arranged alphabetically by topic, be aware that the topic name might not appear on the spine, which only lists the first and last topics in the volume. Also, some topics may span more than one volume; in this case, make sure you select the volume that covers not only your topic but also the relevant section(s).

Open the relevant volume and go to the correct topic. The front of the volume lists all the topics it contains and the page numbers on which they start. The topic title can also be found at the top of each right-hand page. Within the correct topic, turn to the relevant section number. Section numbers appear in bold headings within the text of the topic. The number of the first section, or partial section, on the left-hand page will appear at the top of that page, and the number of the last section, or partial section, on the right-hand page will appear at the top of that page.

The back of each volume provides a partial index, covering only the topics in that volume. This index can be a handy reference when you have already put the general index away or if the general index volume you need is not available.

The Welch Matter

You can use the general index encyclopedia research process to learn about the hypothetical grandparents' visitation rights scenario.

Figure 3-5. One approach to beginning encyclopedia research is to use the general index to look up research terms. In the Welch case, logical terms include grandparents and child custody. As shown in Figure 3-5, the term Grandparents in the general index refers you to the subject heading Grandchildren and Grandparents. That subject heading has a subheading "visitation," which leads to the relevant topic and section number: Divorce § 895.

Figure 3-6. To determine whether the topic Divorce was a shortened version of a longer name, check the table at the front of the set. You find that Divorce stands for Divorce and Separation. Then look at the spines of the books to locate the AmJur volume that includes Divorce and Separation § 895.

Figure 3-4. Opening the AmJur volume to the correct section, you see a number of research references to other sources that might be useful. You can also begin to read a general description of how different states handle visitation rights for grandparents and obtain case citations in the footnotes. Although there are not any Iowa cases cited, you do pick up a significant research lead that many states have statutes on this issue that the courts have interpreted. Because you are a savvy print researcher, you remember to check the pocket part, too, where you find additional secondary source references and cases from other jurisdictions. (The pocket part is not pictured.)

---

2. Using the Topic Outline to Find Encyclopedia Articles

In each encyclopedia, the topics begin with an outline, or table of contents, that lists the main headings and subheadings of the topic. A subsequent *scope note* provides a narrative description of what the topic covers. Each title also references related topics that are covered in other encyclopedia topics. Before the narrative text begins, AmJur also offers general research references to West's key numbers (described in Chapter 5), primary law, and other secondary materials. These references can most easily be accessed electronically through the table of contents under the "Summary" heading listed first under the topic. On Lexis, the table of contents view is shown when "American Jurisprudence, Second Edition" is selected as a source using the red search box. You can also access it on Lexis through the browse sources feature. Search for

American Jurisprudence 2d (AMJUR) and the select the table of contents link. Click on the arrows to the left of the topic or section names to open those sections of the table of contents. When you reach a specific AmJur section, it will appear as a link you can click on. With any AmJur section open, use the "Table of Contents" link on the left to open the table of contents surrounding the section you are viewing. On Westlaw, the table of contents can be accessed from the main American Jurisprudence 2d page, or, with any AmJur section open, click on the table of contents link in the upper-right corner to see the table of contents surrounding the section you are currently viewing. In the Westlaw table of contents, find the topic of interest, then click on the topics or subheadings to see the different sections of the topic outline under each heading or open a specific section.

3. Conducting a Keyword Search to Find Encyclopedia Articles

Keyword searching is an option only in the electronic databases. The advantage of this approach is that your search will retrieve every encyclopedia topic that includes a specific term of interest. Your search can also become quite sophisticated, using the many options available in Westlaw and Lexis, and the databases can suggest additional terms you may want to add to your search. The principal disadvantage of this approach is that it requires skill and familiarity with the terms likely to be used in the encyclopedia to construct a precise search that will only retrieve relevant items. You may get many irrelevant results with a simple keyword search, which will pick up your search term(s) anywhere regardless of how important each term is to the topic. Also, you may miss relevant topics or sections with a more complex search or a keyword search that does not use the right terms. For example, attorneys colloquially refer to "slip-and-fall" cases in which someone is injured after falling in an accident at least partially caused by unsafe conditions. However, searching either for the phrase *"slip and fall"* or the words *slip* and *fall* in close proximity to each other may lead to results that miss relevant cases that would be included in the results of searches using broader terms like premises liability or accidental falls.

I. Research Guides

Research guides describe available research sources and suggest search strategies. Particularly when you are unfamiliar with a certain area of law, consulting a relevant research guide can make your research more effective and efficient. Using a research guide can be akin to consulting a travel guide before going on a journey. A research guide familiarizes you with a particular area, notes sources of interest, and provides practical tips from someone who has already done research in this area. Research guides may also indicate what you will not find. For instance, as will be discussed further in Chapter 5, most opinions rendered in state trial-level cases are not published. Therefore, they will likely not be found in either the books or databases of a major law library. Knowing this before you begin a fruitless search can save you significant time and frustration.

Some research guides are simple lists of valuable sources for researching a topic. Others, like this book, are much more developed. In addition to providing in-depth descriptions of how to locate and use research sources in the field, they may provide important background information, such as explaining key concepts and structures. A federal tax research guide, for instance, may explain the various kinds of regulations issued by the Treasury Department, the regulations' numbering scheme, where regulations are published, and how they can be located.

General guides to legal research cover the field broadly and may include sections on specialized but widespread areas, such as employment law or environmental law. Other guides may have a narrower scope, focusing only on a particular area of law or jurisdiction. Still other guides consider a particular research task. For instance, attorneys sometimes want to compare state statutes on an issue. Before diving directly into all fifty states' codes, you could save a significant amount of time if you first check *Subject Compilations of State Laws*, a guide to sources that have already compiled this kind of information.[24]

Research guides are often written by librarians, lawyers, and professors. They may be formally published as books or journal articles or informally published on the web. Whatever source you use, be aware of the date the guide was created. For instance, in the grandparent visitation hypothetical, you could begin your research by consulting M. Kristine Taylor Warren's *Grandparent Visitation Rights: A Legal Research Guide*. Because the book was published in 2001, you will have to update the key statutes and cases it cites. (See Chapter 9 for information about updating.) However, it will still help you understand the scope of the issue, recommend other secondary sources, and provide research tips, including the suggestion to start with a state's statutes.

---

24. *Subject Compilations of State Laws* is available in print volumes and as a database on HeinOnline.

Table 3-5. Selected Internet Sources for Legal Research Guides

Site	Address
Drake University Law Library	http:// http://libguides.law.drake.edu/
University of Iowa Law Library	http://libguides.law.uiowa.edu/
Georgetown Law Library	http://guides.ll.georgetown.edu/home
GlobaLex (international, foreign, and comparative guides)	http://www.nyulawglobal.com/globalex/index.html
University of Washington Gallagher Law Library Legal Research Guides	http://lib.law.washington.edu/ref/guides.html

Ways to access different legal sources change over time, especially as an increasing number of primary law collections become available on the open web. Because legal research guides may be published on the web, as books, or as journal articles, they can be found using the best corresponding search tools: a web search engine, a law library catalog, and law journal article indexes.

1. Finding Guides Using Web Search Engines

Law library web pages and other legal research sites often provide a variety of law-related guides. Table 3-5 includes examples of internet sites for locating legal research guides. Use your favorite search engine to find more web-based guides. Using search terms like *"research guide" or pathfinder or bibliography* along with your subject, e.g., *"environmental law,"* will likely return a large number of potentially valuable resources, as well as some less useful ones. To remove some of the lower quality sites, try adding the term *"law library"* and/or limiting the search to educational domain sites, e.g., *site: .edu* in Google.

2. Finding Guides Using Law Library Catalogs

Search the catalog of an academic law library collection, as described in Chapter 2, to locate research guides published as books or book chapters. (Hint: Use the phrase *"legal research"* as a subject search term along with a keyword for your topic of interest.) Issue-oriented guides range from the broad, such as Albert P. Melone's *Researching Constitutional Law*, to the very narrow, such as Amy R. Stein's *Illegal Sex Discrimination or Permissible Customer Preference?: Refusal to Hire and Employ Male Gynecologists: A Legal Research Guide.*

3. Finding Guides Using Law Journal Article Indexes

Law articles can include research guides. To find these guides, search law journal indexes, described in Section II.D. Search for the area of law of interest and add the subheading *bibliography* or the keywords *"research guide."* For example, conduct a subject search for *Environmental Law — bibliography.*

Chapter 4

The Constitution

I. Introduction

The United States Constitution serves as the country's preeminent legal authority. It establishes the three-branch form of federal government and grants powers to that government. The Iowa Constitution also creates a three-branch system of state government. However, rather than granting power to the state government, Iowa's constitution, like that of most states, imposes limitations on what the state can do.[1] The state legislature must be cognizant of constitutional requirements and avoid enacting laws not permitted under either the federal or state constitutions.

As the supreme law of the state, the Iowa Constitution may be one of the first places for a researcher to look in certain legal situations. For example, if an Iowa citizen thinks his or her rights have been abridged, a review of the provisions in the Iowa Constitution will be an essential first step for the lawyer assessing the case. The Iowa Constitution plays a key role in the development of the law, providing a lens through which the courts consider the validity of legal principles. For example, the Iowa Supreme Court was asked to review a statute setting the requirements for grandparent visitation and ruled that a key provision of the statute violated Article 1 of the Iowa Constitution.[2]

---

1. For example, the U.S. Constitution grants Congress the power to borrow money and regulate commerce (Art. 1, § 8). Some limitations in the Iowa Constitution include the following: each branch of government is prohibited from exercising a function over another (Art. III, § 1), a legislator can't have a lucrative job with the U.S. government (Art. III, § 22) or be collecting public monies (Art. III, § 23), and the legislature cannot grant a divorce (Art. III, § 27).

2. In *Santi v. Santi*, 633 N.W.2d 312 (Iowa 2001), the Court found that Iowa Code § 598.35(7) was unconstitutional on its face because the statute authorized grandparent visits without a threshold finding that the parents were unfit or their decision to deny visits posed substantial harm to the child. The statute could not withstand strict

Table 4-1. Articles of the Iowa Constitution

I.	Bill of Rights
II.	Right of Suffrage
III.	Of the Distribution of Powers
	Legislative Department
IV.	Executive Department
V.	Judicial Department
VI.	Militia
VII.	State Debts
VIII.	Corporations
IX.	Education and School Lands
	1st—Education
	2nd—School Funds and School Lands
X.	Amendments to the Constitution
XI.	Miscellaneous
XII.	Schedule

Even with a number of amendments, Iowa's Constitution of 1857 remains substantially the same as it was when enacted and is one of the older state constitutions still in force.[3] As shown in Table 4-1, twelve articles comprise the Iowa Constitution. These are preceded by a brief preamble and description of the state's geographic boundaries.

II. Historical Context and Constitution of 1857

Over the years, three constitutions have been drafted for Iowa, with two of those being adopted. In drafting each version of the constitution, Iowa legislators examined the federal constitution and the foundational documents of

scrutiny under Art. I, §§ 8, 9. The legislature repealed that provision and replaced it with Iowa Code § 600C.

3. For a brief history of the Iowa Constitution, see the article by Steven C. Cross, *The Drafting of Iowa's Constitution*, in the *Iowa Official Register* at http://publications. iowa.gov/135/1/history/7-6.html.

other states and territories. The geographic area that became Iowa had been founded under the "Organic Act for the Wisconsin Territory,"[4] so that act served as the basis for some of the initial provisions for the Iowa Constitution, including a Bill of Rights.

The first constitution of 1844 was rejected due to a disagreement regarding boundaries. The 1846 constitutional convention produced and approved a document similar in most respects to the rejected 1844 version but modified mainly to adopt the geographic boundaries of Iowa that are in effect today.[5] The 1857 constitutional convention was called to address some deficiencies apparent in the 1846 document, such as the lack of a lieutenant governor and provisions for election of judges. This 1857 version is still the Iowa Constitution, although it has been amended. In 1868 following the Civil War, for example, the first amendments to the constitution were approved by voters, striking the word white preceding the word male in several provisions. This change gave men of color the right to vote, something voters had rejected in 1857.

III. Constitutional Amendments

As detailed in Article 10, the Iowa Constitution can be changed only by amendment initiated in the legislature and approved by voters. In establishing an amendment process in 1857, the drafters of the Iowa Constitution required that amendments first be passed by both houses of the General Assembly and then passed again by both houses in the next elected General Assembly before being submitted to the voters for approval. Because each General Assembly lasts two years, it can take several years for an amendment to reach the voters. This long and sometimes difficult method of amending the constitution may help ensure that an amendment reaching the voters has been thoroughly debated and considered. This long process also makes it possible for voters to reflect on the prior legislature's work and indicate through the ballot box who they want making constitutional decisions for the next legislative session.

Voters have approved 46 amendments, most recently in 1998 when Amendment 45 affirmed equal rights for men and women and Amendment 46 indicated when a grand jury is required. When researching the Iowa Constitution,

---

4. An Act Establishing the Territorial Government of Wisconsin, ch. 54, 5 Stat. 10 (1836).

5. The geographic boundaries in the 1844 version included much of what is currently Minnesota. The 1846 version adjusted the geographic boundaries to those in effect today.

you can choose to review the codified version with the amendments integrated into the text or the original with amendments separately listed at the end. Versions with separate amendments can be found in the *Code of Iowa* or *Iowa Code Annotated*. Both present the amendments in chronological order and are helpful in understanding the historical context of the amendments. In 1988, for example, Amendment 41 provided for the joint election of governor and lieutenant governor, eliminating the possibility that these officials could be from different political parties. Voters in 1992 approved the deletion of the dueling prohibition in Article 1, § 5, which no longer seemed germane.

Interest in amending the Iowa Constitution may sometimes be spurred by hot-button issues of the day. For example, in the 2009 case *Varnum v. Brien*,[6] the Iowa Supreme Court ruled unanimously that an Iowa Code provision prohibiting same-sex marriage violated the equal protection clause of the Iowa Constitution.[7] Following the decision, groups unsuccessfully lobbied the legislature to move forward on a constitutional amendment that would permit marriage only between a man and a woman.

IV. Interpreting the Iowa Constitution

When analyzing the Iowa Constitution and its interpretation by the Iowa Supreme Court, it is helpful to consider how the Iowa Court has interpreted the original intent of the drafters. The Court has emphasized the state motto, which is emblazoned on the state seal and flag and provides: "Our liberties we prize and our rights we will maintain."[8] From that statement, it should come as no surprise that the very first article of the Iowa Constitution is the Bill of Rights. As the Court has interpreted the constitution, it has been mindful of those rights. The Court explained that historical background in the *Varnum* case:[9]

> In [this court's] first reported case . . . , *In re Ralph* (1839), we refused to treat a human being as property to enforce a contract for slavery and held our laws must extend equal protection to persons of all races and conditions. This decision was seventeen years before the United States Supreme Court infamously decided *Dred Scott v. Sandford*, which upheld the rights of a slave owner to treat a person as prop-

---

6. 763 N.W.2d 862 (Iowa 2009).

7. Iowa Const. art. I, § 6.

8. Iowa Code §§ 1A.1, 1B.1 (2009) (cited in *Varnum v. Brien*, 763 N.W.2d 862, 872 (Iowa 2009)).

9. 763 N.W.2d at 877.

erty. Similarly [in 1868 and 1873], we struck blows to the concept of segregation long before . . . *Brown v. Board of Education* (1954). Iowa was also the first state in the nation to admit a woman to the practice of law, doing so in 1869. Her admission occurred three years before the United States Supreme Court affirmed the State of Illinois' decision to *deny* women admission to the practice of law, and twenty-five years before the United States Supreme Court affirmed the refusal of the Commonwealth of Virginia to admit women into the practice of law. In each of those instances, our state approached a fork in the road toward fulfillment of our constitution's ideals and reaffirmed the "absolute equality of all" persons before the law as "the very foundation principle of our government."

Iowa Courts are frequently asked to determine the meaning of the Iowa Constitution. Perhaps the most notable recent exercise of that authority was the *Varnum* case. In that case, Justice Mark Cady discussed the court's role in interpreting the Constitution:

> The Iowa Constitution is the cornerstone of governing in Iowa. * * *
> A statute inconsistent with the Iowa Constitution must be declared void, even though it may be supported by strong and deep-seated traditional beliefs and popular opinion. Iowa Const. art. XII, § 1 (providing any law inconsistent with the constitution is void). * * *
> It is also well established that courts must, under all circumstances, protect the supremacy of the constitution as a means of protecting our republican form of government and our freedoms. As was observed . . . in reference to the United States Constitution, the very purpose of limiting the power of the elected branches of government by constitutional provisions like the Equal Protection Clause is "to withdraw certain subjects from the vicissitudes of political controversy, to place them beyond the reach of majorities and officials and to establish them as legal principles to be applied by the courts." * * *
> In fulfilling this mandate . . . , we look to the past and to precedent. We look backwards, not because citizens' rights are constrained to those previously recognized, but because historical constitutional principles provide the framework to define our future as we confront the challenges of today.
> Our responsibility, however, is to protect constitutional rights of individuals from legislative enactments that have denied those rights, even when the rights have not yet been broadly accepted, were at one

time unimagined, or challenge a deeply ingrained practice or law viewed to be impervious to the passage of time. The framers of the Iowa Constitution knew, as did the drafters of the United States Constitution, that "times can blind us to certain truths and later generations can see that laws once thought necessary and proper in fact serve only to oppress," and as our constitution "endures, persons in every generation can invoke its principles in their own search for greater freedom" and equality. * * *

Finally, it should be recognized that the constitution belongs to the people. . . . While the constitution is the supreme law and cannot be altered by the enactment of an ordinary statute, the power of the constitution flows from the people, and the people of Iowa retain the ultimate power to shape it over time. *See* Iowa Const. art. X.[10]

V. Researching the Iowa Constitution

As the supreme law of the state, the Iowa Constitution is the definitive source in many areas of the law. The Iowa Constitution's twelve articles outline the rights of the people and the structure of government. If a topic of law you are investigating could be governed by the constitution, you need to know that early in the research process.

The first article contains the Bill of Rights and includes many provisions also found in the U.S. Constitution. Table 4-2 notes which Iowa provisions correspond to those in the federal constitution. This table can be helpful as you look for cases interpreting a provision.

The Iowa Constitution can be found in a number of sources in print and online. Annotated versions are among the most helpful because they include a court's interpretation of constitutional provisions and other explanatory materials. The following sections will explain those sources.

A. Print Sources for the Iowa Constitution

1. *Iowa Code Annotated*

An excellent starting point for researching the Iowa Constitution is West's *Iowa Code Annotated* (ICA), which includes the constitution in the first two volumes. The ICA includes the current constitution and its amendments with annotations of cases interpreting the constitution. Volume 2 provides numerous

---

10. *Id.* at 875–76.

Table 4-2. Iowa Bill of Rights and Corresponding
U.S. Constitutional Provisions

Article 1. Iowa Bill of Rights	U.S. Constitution
§ 1. Rights of persons.	Amendments 1, 5, & 14 § 1
§ 2. Political power.	
§ 3. Religion.	Amendment 1
§ 4. Religious test—witnesses.	Article 6, clause 3
§ 5. Dueling. [Repealed]	
§ 6. Laws uniform.	Amendment 14 (equal protection); Article 4 § 2 (privileges and immunities)
§ 7. Liberty of speech and press.	Amendment 1
§ 8. Personal security—searches and seizures.	Amendment 4
§ 9. Right of trial by jury—due process of law.	Amendments 5 & 1 § 1 (due process); Amendment 6 & Article 3 § 2 (jury trial)
§ 10. Rights of persons accused.	Amendments 7 (jury trial) & 6 (speedy trial)
§ 11. When indictment necessary —grand jury.	Amendment 5
§ 12. Twice tried—bail.	Amendment 5 (double jeopardy)
§ 13. Habeas corpus.	Article 1 § 9
§ 14. Military.	Article 1 § 8; Article 6 § 1 et seq.; Amendment 2
§ 15. Quartering soldiers.	Amendment 3
§ 16. Treason.	Article 3 § 3; Article 4 § 3
§ 17. Bail—punishments.	Amendment 8
§ 18. Eminent domain—drainage ditches and levees.	Amendments 5 (just compensation) & 14 § 1 (limits on state power)
§ 19. Imprisonment for debt.	
§ 20. Right of assemblage— petition.	Amendment 1
§ 21. Attainder—ex post facto law —obligation of contract.	Article 1 §§ 9–10
§ 22. Resident aliens.	Article 6 (treaties are supreme law of the land)
§ 23. Slavery—penal servitude.	Amendments 13–14
§ 24. Agricultural leases.	
§ 25. Rights reserved.	

historical documents, including the 1846 and 1857 constitutions as originally enacted.

The comprehensive index in the back of volume 2 directs you to relevant provisions. The volume also includes a separate index to the U.S. Constitution, so be sure to select the one for the Iowa Constitution. When you look for a topic, such as freedom of speech, the index refers to the provision that is applicable, such as Const. Art. 1, § 7. Retrieve the provision and carefully read the actual language of the text. Then consult the annotations, which will help you understand the way the text has been applied. Figure 4-1 illustrates a single section of the Iowa Constitution in ICA, followed by its annotations as explained below.

As illustrated in Figure 4-1, following the original text is a *Historical Note* helping identify the origin of the section and *Cross References* to related sections of interest. The heading for *Law Review and Journal Commentaries* is next with a list of articles on the topic, primarily from Iowa-based periodicals, such as the *Drake Law Review* and the *Iowa Law Review*. Entries under *Library References* then indicate where to find similar information in other West resources, such as using the topic and key number in a digest or on Westlaw or consulting legal encyclopedias such as *Corpus Juris Secundum* (CJS). *Research References* guides you to ALR annotations and treatises, such as the *Iowa Practice Series*, that may be helpful. For the Bill of Rights sections, there also may be a heading for the *United States Code Annotated* (USCA) noting the corresponding sections in the United States Constitution volumes of the USCA. The following heading may be of related decisions by the *United States Supreme Court*.

The final heading, called *Notes of Decisions*, is one of the most important sections in the annotations. Here you find annotations for relevant cases interpreting that section of the constitution. The notes begin with a table of contents of the decisions showing their organization by subject. As an example, assume a church and its members are disputing who owns the church property. You check the Iowa Constitution and find that Section 3 of the Bill of Rights covers religion. When you look at the *Notes of Decisions* under that section, as illustrated in Figure 4-1, one of the entry headings is "Church property disputes" followed by the number 22. You could then skim through case summaries in the notes until you see the bold-faced heading for **22 Church property disputes**, which would have annotations of the key cases on the topic. Figure 4-2 provides an example of a case annotation. That annotation ends with a reference to the relevant digest topic and key number, Religious Societies ⇐ 23(3), so that you could find additional cases on church property issues in the *Iowa Digest* (discussed in Chapter 5) or on Westlaw.

Figure 4-1. Excerpt of Iowa Constitution from *Iowa Code Annotated* v. 1

Iowa Constitution Art. 1, § 3. Religion

The General Assembly shall make no law respecting an establishment of religion, or prohibiting the free exercise thereof; nor shall any person be compelled to attend any place of worship, pay tithes, taxes, or other rates for building or repairing places of worship, or the maintenance of any minister, or ministry.

Historical Note

Prior Constitution: Const.1846, Art. 1, § 3.

Cross References

Compulsory education, attendance requirements, exceptions for religious services or instructions, see § 299.2.

* * *

University of Iowa not to be under control of religious denomination, see § 263.1

Law Review and Journal Commentaries

Attorney's right to religious freedom: A critical look at the clerical collar. 61 Iowa L.Rev. 899 (1976).

Contempt—enforcement of divorce decree—duty to raise child in particular religion. 42 Iowa L.Rev. 617 (1957).

* * *

Library References

Constitutional Law ⟵ 1295, 1303.

Westlaw Topic No. 92.

C.J.S. Constitutional Law §§ 750 to 758.

Research References

ALR Library

26 ALR 6th 145, State Constitutional Challenges to the Display of Religious Symbols on Public Property.

* * *

Source: Iowa Code Annotated. Published with permission of West, a Thomson Reuters business.

Figure 4-1. Excerpt of Iowa Constitution from *Iowa Code Annotated* v. 1,
continued

Treatises and Practice Aids

4A Iowa Practice Series § 36:1, Scope of the First and Second Amendments.

Restatement (2d) of Property, Don. Trans. § 8.1, Provisions Concerning Religion.

United States Code Annotated

Freedom of religion, see U.S.C.A. Const. Amend. 1.

United State Supreme Court

Charitable tax deductions, payments for religious auditing and training services, see Hernandez v. C.I.R., 1989, 109 S.Ct. 2136, 490 U.S. 680, 104 L.Ed.2d 766.

Colleges and universities, funding of student newspapers with Christian editorial viewpoint, see Rosenberger v. Rector and Visitors of University of Virginia, 1995, 115 S.Ct. 2510, 515 U.S. 819, 132 L.Ed.2d 700.

* * *

Notes of Decisions

Burden of proof, government aid 14, 20

Church property disputes 22

Construction and application 1

* * *

Figure 4-2. Sample Case Annotation from ICA

---

22 Church property disputes

Where provisions of constitution of hierarchical church gave hierarchical church exclusive ultimate control of uses and disposition of local church property, . . . hierarchical church could properly take over local church government to control use and disposition of local church property after local church disaffiliated itself from hierarchical church. Fonken v. Community Church of Kamrar, 1983, 339 N.W.2d 810. Religious Societies ☞ 23(3)

Source: Iowa Code Annotated. Published with permission of West, a Thomson Reuters business.

After finding a case that appears to be helpful, retrieve the full text of the case. Read the entire case to ensure that the editorial summary in the annotation accurately reported the decision and to fully understand and analyze the wording of the court. See Chapter 5 for more detailed information on researching and analyzing case law.

As with other ICA volumes, the constitution volume is supplemented by an annual pocket part in the back of the volume and an interim pamphlet between the annual publication dates. Checking that supplementation is essential to make sure new cases or changes are not overlooked. See Chapter 6 for more detailed information about publication formats and research information on the *Iowa Code Annotated.*

2. Code of Iowa

The official *Code of Iowa* is published by the state and includes the codified 1857 Constitution as well as the original 1857 Constitution and the amendments presented separately. However, the *Code of Iowa* does not contain the case annotations, cross-references, law review citations, and other tools found in the ICA. Thus, it is a less helpful research tool.

B. Free Online Sources of the Iowa Constitution

Several websites provide access to the Iowa Constitution free of charge. The Iowa General Assembly website[11] is one of the easiest to use. The constitution and historical information can also be found in the *Iowa Official Register* at the Iowa Publications Online website.[12] Copies of the original constitution also can be found in books that have been digitized to the web, such as Shambaugh's *Constitution of the State of Iowa.*[13] The state also has digitized the *Debates of the Constitutional Convention,* so those documents are easily accessible.[14]

C. The Iowa Constitution in Westlaw, Lexis, and Bloomberg Law

1. Finding Relevant Provisions

Westlaw and Lexis provide ready access to the Iowa Constitution, including annotations. In most instances, you would choose the annotated version of the database to also access cases interpreting the Iowa Constitution. On Westlaw, the Iowa Constitution is found in the statutory databases and cor-

---

11. The legislature's website provides access to the Iowa Constitution on its Iowa Law page at https://www.legis.iowa.gov/law/statutory/constitution.

12. The address is http://publications.iowa.gov/id/eprint/16716. Print editions of the *Official Iowa Register* are referred to as the "Redbook."

13. See Google Books for several of these works on the Iowa Constitution at http://books.google.com/books.

14. The address is http://www.statelibraryofiowa.org/services/collections/law-library/iaconst.

responds to the print *Iowa Code Annotated*.[15] Once you click open the constitution, the Table of Contents allows you to see the headings and find sections and subsections of the constitution. If you want to retrieve a specific section of the constitution, you can do that from Westlaw's search box as well (e.g., enter *ia const art 1 s 1* to retrieve Const. Art. 1, § 1.).

In Lexis, you can use the browse sources function or enter Iowa Constitution in the red search box, then select the identified source "IA- LexisNexis Iowa Annotated Constitution." By selecting the Table of Contents link and opening menus, you will find checkboxes to help you easily narrow your search to particular articles or sections. Otherwise, you can add the Iowa Constitution as a filter or choose to "Get Documents" and then search the entire constitution.

Bloomberg Law provides the text of the Iowa Constitution by going to State Law > Iowa > Iowa Legislative > Iowa Constitution. Annotations are not provided.

2. Using a Citator

You always want to make sure that you find the most current authorities interpreting the Iowa Constitution. Shepard's on Lexis and KeyCite on Westlaw provide cases and other authorities citing the Iowa Constitution and can be used to make sure any cases you find are still good law. Bloomberg Law's BCite can be used for court opinions but not for the Iowa Constitution. Some researchers find it helpful to use a citator early in their research once they locate a relevant provision of the constitution. Doing so gives them a quick overview of the authorities interpreting that part of the constitution. Chapter 9 provides more details on using citators. After searching for cases interpreting the Iowa Constitution, whether via citator or otherwise, you may want to look for federal cases on the topic; as shown in Table 4-2 some provisions are similar in both constitutions.

The Welch Matter

As noted in Section I of this chapter, the Iowa Supreme Court declared unconstitutional a prior statute regarding grandparents' visitation rights. In the Welch hypothetical introduced in Chapter 1, you are representing a client on such a matter.

---

15. From the Westlaw homepage go to: State Materials > Iowa > Iowa Statutes & Court Rules > Constitution of the State of Iowa (Annotated).

Table 4-3. Selected Websites Providing Access to the U.S. Constitution

Cornell's Legal Information Institute	http://topics.law.cornell.edu/constitution
— offers an annotated constitution	
FindLaw	http://constitution.findlaw.com
— features extensive annotations and hyperlinks	
GPO FDsys	http://www.gpo.gov/fdsys/browse/collec tiontab.action
— analysis and interpretations include case annotations	
Congressional Constitution Caucus	http://congressionalconstitutioncaucus-garrett.house.gov/resources/us-constitution
— analysis and interpretations include link to Heritage Guide	

As such, you may want to research the Iowa Constitution to understand the provisions the court believed the earlier law violated.

If you start in Westlaw's "Iowa Statutes and Court Rules" database, the *Iowa Code Annotated* equivalent, you might run this search: *grandparent /3 visitation*. Two results are citations to the Iowa Constitution (Sections 8 and 9 of Article I). Those documents reference the aforementioned Iowa case involving grandparent rights: *Santi v. Santi*, 633 N.W.2d 312 (Iowa 2001). You can read that case to learn what the constitutional issues were with that Iowa statute and with one mouse click you find the current statute on grandparent visitation.

VI. United States Constitution

The United States Constitution can be found in volume 1 of the *Code of Iowa* and Volume 2 of the *Iowa Code Annotated*. An index to the U.S. Constitution follows the index to the Iowa Constitution in the back of ICA volume 2. Researching the U.S. Constitution is perhaps best approached using an annotated version which includes cases interpreting the provisions. The *United States Code Annotated* (USCA) and *United States Code Service* (USCS) provide that coverage in their initial volumes. Comparable versions can be found online on Westlaw (USCA > Constitution) and Lexis (Browse for USCS Constitution). On Bloomberg Law the text of the U.S. Constitution can be found by going to Federal Law > Federal Legislative > U.S. Constitution. Table 4-3 details some reliable websites that provide access to the U.S. Constitution.

Chapter 5

Judicial Opinions, Reporters, and Digests

I. Introduction

The United States and individual states, including Iowa, operate under the *common law system*, in which established court decisions help determine future court decisions.[1] In contrast, the *civil law system* is primarily based on legislation. The common law system originated in England and spread to those countries England settled or controlled. The civil law system, based on Roman law, predominates in continental Europe and other Western countries.[2]

Case law refers to the body of prior court decisions.[3] In the common law system, previously decided cases have *precedent*, meaning prior courts' decisions on similar questions or issues influence how current courts rule on those same issues. Note, however, that not all decisions become precedent. Only cases a court designates for publication become binding authority for the jurisdiction in which the case was decided.[4] The researcher can be fairly confident precedent will be upheld due to the doctrine of *stare decisis*, which compels courts to abide by or adhere to previously decided cases. This doctrine also allows the court system to be fairly confident that people in similar situations are treated the same under the law.

---

1. Common law is defined as "[t]he body of law derived from judicial decisions, rather than from statutes or constitutions." *Black's Law Dictionary* 334 (Bryan A. Garner ed., 10th ed. 2014).

2. Note that Louisiana developed under French rule and operates under a mixture of civil and common law.

3. Caselaw is defined as "the law to be found in the collection of reported cases that form all or part of the body of law within a given jurisdiction." *Black's Law Dictionary* 259 (Bryan A. Garner ed., 10th ed. 2014).

4. "Opinions designated 'not for publication', even though available on Lexis and Westlaw, are not binding precedents or even persuasive authority." Neil Duxbury, *The Nature and Authority of Precedent* 6 n. 12 (2008).

Although most legal research projects typically require an examination of case law at some point in the process, researchers do not often begin the research process with case law, beginning instead with secondary sources, as discussed in Chapter 3. This is especially true in situations when the researcher is not familiar with the applicable area of law.

This chapter describes the structure of the state and federal court systems, expanding on the brief introduction in Chapter 1, Section IV, and the organization of published court opinions in reporters. It also explains how to find relevant cases on a legal issue using print digests. The chapter also addresses electronic research sources including Lexis, Westlaw, Bloomberg Law, Fastcase, and Google Scholar. Finally, the chapter briefly addresses how to access cases for relevance.

II. Court Systems

To find case law effectively, a researcher must first understand the structure of the court system both in Iowa and in the United States. Whether at the federal or state level, the basic court structure moves from the trial court level to the intermediate court of appeals, and finally to the ultimate appellate court, often, but not always, called the "supreme" court. The *jurisdiction* of the trial court — the authority of the court to issue decisions — may be based on geography (e.g., U.S. District Courts on the federal level or county courts on the state level) or subject (e.g., U.S. Tax Courts, state family courts, or probate courts).

A. Iowa Courts

Iowa's trial courts are known as *district courts*. Iowa has two appellate courts: the Court of Appeals and the Supreme Court. The website for the Iowa judiciary[5] contains a great deal of information, including judicial opinions, court rules and forms, a map of Iowa's judicial districts, an explanation of court structure, and information about jury service.

1. Iowa District Courts

Iowa's district courts serve as the state's trial courts. There is one district court in each of Iowa's 99 counties; the counties are organized into eight judicial districts for administrative purposes.[6] Each of the eight judicial districts

---

5. The website for the Iowa Judicial Branch is http://www.iowacourts.gov.

6. A map of the districts is available at http://www.iowacourts.gov/About_the _Courts/District_Courts/.

has a chief judge who is appointed by the Iowa Supreme Court. District courts have *general jurisdiction*, authorizing them to hear all civil and criminal cases.[7] District courts have divisions for Juvenile Court, Probate Court, and Small Claims. Different types of judges in the district court system have varying amounts of jurisdiction. District Judges have general jurisdiction over all types of cases in the district courts. Judicial officers with more *limited jurisdiction*, authorizing them to hear only certain types of cases, include District Associate Judges, Associate Juvenile Judges, Associate Probate Judges, and Judicial Magistrates.

2. Iowa Court of Appeals

The Iowa Court of Appeals is an intermediate appellate court that consists of nine judges who are appointed by the governor and confirmed to six-year terms by election after they have served for one year. The Court of Appeals typically hears cases in Des Moines in panels of three judges. Cases come to the Court of Appeals from the Iowa Supreme Court, which transfers certain district court cases that have been appealed. The majority of district court appeals are decided by the Court of Appeals, and its decisions are final unless reviewed by the Iowa Supreme Court on grant of further review. Some of the opinions of the Iowa Court of Appeals are published and become precedent for subsequent cases.

3. Iowa Supreme Court

The Iowa Supreme Court is an appellate court consisting of seven justices who are appointed by the governor and confirmed to eight-year terms by judicial election once they have served for one year. The Iowa Supreme Court hears cases *en banc*—with all justices present—typically in Des Moines. As the *court of last resort* in Iowa, it hears the final appeals of cases in the state, and its opinions are binding on all other Iowa state courts. The court also admits attorneys to practice in Iowa and is responsible for prescribing rules on attorney conduct and for disciplining attorneys. The court promulgates rules of procedure and practice used in the state court system. It also has supervisory and administrative authority over the judicial branch and its officers and employees.

---

7. District courts have jurisdiction over all matters unless specifically accorded by the legislature. Iowa Code § 602.6101 (2015) (noting that "[t]he district court has exclusive, general, and original jurisdiction of all actions, proceedings, and remedies, civil, criminal, probate, and juvenile, except in cases where exclusive or concurrent jurisdiction is conferred upon some other court, tribunal, or administrative body").

B. Federal Courts

Trial courts in the federal judicial system are called United States District Courts. There are ninety-four federal judicial districts, including at least one district in each state, as well as the District of Columbia and Puerto Rico. Some states are subdivided into smaller geographic regions, while others are not. The entire state of Minnesota, for example, makes up the federal District of Minnesota. Iowa, in contrast, has two federal districts. The United States District Court for the Northern District of Iowa[8] has jurisdiction over fifty-two of Iowa's ninety-nine counties. It is headquartered in Cedar Rapids, with a satellite facility in Sioux City. The United States District Court for the Southern District of Iowa[9] has jurisdiction over forty-seven of Iowa's ninety-nine counties. It is headquartered in Des Moines, with satellite facilities in Council Bluffs and Davenport. Cases from both the Northern and Southern Districts of Iowa are appealed to the United States Court of Appeals for the Eighth Circuit.

The federal courts are administratively structured in thirteen circuits, each of which has its own United States Court of Appeals, the intermediate appellate court that hears appeals from federal agencies and district courts.[10] Twelve of the circuits are regional. Iowa is in the Eighth Federal Circuit, which also includes Arkansas, Minnesota, Missouri, Nebraska, North Dakota, and South Dakota.[11] The thirteenth circuit, the Federal Circuit, hears cases from throughout the nation arising in specialized subjects, such as patents and international trade.

The United States Supreme Court is the nation's highest court. It stands at the head of the judicial branch and provides the ultimate interpretation of the U.S. Constitution and federal statutes, although not on matters of state law as stated in Chapter 1. The website for the federal judiciary contains much useful information such as maps, addresses, definitions, and more.[12]

---

8. The website for the United States District Court for the Northern District of Iowa is http://www.iand.uscourts.gov.

9. The website for the United States District Court for the Southern District of Iowa is http://www.iasd.uscourts.gov.

10. There are eleven numbered circuits covering all the states as well as a twelfth circuit for the District of Columbia. A map of the circuits is available at http://www.uscourts.gov/about-federal-courts/federal-courts-public/court-website-links and may also be found at the front of bound volumes for both the *Federal Supplement* and the *Federal Reporter*.

11. The website for the Eighth Circuit is http://www.ca8.uscourts.gov.

12. The website is http://www.uscourts.gov.

C. Courts of Other States

While the court systems of many states follow the three-tier system of Iowa and the federal judiciary, some deviate from this structure. Some states, such as Rhode Island and South Dakota, do not have an intermediate appellate court.[13] In New York and Maryland, the highest court is the Court of Appeals; also in New York, the "supreme" court is the trial level court. In Maine and Massachusetts, the highest court is the Supreme Judicial Court.

When working with an unfamiliar jurisdiction, verify the court structure and hierarchy. Court websites and citation manuals are both excellent references for locating this information, as discussed in Chapter 1.

III. Published Case Law[14]

When appellate courts decide cases, they usually write opinions that summarize the facts of the case, detail existing laws, and explain how and why they resolved the case.[15] More specifically, opinions usually contain the following information, although not necessarily in this order: an introduction to the case where the court may briefly discuss key facts and issues; a statement of the case, which includes the facts of the case and its procedural history; a statement of the issues the court will address; the applicable law, which may also include previously decided cases; an analysis of the case; and the disposition of the case, which includes the court's resolution of the case and how that may affect other courts in its jurisdiction.

If the opinion is written by a majority of judges, it will be referred to as a *majority opinion*. Judges who do not share the majority opinion may write a *concurring* or *dissenting opinion*. A concurring opinion means that the judge agrees with the decision but for different reasons than those stated in the majority opinion. A dissenting opinion means a judge does not agree with the majority.

---

13. Iowa did not have an intermediate appellate court until 1977.

14. This Section notes many sources for judicial opinions, including freely accessible websites whose addresses may change. For this reason, it can be helpful to consult an online research guide that indicates sources of case law. Unlike a book, online guides can be easily updated to reflect changes. The Drake Law Library offers a case law guide at http://libguides.law.drake.edu/caselaw.

15. Trial courts may also issue such detailed opinions. However, particularly at the state level, trial courts may also issue decisions in an abbreviated form that does not include detailed analysis of how the court came to its conclusion but simply reports the jury verdict or judge's findings.

Significantly, the vast majority of court cases are unpublished, in the sense that they are not printed in case reporters or available as precedent even if found online.[16] This is especially true of state trial court cases. If you want to read the decision of a highly publicized trial, there is likely no "published" decision as such. There may be a brief court order or memorandum in the case file. A trial transcript may or may not be included in the case file. You must contact the clerk of court directly to find out whether they will allow you to copy or view the file. Docket information — the official schedule of proceedings in a court of law — may be available in federal cases through PACER,[17] which may also provide access to court documents, and in Iowa through Iowa Courts Online.[18] In addition, Bloomberg Law provides docket access to federal courts and many state courts, not including Iowa.[19]

Published cases are released in three stages: slip opinions, advance sheets, and reporters. These are explained more fully in the following sections. Today, most legal researchers access case law electronically as either slip opinions or in their final form, similar to the opinion you would find in a print reporter.

A. Slip Opinions

A case first appears as a *slip opinion*. These are individual pamphlets issued directly by the court that are published as a single opinion. Slip opinions are often freely available from court websites but do not have any editorial information that can help the researcher determine the court's intent or highlight the legal issues addressed. Slip opinions can also be difficult to cite because they do not have final page numbers and may be referred to by their *docket number*.[20]

B. Advance Sheets

In print, slip opinions released for publication are compiled into a softcover book called an *advance sheet*. When most researchers relied on print reporters, advance sheets served the important purpose of making opinions

---

16. Although unpublished opinions are not binding authority, they can still be cited in a brief. Barry A. Lindahl, 12 *Iowa Practice: Civil and Appellate Procedure* § 45:5 (2015 ed.).

17. PACER's website is http://www.pacer.gov.

18. Iowa Courts Online can be accessed at http://www.iowacourts.state.ia.us.

19. Follow this path on Bloomberg Law: Home > Dockets.

20. A docket number is a unique number that identifies a specific case on the court's calendar.

more quickly accessible, in advance of the publication of the reporters. Today electronic case law sources tend to serve this purpose. If you do need to use an advance sheet, know that page numbers of advance sheets mirror the page numbers of bound reporters so, if you cite to a case in an advance sheet, that citation will also be accurate for the reporter.

C. Reporters

The contents of multiple advance sheets are compiled into a bound *reporter.* Once the reporter has been published, most libraries and law firms discard the advance sheets. Reporter volumes are consecutively numbered. When the volumes of an initial reporter reach an arbitrary number, such as 300, the publisher starts over with volume 1, second series. Some reporters are now in their third or later series. Reporters include editorial features that make it easier to find and understand the decision. See Section III.C.1 for an example.

Two types of reporters are published: official and unofficial. State and federal governments designate the *official reporters* for their judicial opinions. Originally these tended to be published by the governments themselves, and there was often a large time delay between when a case was decided and when the decision was officially published. To remedy this situation, in the 1880s the West Publishing Company began publishing *unofficial reporters* that cover the state and federal courts in the United States. These publications comprise the National Reporter System. Sometimes decisions are published in both official and unofficial reporters; other times a state may give up publishing its own reporter and designate a commercial source as its official reporter. For instance, Rules 21.22 and 21.23 of the Iowa Court Rules designate West[21] as the publisher of the official opinions of the Iowa Supreme Court and Iowa Court of Appeals. Other states may only release their official case reports electronically, as Nebraska began doing in 2016.[22]

Unlike official reporters published by a state and only covering that state, the National Reporter System divides the fifty states into seven regions. Under the reporter system, each region has a separate reporter that contains opinions from the states' highest court and courts of appeals.[23] The seven regions

---

21. Thomson Reuters owns West.

22. Nebraska took this path, in part, to facilitate public access to its court opinions. See https://supremecourt.nebraska.gov/17389/access-court-opinions-expands for more information.

23. In California and New York intermediate appellate cases have separate reporters. The *Pacific Reporter* contains Supreme Court opinions from California, but

Table 5-1. West's National Reporter System

Regional Reporter	Abbrevia- tions	States Included
Atlantic Reporter	A., A.2d, A.3d	Connecticut, Delaware, District of Colum- bia, Maine, Maryland, New Hampshire, New Jersey, Pennsylvania, Rhode Island, and Vermont
North Eastern Reporter	N.E., N.E.2d, N.E.3d	Illinois, Indiana, Massachusetts, New York, and Ohio
North Western Reporter	N.W., N.W.2d	Iowa, Michigan, Minnesota, Nebraska, North Dakota, South Dakota, and Wisconsin
Pacific Reporter	P., P.2d, P.3d	Alaska, Arizona, California, Colorado, Hawaii, Idaho, Kansas, Montana, Nevada, New Mexico, Oklahoma, Oregon, Utah, Washington, and Wyoming
South Eastern Reporter	S.E., S.E.2d	Georgia, North Carolina, South Carolina, Virginia, and West Virginia
South Western Reporter	S.W., S.W.2d, S.W.3d	Arkansas, Kentucky, Missouri, Tennessee, and Texas
Southern Reporter	So., So. 2d, So. 3d	Alabama, Florida, Louisiana, and Mississippi

are Atlantic, North Eastern, North Western, Pacific, Southern, South Eastern, and South Western. See Table 5-1 for the states included in each region. Note that the coverage of each regional reporter is not the same as the composition of the federal circuits. For example, Michigan and Wisconsin are included with Iowa in the *North Western Reporter* but are not in the same federal circuit as Iowa. Iowa is in the Eighth Circuit while Michigan and Wisconsin are in the Sixth and Seventh Circuits, respectively.

---

the *West California Reporter* has both the California Supreme Court and California intermediate appellate court opinions. The *North Eastern Reporter* contains decisions for the Court of Appeals (the state's highest court) from New York, and the *New York Supplement* has both the New York Court of Appeals opinions as well as the opinions of New York's intermediate appellate courts.

To find a case in a reporter, you must have a citation, e.g., 484 N.W.2d 864.[24] See Table 5-1 for a list of regional reporter abbreviations. In order to locate a case without a citation, you can begin your research with a digest or online, as described in Section IV of this chapter.

1. Features of a Reported Case

A case printed in a reporter, or available through a database such as West-law, contains the text of the court opinion. However, it also contains editorial enhancements that can aid researchers. Some of the information is gathered from court records while other information is written by the publisher's editorial staff. Cases found online on other legal research platforms may include similar editorial enhancements or they may only offer the text of the opinion.

The following description refers to the *North Western Reporter 2d*. It may be helpful for you to consult a volume while reading this description. Figure 5-1 shows a case as it appears in N.W.2d (the numbers in boxes in Figure 5-1 correspond to the bracketed numbers below). Figure 5-2 shows the same case as it appears on Westlaw. Editorial enhancements will be different, and sometimes absent, in official reporters and in non-West publications and databases; however, the text of the opinion will be identical.[25]

Citation information. {1} Above the text is the title of the case along with citation information. You need this citation information to refer to the case in legal documents.

Parties and procedural designations. {2} At the beginning of the case, all parties are listed with their procedural designations.

Docket numbers. {3} The number assigned to a case by the court is called a docket number. Docket numbers can aid in locating briefs, court orders, and other documents related to the case. Sometimes these materials are available in online databases; other times you need to contact the court directly. When citing to a published case, you do not cite the docket number, but rather the reporter citation.

Court and date information. {4} The name of the court that decided the case as well as the date it was decided appear below the docket number.

---

24. As explained in Chapter 2, 484 is the volume, N.W.2d refers to the *North Western Reporter* 2d series, and 864 is the page number.

25. In the rare case that a discrepancy does exist between the text of a case in an official reporter and an unofficial reporter or database, the official reporter is the final authority.

Figure 5-1. Case Excerpt from *North Western Reporter 2d*

IN RE MARRIAGE OF HOWARD   Iowa **183**
Cite as 661 N.W.2d 183 (Iowa 2003)

after the settlement will be free from a claim of indemnity by the employer or its insurer.

V. Conclusion.

We conclude a settlement under section 85.35 bars an employer's or insurer's statutory right to indemnification under section 85.22(1). We reverse the judgment of the district court and remand the case for entry of judgment for Stanley.

REVERSED AND REMANDED.

All justices concur except CARTER, J., who takes no part.

🔑 KEY NUMBER SYSTEM

In re the MARRIAGE OF Charitie
S. HOWARD and Dennis M.
Howard, Jr.

Upon the Petition of Charitie
S. Howard, **Appellant,**

and

Concerning Dennis M. Howard,
Jr., **Respondent,**

Dennis Howard, Sr., and Connie
Howard, **Intervenors–
Appellees.**

No. 02–0211.

Supreme Court of Iowa.

May 7, 2003.

Ex-wife appealed from decision of the District Court for Polk County, George W. Bergeson, J., granting paternal grandparents visitation. The Supreme Court, Cady, J., held that section of the grandparent

visitation statute permitting a petition for grandparent visitation when the parents of a child are divorced failed on its face to comport with the due process clause.

Reversed and dismissed.

1. Child Custody ⇐4

Supreme Court would apply strict scrutiny analysis when determining if section of grandparent visitation statute, permitting a petition for grandparent visitation when the parents of a child are divorced, was unconstitutional. I.C.A. § 598.35, subd. 1.

2. Child Custody ⇐4

Because section of grandparent visitation statute permitting a petition for visitation when the parents of a child are divorced interfered with a fundamental interest, a compelling interest of the State had to be demonstrated for the section to withstand constitutional scrutiny. I.C.A. § 598.35, subd. 1.

3. Parent and Child ⇐1

Divorce can alter the decision-making ability of parents to a point that may generate a sufficient state interest to intervene in areas not affecting fundamental rights, or to invoke the need for special considerations to protect children.

4. Child Custody ⇐8

Divorce, by necessity, permits the State to intervene to resolve immediate and direct disputes that arise between parents over custody and visitation.

5. Child Custody ⇐8

Divorce is not the sine qua non of a compelling state interest when non-parents seek to challenge parental decision-making; instead, a compelling state interest arises when substantial harm or potential harm is visited upon children.

Source: In re Marriage of Howard, 661 N.W.2d 183, 185 (Iowa 2003). Published with permission of West, a Thomson Reuters business.

Figure 5-1. Case Excerpt from *North Western Reporter 2d, continued*

IN RE MARRIAGE OF HOWARD   Iowa **185**
Cite as 661 N.W.2d 183 (Iowa 2003)

tion of fitness to parents rendered it unconstitutional on its face. I.C.A. § 598.35, subd. 1.

―――――

West Codenotes

Held Unconstitutional
I.C.A. §598.35(1).

Recognized as Unconstitutional
I.C.A. §598.35(7).

―――――

Anjela A. Shutts of Whitfield & Eddy, P.L.C., Des Moines, for appellant.

Eric R. Eshelman, Des Moines, for appellees.

CADY, Justice.

In *Santi v. Santi*, 633 N.W.2d 312 (Iowa 2001), we determined that at least one subsection of the Iowa grandparent visitation statute was unconstitutional on its face. In this appeal, we revisit the question of the statute's constitutionality to determine whether the section of the statute permitting a petition for grandparent visitation when the parents of a child are divorced is also unconstitutional. We conclude that it is unconstitutional on its face, and we reverse the decision of the district court and dismiss this petition for grandparent visitation.

I. Background Facts and Proceedings.

Delainey Howard (Delainey) was born on April 28, 1999. Her parents, Charitie

Howard (Charitie) and Dennis Howard, Jr., (Dennis) were in the process of dissolving their marriage. The pending dissolution prompted Dennis' parents, Connie and Dennis Howard, Sr., (Howards) to file a petition for grandparent visitation to establish their right to visitation with Delainey. *See* Iowa Code § 598.35(1) (permitting a petition for grandparent visitation when "[t]he parents of the child are divorced."). A final decree was issued in the dissolution action on February 16, 2000. One of the issues decided by the decree was the visitation arrangement under which Dennis and the Howards were to have subsequent contact with Delainey. The district court granted Dennis joint legal custody and unsupervised visitation, but made the exercise of his visitation right contingent on his resumption of drug treatment and counseling. The court did not grant the Howards independent visitation, choosing instead to allow them visitation through their son.

Unfortunately, Dennis failed to pursue drug treatment and counseling as ordered. In March 2000, Charitie filed an application to alter his visitation privileges. In response, the Howards filed a motion for intervention, requesting again that they be granted visitation independent of their son. The district court ordered Charitie and Dennis to participate in mediation to settle on an agreeable revised visitation schedule.[1] When Dennis failed to show for the mediation, the court put in place its own supervised visitation schedule that again did not provide for independent visitation for the Howards. The visitation alteration made no real difference to Dennis—his

1. At this point in the proceedings, Charitie had already appealed from the court's original decree order. Therefore, the court concluded it no longer had jurisdiction to rule on the Howards' request for enhanced visitation because they sought to intervene in a matter

that was the subject of a pending appeal. Charitie eventually dismissed her appeal, at which time the Howards filed an application for modification of the decree of dissolution as it related to grandparent visitation.

Figure 5-2. Case Excerpt from Westlaw

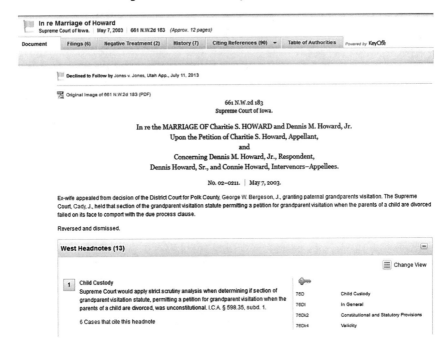

Source: In re Marriage of Howard, 661 N.W.2d 183 (Iowa 2003) on Westlaw. Published with permission of West, a Thomson Reuters business.

Background. {5} This is a brief synopsis of the case as written by the editors at West. As this information is not from the court, you should never cite or quote to background information as primary authority.

Holdings. This is another West editorial addition that is not always present. For instance, there are no holdings in Figure 5-1. A *holding* is the legal principle or principles derived from the opinion. In a reporter, West may summarize these holdings in a bullet point or number format. The same citation warning for background information applies here as well.

Headnotes. {6} A headnote is a sentence or short paragraph that sets out a single point of law in a case. The headnote is then assigned a preexisting West topic and key number (explained in Section IV.A.1) that enables researchers to easily find cases on that point of law. Most cases will have more than one headnote.

Attorney Information. {7} The names of the attorneys who argued the case are listed before the official opinion of the case.

Opinion. {8} The name of the judge who wrote the opinion is followed by the official text of the case as originally reported by the court. This text is primary authority and can be cited as such.

The Welch Matter

As noted in Chapter 4, in the *Santi* case, the Iowa Supreme Court declared unconstitutional part of an Iowa statute on grandparents' visitation rights. A few years later, the court revisited the issue in *Howard*, which effectively overturned Iowa Code § 598.35. Figures 5-1 and 5-2 illustrate this seminal decision. Figure 5-1 shows the decision as it is printed in the *North Western Reporter*, while Figure 5-2 shows the start of the case as it appears on Westlaw.

---

2. Other Features of a West Reporter

Beyond the editorial enhancements of individual cases, each reporter contains other useful information, such as Parallel Citation Tables,[26] if applicable; Table of Cases Reported; Table of Cases Arranged by States; Words and Phrases; and Key Number Digest. Of these, the Table of Cases and Words and Phrases are the most useful because they give you a succinct list of key terms defined by the court and a list of cases you will find in the volume. Each is explained in full in Sections IV.B.1 and IV.B.4, respectively. In a reporter, Words and Phrases and the Table of Cases are only applicable to that volume. However, both are published in full as part of the reporter's respective digest.

D. Reporters for Iowa Cases

Iowa appellate court case decisions from 1879 to 1942 are reported in the *North Western Reporter,* cited as N.W. Cases from 1942 to the present are published in the *North Western Reporter, Second Series,* cited as N.W.2d.

From 1855 to 1968, *Iowa Reports* was the official reporter of Iowa Supreme Court opinions. In 1968, the Iowa Supreme Court designated West Publishing Company as the official reporter of Iowa decisions. Cases prior to 1968 may contain a parallel citation to *Iowa Reports.*

Cases published prior to the reporter system can be found in the reports of Bradford (1838–1841), Morris (1839–1846), and Greene (1847–1854). Prior to

---

26. Reference Chapter 2 for information about Parallel Citation Tables.

the systematic official publication of Iowa case law, various individuals privately published court decisions compiled from their observations and notes. These early publications are referred to by the names of those who published them and are called *nominative reporters*. If at an Iowa law library, these volumes can be found with *Iowa Reports* and the *North Western Reporter*.

E. Other Sources for Finding Iowa Cases

Court decisions are available from the Iowa Supreme Court website. The full text of cases from 1998 to the present is available for both the Iowa Supreme Court[27] and the Iowa Court of Appeals[28] in the form of slip opinions. Bloomberg Law,[29] Fastcase,[30] Google Scholar,[31] Lexis,[32] and Westlaw[33] all offer collections of Iowa court decisions. In addition to the text of the opinions, Lexis and Westlaw include extensive editorial enhancements, as described in Section III.C.1. Bloomberg Law includes headnotes with topic classification for a subset of Iowa cases. For opinions from 2011 and later, Fastcase includes summaries taken from Justia.[34]

F. Reporters for Federal Cases

Federal reporters are similar in many respects to Iowa reporters. Table 5-2 lists the federal courts and their respective reporters and the reporters' abbre-

---

27. Iowa Supreme Court opinions are located at http://www.iowacourts.gov /About_the_Courts/Supreme_Court/Supreme_Court_Opinions/index.asp.

28. Iowa Court of Appeals opinions are at http://www.iowacourts.gov/About _the_Courts/Court_of_Appeals/Court_of_Appeals_Opinions/index.asp.

29. On Bloomberg Law, follow this path: Home > Court Opinions > State Court Opinions > Iowa.

30. On Fastcase, follow this path: Home > Advanced Caselaw Search > Individual Jurisdictions > State Supreme and Appellate Courts > Iowa.

31. From https://scholar.google.com/ select the "Case law" option. If "Iowa Courts" is not immediately listed as a choice, click on the "Select courts" link and check the box next to Iowa or the specific Iowa court you want to search.

32. On Lexis, you can browse "Explore Content," or use the red search box to bring up the following source names: IA Court of Appeals Cases from 1977, IA Supreme Court Cases from 1839, and IA District Courts — Trial Level Orders.

33. On Westlaw, follow this path: Home > Cases > Iowa.

34. You can read more about this partnership at http://www.fastcase.com/fastca se-partners-with-justia-to-provide-opinion-summaries-for-free/.

Table 5-2. Reporters for Federal Court Cases

Court	Reporter Name	Reporter Abbreviation
U.S. Supreme Court	*United States Reports* (official)	U.S.
	Supreme Court Reporter	S. Ct.
	United States Supreme Court Reports, Lawyers' Edition	L. Ed., L. Ed. 2d
U.S. Courts of Appeal	*Federal Reporter*	F., F.2d, F.3d
	Federal Appendix (unpublished cases)	Fed. Appx.
U.S. District Courts	*Federal Supplement*	F. Supp., F. Supp. 2d, F. Supp. 3d
	Federal Rules Decisions	F.R.D.

viations. Bloomberg Law,[35] Fastcase,[36] Lexis,[37] and Westlaw[38] contain all available levels of federal court opinions back to the beginning of the court system in 1789. As with Iowa cases, the editorial enhancements for federal cases are most robust with Westlaw and Lexis, with Bloomberg Law offering select headnotes and classification and Fastcase including summaries from Justia for 2011 and later cases.

In addition to these subscription databases, federal opinions are available from a variety of freely accessible web sources, as detailed in the following sections. These open web opinions could be located via a general search engine,

---

35. On Bloomberg Law, follow this path: Home > Federal Law > Federal Court Opinions. You can then narrow further if you only want to search a particular level of the federal courts, such as all U.S. Circuit Courts of Appeals, or a particular court, such as the Eighth Circuit Court of Appeals.

36. On Fastcase, click "Advanced Caselaw Search," then select the courts you want to search. You can search all federal appellate, all bankruptcy, all district courts, or one or more individual courts.

37. On Lexis, click the drop-down menu to the right of the main search box and then select "Jurisdiction" to select and limit your search to the desired court. This option does not let you limit to one or more particular federal district courts, but you can use a post-search filter to do that by setting your "Category" to "Cases." The "Explore Content" feature will enable you to select federal districts by state within each circuit.

38. On Westlaw, follow this path: Home > Cases > All Federal Cases. You can then search across all federal cases or narrow further to a particular court, level of courts (e.g., all federal district courts), circuit, or state.

e.g., Yahoo or Google (but not Google Scholar, which has a case law search tool). However, that approach would likely yield an overwhelming number of results, most irrelevant, and would therefore be a very ineffective way to perform case law research. Using one of the identified sites that contain case law in the jurisdiction you are researching will be more efficient. Nevertheless, even using open web sources has some drawbacks. These sites typically provide just the court opinion with no editorial enhancements, and site searching will likely be restricted to simple keyword searches.

1. United States District Courts Cases

Originally, the *Federal Reporter* covered decisions of both district and circuit courts. In 1932, West began the *Federal Supplement*, which publishes selected U.S. District Court decisions, leaving the *Federal Reporter* to cover U.S. Court of Appeals decisions.

In 1940, West began publishing *Federal Rules Decisions*. This series contains a limited number of U.S. District Court decisions dealing with procedural issues under the Federal Rules of Civil Procedure and the Federal Rules of Criminal Procedure.

Some district court cases are also available online outside of subscription databases. Opinions may be available directly from the court site, as is the case with the U.S. District Court for the District of Columbia.[39] Other sources that provide access to cases from multiple federal district courts are shown in Table 5-3.

2. United States Court of Appeals Cases

Cases decided by the federal intermediate appellate courts are published in the *Federal Reporter*. The decisions of all thirteen circuits are available in this source. In general, a decision is published if it lays down a new rule of law or alters an existing rule, criticizes existing law, resolves a conflict of authority, or involves a legal issue of public interest. From 2001 to the present, West's *Federal Appendix* has published U.S. Court of Appeals decisions that are not released for publication in the *Federal Reporter*. Opinions are included from all circuits except for the Fifth and Eleventh, which do not provide their "unpublished" opinions to any publisher.

While not as ubiquitous as Supreme Court cases, Court of Appeals decisions are also available online. Table 5-3 provides a selected list of free web-

---

39. These opinions are available at http://www.dcd.uscourts.gov/dcd/court_opinions.

Table 5-3. Selected List of Free Internet Sources Containing Court of Appeals and District Court Decisions

Source	Address	Content
Cornell's Legal Information Institute	http://www.law.cornell.edu/federal/districts.html	District Court and Bankruptcy Court Decisions.
FindLaw: District Courts	http://www.findlaw.com/casecode/district-courts.html	A list of U.S. District Court websites with descriptions of their content.
FindLaw: Federal Courts of Appeals	http://www.findlaw.com/casecode/courts/	U.S. Courts of Appeals decisions from 1990's–present. Beginning date varies by circuit.
Google Scholar	https://scholar.google.com/	State appellate and supreme court cases since 1950 as well as federal district, appellate, tax, and bankruptcy court cases since 1923.
Justia	http://law.justia.com/cases/federal/district-courts/	U.S. Federal District Courts Case Law. Select coverage back to 1924.
Open Jurist	http://openjurist.org/	First, second, and third series of the *Federal Reporter* (1880–2007).
Public Access to Court Electronic Records (PACER)	https://www.pacer.gov/	Case and docket information from federal appellate, district, and bankruptcy courts. (You need to register to use PACER, and you will incur charges. However, if these are less than $15/quarter, they will be waived.).
Public Library of Law	http://www.plol.org/	U.S. Courts of Appeals opinions back to 1950 (except for the 11th Circuit, which has coverage from 1981).
U.S. Courts site	http://www.uscourts.gov/court-locator/	Links to websites for U.S. Supreme Court, Courts of Appeals, District Courts, and Bankruptcy Courts.

**Table 5-4. Selected List of Free Internet Sources of
Supreme Court Opinions**

Source	Address	Dates
Cornell's Legal Information Institute	http://www.law.cornell.edu/supct/	1990–present; selective coverage prior to 1990
FindLaw	http://caselaw.findlaw.com/court/ us-supreme-court	1760–present
Google Scholar	https://scholar.google.com/	1759–present
Justia.com	http://supreme.justia.com/	1759–present
Open Jurist	http://openjurist.org/	1790–present
Oyez	http://www.oyez.org/	1995–present (audio recordings of oral arguments); 1955–1995 (selected audio)
Public Library of Law	http://www.plol.org/	1754–present
Supreme Court of the United States	http://www.supremecourt.gov/	1991–present

sites. Note that decisions are also often available through the website of each individual circuit court.

3. United States Supreme Court Cases

Cases decided by the U.S. Supreme Court can be found in numerous places. The official reporter of the Supreme Court is *United States Reports*. However, after a case is decided, it can take upwards of two years for the official reports to appear in bound volumes, although the advance sheets are available much sooner. Two unofficial reporters publish decisions in a more timely fashion: *Supreme Court Reporter*, published by West, and *United States Supreme Court Reports, Lawyers' Edition*, published by LexisNexis.

Many online sources offer access to Supreme Court opinions. The website of the Supreme Court[40] publishes slip opinions as soon as they are decided. The website may also include supplementary material, such as court briefs which provide the parties' written arguments in the case. In addition to the subscription databases offering access to all federal court opinions, described in the introduction to Section III.F, HeinOnline contains the full text in PDF

---

40. The U.S. Supreme Court site is located at http://www.supremecourt.gov.

format of *United States Reports* from volume 1 to the present. Table 5-4 lists some of the other internet sites that make U.S. Supreme Court opinions freely available.

IV. Finding Cases

Case research can be difficult because the courts issue numerous opinions each year, and cases are published chronologically as they are decided, not by subject matter. You can find cases that address your legal issues through a variety of techniques. First, you can take advantage of case headnotes and editorially assigned subject classifications to find cases by topic. In print, this approach is done through a digest. Westlaw and Lexis allow similar searching online for Iowa cases.[41] Second, you can use electronic databases to search for specific terms. Third, you can start with a secondary source, which will point you to primary authorities, including case law, as described in Chapter 3. Finally, starting with at least one relevant case, you can use a citator, explained in Chapter 9, to find other cases that have cited your starting case. The next sections will explain the first two methods in more detail.

A. Digest/Topic Analysis Concepts

Digests, and their electronic equivalents, essentially provide an indexed approach to finding cases. A digest arranges each case's points of law, represented in headnotes, by subject categories and provides summaries of cases that discuss the law on that subject. Whether working in print or online, you need to understand two basic concepts to research effectively using a digest approach: subject classification of law and headnotes. When researching in print, you also have to understand which digest to use.

1. Subject Classification

West created the first widespread system to organize American law into subject categories, which it calls the West Key Number System. Published in print as *West's Analysis of American Law*, the system can also be accessed on Westlaw.[42] The system divides American law into over 400 broad subject categories referred to as *topics*. It then divides each topic into narrower subdivi-

---

41. Bloomberg law offers headnotes and classification in some of its collections, but not for most Iowa opinions.
42. On Westlaw, select the "Key Numbers" link from the homepage.

sions to make the topic easier to navigate. Specific *key numbers* address a particular point of law within that topic. For instance, the topic Antitrust and Trade Regulation is broken into 29 subtopics ranging from attempts to monopolize to unfair competition. Each subtopic contains related key numbers, such as key number "43 Misappropriation" under the subtopic of "Unfair competition." In all, the Antitrust and Trade Regulation topic includes over 1000 distinct key numbers, each representing a different legal issue. Topics are listed alphabetically in the key number system. At the beginning of each topic entry is a scope note, an explanatory section detailing which subjects are included under that topic and which topics are excluded and covered by other topics. On Westlaw, this information appears in an information link next to the topic name. Although the search tools are simply called "key numbers," in reality you need to know both the topic name and the specific key number to use these classification references in your research. Figure 5-3 illustrates the beginning of the child custody topic in the *North Western Digest*, including its scope note and first few subtopics.

Lexis offers its own subject classification of American law.[43] After selecting a starting point from one of forty-four practice areas, you can continue narrowing that area of law until reaching a specific legal issue. For instance, starting with torts, you could keep choosing smaller relevant areas until arriving at the smallest topical subdivision, as seen in this path: Torts > Negligence > Defenses > Comparative Fault > Intentional & Reckless Conduct. Bloomberg Law also offers a classification system, but it does not comprehensively cover case law.[44]

2. Headnotes

As noted in Section III.C.1, a headnote is an editorial enhancement that appears above the court opinion, providing a sentence or short paragraph that sets out a single point of law in a case. When editors create a headnote, they also determine where that point of law fits in the classification system. That is, West editors assign a particular topic and key number to each headnote and label it accordingly. For instance, in the *Howard* case, the first headnote was

---

43. Access the classification through the Browse link, choosing to browse topics.

44. Access a form for searching case law on Bloomberg Law through this path: Home > Court Opinions. You can browse and select a topic using the "Select Topic" toolbar. A more detailed version of the classification system is available through this path: Home > Litigation & Dockets > BNA Outlines & Headnotes. This classification system was originally developed by the Bureau of National Affairs (BNA), now part of Bloomberg Law.

Figure 5-3. Example of the Analysis Outline from the *North Western Digest*

CHILD CUSTODY

SUBJECTS INCLUDED

Child custody rights pending or following divorce or dissolution of marriage

Visitation rights of parents, grandparents, and others

Extent of custody rights

Geographical limitations imposed on custodians

Enforcement of custody rights

Interstate and international custody disputes

SUBJECTS EXCLUDED AND COVERED BY OTHER TOPICS

Custody and access to dependent, neglected, abandoned, or delinquent children, see INFANTS

Issues peculiar to children born out-of-wedlock, see CHILDREN OUT–OF–WED-LOCK

Issues peculiar to custody of Native American children, see INDIANS

Parent and child relationship generally, rights of parents to control their children, and duty of parents to protect and supervise their children, see PARENT AND CHILD

For detailed references to other topics, see Descriptive-Word Index

---

Analysis

I. IN GENERAL, ⚎1–9.

II. GROUNDS AND FACTORS IN GENERAL, ⚎20–88.
   (A) IN GENERAL, ⚎20–37.
   (B) FACTORS RELATING TO PARTIES SEEKING CUSTODY, ⚎41–68.
   (C) FACTORS RELATING TO CHILD, ⚎75–88.

Source: 4D *North Western Digest 2d* 1 (Thomson/West 2004). Published with permission of West, a Thomson Reuters business.

assigned the topic Child Custody and key number 4, as illustrated in Figure 5-1. On Westlaw, that same key number would appear in a slightly different manner, as seen in Figure 5-2. Note that, to the right of the first headnote, you see its place in the classification outline. The topic, Child Custody, is assigned the number 76D. At the bottom of the outline list, you see the specific key number, for the concept of Validity. The entire topic and key number is represented on Westlaw as 76Dk4. Note, too, that West periodically revises its topic and key number system. When references change, the headnote classifications on Westlaw reflect these updates, but the print materials, of course, remain static, still showing the topic name and key number originally assigned to the headnote.

On Lexis, editors create their own headnotes for cases, using the text of each case or cases and determine where these fit into the Lexis topic classification. These indicate the path you would follow if browsing a topic to reach the relevant point of law, such as Family Law > Child Custody > Visitation > Visitation Awards > Third Parties > Grandparent Visitation. Bloomberg Law only assigns headnotes to a relatively small subset of Iowa cases; this means that accessing cases through the Bloomberg Law classification system will only be discussed in this chapter where headnotes are not relevant.

Because each headnote is individually classified, you can easily retrieve all headnotes with a particular West topic and key number or Lexis topic classification string. This means that you can generate a list of cases addressing the legal issue of interest. Section IV.B describes the specific techniques for doing so.

3. Print Digests

The Lexis topic classification does not have a print counterpart. West key numbers, however, can be identified and used to find relevant cases using print digests. Determine the jurisdiction for which you need to find cases, and then consult a digest that covers that jurisdiction. See Table 5-5 for a list of digests and jurisdictions. Always work with the narrowest jurisdiction possible so you are not searching through irrelevant information.

North Western Digest and *North Western Digest 2d* contain information about cases published in the *North Western Reporter* and *North Western Reporter 2d*, respectively. Remembering the states included in the *North Western Reporter*, this means that the *North Western Digest* will contain information about state and federal cases from Iowa, Michigan, Minnesota, Nebraska, North Dakota, South Dakota, and Wisconsin. *Iowa Digest* contains summaries of points of law in Iowa cases published in *Iowa Reports*, *North Western Reporter*, and *North Western 2d*, as well as Iowa cases decided in the Supreme Court of the United States, U.S. Court of Appeals, and U.S. District Courts.

B. Finding Cases Using a Digest/Topical Analysis Approach

In order to use a West topic and key number or Lexis topic classification string to find cases, you must first identify the relevant topic classification. Note that, although they may share similarities, these two classification systems are unique. If you want to search both Westlaw and Lexis using this approach, you separately have to identify the right classification for each system.

Table 5-5. West Digest System

Court or Jurisdiction	Reporter	Digest
United States Supreme Court	*Supreme Court Reporter*	*West's United States Supreme Court Digest*
Federal Courts	*West's Federal Reporter* *West's Federal Supplement*	*West's Federal Practice Digest*
State Courts		All states *except* Delaware, Nevada, and Utah. *Virginia Digest* covers Virginia and West Virginia. *Dakota Digest* covers North Dakota and South Dakota.
Regional	*Atlantic Reporter*	*Atlantic Digest*
	North Eastern Reporter	*West's Illinois Digest, West's Indiana Digest, West's Massachusetts Digest, West's New York Digest, West's Ohio Digest. (N.E. Digest* is no longer published.)
	South Eastern Reporter	*South Eastern Digest*
	Southern Reporter	*West's Alabama Digest, West's Florida Digest, West's Louisiana Digest, West's Mississippi Digest. (So. Digest* is no longer published.)
	South Western Reporter	*Arkansas Digest, West's Kentucky Digest, West's Missouri Digest, West's Tennessee Digest, West's Texas Digest.* (No *S.W. Digest* exists.)
	North Western Reporter	*North Western Digest*
	Pacific Reporter	*Pacific Digest*
Combined State & Federal		*General Digest*, 15th Series (2016–present); *Decennial Digest*, Century through Twelfth (1658–2016)*

* Note that, as most academic law libraries have access to Westlaw in which to search all jurisdictions, many libraries no longer carry recent *Decennial* and *General Digests.*

There are three basic strategies you can employ. One is to begin with a relevant case. A second is to use keywords to find the classification. The third is to browse the classification system. In addition, West digests provide a special tool, called "Words and Phrases," to help you identify cases that define terminology. Each of these approaches is discussed below. Regardless of which method you choose, always update your research, as noted in Section V.

1. Beginning with a Relevant Case

One of the easiest strategies for digest research is to begin with a relevant case that you found through other methods, such as using secondary sources, speaking with a colleague, or finding relevant enacted law.

If you have a citation to a particular case, each major legal research platform easily lets you retrieve it by entering the brief citation, e.g., *661 N.W.2d 183*, in the main search box. If you know of a relevant case, but do not have the necessary citation information, just the parties' names, you can try to identify the case by searching one of the online collections of Iowa case law noted in Section III.E (or Section III.F for federal cases). Most platforms offer a way to limit your keyword to the party name field,[45] but this approach can still lead to a large number of results. Print digests have a *Table of Cases* that can help you identify the full citation. The *Table of Cases* is just what the name implies: an alphabetical list of all the cases reported in that digest's respective reporter, i.e., the *North Western Digest Table of Cases* lists only those cases that appear in the *North Western Reporter*. This table is another multi-volume set that is appended to West digests. The *Table of Cases* can be invaluable if you know the name of either the plaintiff, the defendant, or both but do not have a case citation. In that situation, you can look up the parties in the *Table of Cases* and the entry will list the reporter citation and a few topics and key numbers associate with the case.

Once you have a citation to a case that appears to be relevant, locate and read the case and its headnotes in its respective West reporter or on Westlaw or Lexis. This step both verifies that the case is on point and provides citations to cases upon which the judge relied when writing the opinion that may also be applicable to your issue. The relevant headnote(s) will have one or more associated classifications. For West reporters and on Westlaw, you will see a topic and key number. On Lexis you will see the topic string. Online, click on

---

45. See Section IV.C. for more detail on keyword searching for case law.

the hyperlinked classification to bring up other cases that share that classification.[46]

In a print digest, you will look up the topic and key number in the appropriate digest volume. Topics are arranged alphabetically and noted on the spines of the volumes, so you can pull the correct volume. As noted earlier, key numbers can change, so you may want to start with a recent case. Otherwise, you may have to use a conversion table to translate the old key number into the new one. After locating your topic and key number, you will find headnote summaries of other relevant cases. These are listed according to the court that decided the case. In a state digest, federal cases are listed first, followed by state cases. Within each system, cases are listed according to hierarchy, so cases from the final appellate courts are listed first, followed by decisions from the intermediate appellate courts and finally trial court cases. Cases are listed in reverse chronological order within each level of court, so the most recent cases of a court will appear first. A pocket part in the back of the volume will have the latest cases. Remember, never rely upon headnotes, digest paragraphs, or references alone; always read a case completely and update it before relying on it.

In the hypothetical Welch case, a key point of law is Grandparent Visitation and Access to Child, found under West's topic and key number Child Custody 282. More specific subdivisions of this topic follow at key numbers Child Custody 283–289, including ones that address this issue in general (283), conduct or status of child's parent or custodian (285), and objections of parent (286). Figure 5-4 illustrates a page from the *North Western Digest 2d*, showing the topic Child Custody and several of its key numbers, including 282 and the start of 283. Note that under key number 283, the first three entries are all from *Howard*. This is because the print digest does not list individual cases, but individual headnotes, labeled with the relevant topic and key number. As with *Howard*, a case may have more than one headnote with the same classification.

2. Browsing the Classification System

As discussed in Section IV.A.1, you can view each platform's classification system on Westlaw and Lexis, as well as seeing the West system in the print

---

46. In Lexis, you also will have the choice to either view that classification in the topic index or set up an alert that would notify you when new cases with this classification were added to Lexis.

Figure 5-4. Example from the *North Western Digest 2d*

⬅279 **CHILD CUSTODY**   4D N W D 2d—32

For later cases, see same Topic and Key Number in Pocket Part

In habeas corpus proceedings by a father to obtain the custody of his infant children, it was admitted on the trial that he was not a fit person, and it appeared that the mother was of good character and, although in straitened circumstances, was industrious and able to care for them. Held, that it was a wise exercise of discretion to refuse to take them from their mother in order to give them to their paternal grandfather, who was wealthy, although it further appeared that the mother had at times been passionate and profane of speech under provocation of shameful misconduct on the part of her husband, and that her mother, with whom she lived, was a person of coarse and vulgar speech and conduct.

Johnston v. Johnston, 62 N.W. 181, 89 Wis. 416.

⬅280. —— **Abandonment by parent or custodian.**

Iowa 1966. Where 12-year-old boy had lived for last 10 years with paternal grandparents, and mother had visited boy only about six times during that period, and boy desired to remain with grandparents and did not wish to live with mother, best interests of boy required that grandparents retain custody; Wooley v. Schoop, 234 Iowa 657, 12 N.W.2d 597 overruled. 58 I.C.A. Rules of Civil Procedure, rule 344(f), par. 15.

Halstead v. Halstead, 144 N.W.2d 861, 259 Iowa 526.

Iowa App. 1986. Best interests of child, whose mother died suddenly, who had no contacts with father for seven years, and who had close relationship with maternal grandparents, would be served by awarding custody to maternal grandparents rather than to father.

Thompson by Thompson v. Collins, 391 N.W.2d 267.

N.D. 1976. Grandparents who raised six-year-old child in their home from birth were entitled to custody, as against father, divorced and remarried, who abandoned child and provided little support or care even when contact was reestablished. NDCC 27-20-1, et seq., 27-20-30.

In Interest [Custody] of D. G., 246 N.W.2d 892.

⬅281. —— **Failure to support or provide for child.**

For other cases see earlier editions of this digest, the Decennial Digests, and WESTLAW.

⬅282. **Grandparent visitation and access to child.**

Rights following adoption, see ⬅313.

⬅283. —— **In general.**

not the mere marital status of parents, and thus, if grandparent visitation is to be compelled by the State, there must be a showing of harm to the child beyond that derived from the loss of the helpful, beneficial influence of grandparents; the problem with a divorce standard is that it either assumes harm occurs in all families when there is no grandparent visitation or it embraces a standard short of harm, and both approaches are rejected. I.C.A. § 598.35.

In re Marriage of Howard, 661 N.W.2d 183.

If grandparent visitation is to be compelled by the State, there must be a showing of harm to the child beyond that derived from the loss of the helpful, beneficial influence of grandparents, and, although the statutory requirement of an established substantial relationship between child and grandparents fails to specify any harm or potential harm to the child, when a grandparent has established a substantial relationship with a grandchild, as required under grandparent visitation statute, an emotional bond can be created that, if severed, can inflict harm on the child. I.C.A. § 598.35, subd. 1.

In re Marriage of Howard, 661 N.W.2d 183.

Divorce is, alone, insufficient to establish a compelling state interest for the State to intervene into the issue of grandparent visitation, and similarly, the best interests of a child requirement is insufficient. I.C.A. § 598.35.

In re Marriage of Howard, 661 N.W.2d 183.

Iowa 1997. Grandparent visitation can be granted when it is authorized by statute, when it is ordered in a guardianship in the best interests of the child, and when it is ordered by a juvenile court as a part of its dispositional or permanency hearing. I.C.A. § 598.35.

McMain v. Iowa Dist. Court for Polk County, 559 N.W.2d 12.

Iowa 1995. Statute designating under what circumstances grandparents may petition for visitation may limit grandparent's visitation rights, but statute does not limit statutory authority of juvenile court to decide grandparent's petition for visitation with child placed in custody of court-appointed guardians. I.C.A. §§ 232.61, 598.35.

In Interest of K.R., 537 N.W.2d 774.

Iowa 1986. Jurisdiction is vested in a district court to award grandparents visitation rights in connection with a dissolution of marriage action. I.C.A. §§ 598.2, 598.21, subd. 8, 598.35, 598.35, subd. 1.

Source: 4D *North Western Digest 2d* 32 (Thomson/West 2004). Published with permission of West, a Thomson Reuters business.

title *West's Analysis of American Law*. Sometimes simply browsing through one of these systems will allow you to select the classification that is most relevant to your problem. You can then click on it to bring up associated cases.

If you are using print and do not have access to *West's Analysis of American Law*, you can browse a digest directly because it is arranged alphabetically by topics, which are printed on the spine of each volume. So, if your topic is related to Navigable Waters, you could proceed directly to the digest volume that contains that term. Once in the correct digest volume, you can browse the beginning of the relevant entry to determine which key number best fits your topic. After you have found a topic and key number, look through the entry to determine which cases are relevant to your research. From there, locate each case in its respective reporter.

In browsing the topic, you can see all the related key numbers. This overview can provide a broader context for your issue and perhaps allow you to identify other issues you might not have considered. However, this method can be very time-consuming if you do not have enough prior knowledge to know which topic is relevant to your research.

3. Searching the Classification System

An alternative to browsing a classification system is to search it online or, for the print digest, use an index. On Westlaw, when you open the key number system and enter keywords to identify relevant topics and key numbers, the search is different from searching the text of the headnotes themselves. On Lexis, the "Browse topics" option includes a search feature in the left column that allows you to search for topics across the entire classification system or within a particular practice area.

Print digests have a set of volumes, the Descriptive-Word Index, where you can look up keywords and find related topics and key numbers. To find a relevant case using the Descriptive-Word Index, you must first identify words or phrases that describe your topic. Using the journalistic or TARPP methods discussed in Chapter 1, think about the parties, places, objects, acts, omissions, defenses, and relief that may be relevant. Sometimes you may find a relevant term quickly. However, if you are having trouble finding on-point information, think about other terms or synonyms that might be used. Indexes have been developed by people who have examined the cases and have assigned terms that describe legal issues and facts. Often a concept can be expressed in many different ways. It is the job of the indexer to choose one term and put all the derivations of the term under the standard heading. See Table 5-6 for an outline for using the Descriptive-Word Index.

Table 5-6. Outline for Digest Research with the Descriptive-Word Index

1.	Develop a list of research terms using the journalistic or TARPP approach as discussed in Chapter 1.
2.	Find the research terms in the Descriptive-Word Index, which will list topics and key numbers relevant to those terms. (Remember to check the pocket part.)
3.	Review each topic and key number in the main volumes of the digest. (Remember to update your digest research by checking pocket parts, supplements, and digests contained in the reporter's advance sheets.)
4.	Read all of the relevant cases your research reveals.

To find cases on your topic, identify the jurisdiction(s) relevant to your research and use the corresponding digest(s). Look for the terms you have identified in the Descriptive-Word Index, located in a volume at either the end or beginning of the digest set. This index will direct you to the topics and key numbers covering your issue. To use the Descriptive-Word Index, look up the subjects you want to research. The subjects will be followed by abbreviations indicating the topics and key numbers relevant to each subject. See Figure 5-5 for an example from the *North Western Digest 2d Descriptive-Word Index.*

The topic headings are arranged alphabetically in the main volumes; within each topic, the key numbers appear sequentially. Once you have found the topic and key number, read the case abstracts that summarize the legal issues involved. The case name and citation are located beneath the summary. If you are unfamiliar with the abbreviations used in the citation, consult the list of reporter abbreviations located at the front of the digest volume. Make sure you refer to the reporter and read the full case for each citation you think is relevant; do not rely on the abstract alone. In the digests, the statement "See topic analysis for scope" directs you to the analysis section that appears at the beginning of each broad topic. This analysis indicates other topics that may be relevant to the issue.

4. Using Words and Phrases

Print digests have Words and Phrases volumes that include headnotes that refer to any instance in which a court has defined or interpreted a legally significant term. Headnotes interpreting the words or phrases from cases reported in the entire West National Reporter System are also included in a

Figure 5-5. *Descriptive-Word Index* Excerpt from *North Western Digest 2d*

```
GRANDPARENTS AND
GRANDCHILDREN

CHILD custody. See heading CHILD
   CUSTODY, GRANDPARENTS.

CHILDREN out-of-wedlock,
   Support, duty to, Child ☞ 21
   Visitation rights, Child ☞ 20

DEATH actions,
   Grandchild rights, Death ☞ 31(8)

DESCENT and distribution,
   Entitlement and shares, Des & Dist ☞ 28,
   36

SUPPORT, duty to,
   Children out-of-wedlock, Child ☞ 21

VISITATION, Child C ☞ 283-289
   Following adoption, Child C ☞ 313

VISITATION rights,
   Children out-of-wedlock, Child ☞ 20

WILLS. See heading WILLS,
   GRANDCHILDREN.

WORKERS' compensation,
   Dependency and relationship, Work Comp
      ☞ 483-485
   Burden of proof, Work Comp ☞ 1486
   Death, marriage, or other change of
      condition, Work Comp ☞ 505
   Evidence,
      Sufficiency, Work Comp ☞ 1486
```

Source: 34 *Descriptive-Word Index, North Western Digest 2d* 554 (Thomson/West 2001). Published with permission of West, a Thomson Reuters business.

master set titled *Words and Phrases*, which provides judicial definitions in cases going back to 1658. Entries in both sets are arranged alphabetically and can be invaluable if you need to know the meaning of a term in a particular jurisdiction. As with most West products, *Words and Phrases* is also available

Figure 5-6. Example from Words and Phrases

GRANDPARENTS

Wis. 1992. Paternal grandparents continued to be considered "grandparents" who could seek visitation with their deceased son's child even following child's adoption by stepfather. W.S.A. 48.92(3), 880.155.—Matter of C.G.F., 483 N.W.2d 803, 168 Wis.2d 62, reconsideration denied H.F. v. T.F., 490 N.W.2d 26, certiorari denied 113 S.Ct. 408, 506 U.S. 953, 121 L.Ed.2d 333.—Child C 313.

Source: 39 Words and Phrases, North Western Digest 2d 530. Published with permission of West, a Thomson Reuters business.

on Westlaw. It can be accessed as a separate source.[47] In addition, you can use a field limiter of words and phrases in a keyword search of cases. To do this, from the homepage, click on "Cases." Use the search box at the top to search across all cases on Westlaw (be sure to note which jurisdiction you have selected in the menu to the right of that box), or select a more specific database of cases, such as Eighth Circuit federal cases or Iowa cases. Then enter the field limiter *wp* followed by the term you want in parentheses. For example, to conduct a words and phrases search for the term grandparents, enter *wp(grandparents)* in the Westlaw search box. See Figure 5-6 for an example from the *North Western Digest* version of Words and Phrases showing the headnote from a Wisconsin case where the court defined the term grandparents.

The Welch Matter

The explanations and figures in this chapter illustrate the digest research process beginning with the Descriptive-Word Index as it relates to the hypothetical grandparent visitation rights scenario.

Figure 5-5. When beginning case research on a topic in print, first go to the Descriptive-Word Index to look up research terms. In this case, logical terms include grandparents and child custody. As you see, the term Grandparents in the Descriptive-Word Index has a subheading "visitation" which leads to the topic and key numbers

---

47. On the Westlaw homepage, click on "Cases." In the right column, click on the "Words & Phrases" link.

that appear on point: Child Custody 283–289. On Westlaw, this topic and key number could be determined by browsing or searching the Key Number System.

Figure 5-6. To determine whether the term *grandparent* had been defined in any special way, a quick look at the Words and Phrases section of the *North Western Digest* shows that the one definition of grandparent is not relevant to our fact pattern. As explained earlier, this search could have been conducted on Westlaw, as well.

Figure 5-4. With the relevant topic and key number, locate the *North Western Digest* volume that covers Child Custody and contains key number range 283–289. Looking through the cases under key number 283, you will find an Iowa case that seems on point, *In re Marriage of Howard.* You could also have retrieved this case by clicking on the Child Custody key number 283 through the West Key Number System on Westlaw.

Figures 5-1 and 5-2. Going to the *North Western Reporter* volume, or online via Westlaw,[48] look for the citation noted in the digest citation: 661 N.W.2d 183. Read the text of the case to see if it is in fact relevant to the hypothetical situation.

C. Keyword Searching

All of the electronic sources for Iowa cases noted in Section III.E offer at least some ability to search by keyword. However, the level of complexity of these search capabilities varies significantly. The opinions available through the Iowa judicial branch website have the simplest search functionality, only allowing you to search for an exact phrase or one or more keywords. Google Scholar also offers similarly simple search options for case law, with the choice to sort results by date or relevance or limit results to a particular time frame or jurisdiction.

As described in Chapter 2, more robust systems offer terms-and-connectors searching with a wide variety of search operators, including more sophisticated options like proximity searching. Such options are available on Bloomberg Law, Fastcase, Lexis, and Westlaw. In addition, all of these platforms except Bloomberg Law offer natural language searching options. As emphasized in Chapter 2, the specific manner in which you create a search query may vary in terms of vendor. Therefore, before beginning your research on one of the products, it is important to carefully review help screens, introductory material, or any available online training materials in order to familiar-

---

48. Note that if you are performing this research through Lexis, the topics will not necessarily be the same as those in Westlaw.

ize yourself with the product to make your research most efficient and effective. As always with keyword searching, be mindful of synonyms. For example, using the search term *children* will not retrieve results if the court consistently used the word juveniles.

Just as you choose the narrowest reporter and digest when conducting print research, selecting a narrow database to search online helps ensure that your search does not return numerous irrelevant results. For instance, on Bloomberg Law, simultaneously searching Iowa Court of Appeals Opinions and Iowa Supreme Court Opinions will result in far fewer results than searching All Federal & State Court Opinions. Carefully selecting the relevant database(s) before you begin is particularly important on Westlaw where the total number of search results shown has a cap of 10,000. This means that by doing a broad initial search across all Westlaw cases and then limiting to Iowa cases will likely mean you do not retrieve as many Iowa opinions as you would if you first selected Iowa cases, or the specific Iowa court of interest, and then entered your keyword search.[49]

On the platforms that offer some form of case classification — Bloomberg Law, Lexis, and Westlaw — try to combine keyword searching and topic classification. This can be accomplished in a variety of ways as the following examples illustrate. On Bloomberg Law, the case search form lets you enter both keywords and limit to a particular topic. On Lexis, click the drop-down menu to the right of the main search box and then select "Practice Areas & Topics" to select and limit your search to one or more practice areas. On Westlaw, you can use a topic and key number as one of your keywords in an advanced search by entering a search string: with the topic number, the letter k, and then the key number. For instance, if you are interested in the age at which people may marry, you could use the topic 253, Marriage, and key number 5, Persons who may marry — age. The search term would be entered as *253k5* and could be combined with other search terms. From Westlaw's home page you also can click on "Key Numbers" and select that topic and key number.

---

49. To try this yourself, on the Westlaw homepage, click on "Cases." Enter *marriage* in the search box at the top. Click the "Search" button. Using the filters on the left, make a note of how many cases in your results are from Iowa courts. (You may have to open the "State" menu under jurisdiction to see this number.) Then follow this path from the Westlaw homepage: Cases > Iowa > All Iowa State Cases. Enter *marriage* in the search box at the top. Click the "Search" button. Note the number of cases retrieved. How do the two figures compare?

Take advantage of post-search filters, where available. Bloomberg Law, Lexis, and Westlaw all offer a variety of options to refine your results using filters found in left-hand menus. In particular, the latter two systems have extensive filters and options to search within the initial result set. You can also change the order in which your results appear. All of these options can save you time as you review your search results.

V. Updating Your Research

The final step of case law research, whether done in print or online, is to update your research. Updating fulfills several important purposes. It tells you whether a case is still good law. It indicates the treatment the case has received in subsequent opinions, e.g., whether the opinion has been questioned, explained, etc. It provides citations to cases that have cited your case and may therefore also be relevant to your issue. Although updating can sometimes still be done in print, online updating is more prevalent and advantageous. Databases are more up-to-date than their print equivalents and more efficient to use, as explained below. Refer to Chapter 9 for complete information about updating with citators.

VI. Reading and Analyzing Cases[50]

Finding a case is only the first step in the process of case law research. After locating a case, you must then read it, understand it, and analyze its potential relevance to the problem you are researching. Novices may spend hours reading and re-reading a single case in order to understand the details. This reading may also include frequent stops to consult secondary sources for definitions or background information.

It can sometimes be difficult to determine if a case is relevant to your research or client situation. If the case concerns the same principles of law as the client's situation, it is likely relevant. If the case contains the same legally significant facts, it is also likely relevant. Legally significant facts are those that affect the court's decision.

The problem is that research rarely reveals a case that addresses a fact pattern that exactly mirrors that of your client. Instead, several cases may have elements that are similar, but that also differ in some respect from that of your

---

50. This part is based on Suzanne E. Rowe, *Oregon Legal Research* (3d ed. 2014).

client's. It is your job to determine whether the facts are similar enough for the court to apply the law in the same way and reach the same decision.

After you have located binding cases involving similar doctrine and facts, you next need to synthesize the cases to state and explain the relevant legal rule, then decide how the rule applies to the client's facts and determine your conclusion.

As you read cases, the following strategies may help you understand them more quickly and thoroughly:

- Review the synopsis to determine if the case appears to be on point. If it is, skim the headnotes to find the particular portion of the case that is relevant. Remember that as one case may discuss several issues of law, only one or two headnotes may interest you. Go to the portion of the case identified by the relevant headnote and decide whether it is important for your research.
- If the headnote is important, skim the entire case to get a feeling for what has happened and why, focusing on the portion of the case identified by the relevant headnote.
- Read the case slowly and carefully. However, you may skip the parts that are obviously not relevant to your situation.
- As you finish reading each paragraph, try to summarize what you just read. If you are unable to do so, read it again.
- The next time you read the case, take notes. These will help you better understand the essential concepts of the case.[51]
- Remember that skimming is often not sufficient for you to fully understand the case.

---

51. For guidance on taking notes on cases, see Chapter 12, Section II.E.2.

Chapter 6

Statutes, Court Rules, and Ordinances

I. Introduction

A *statute* is a law written[1] and enacted by a legislature. Statutes are mandatory authority and binding on a court in the jurisdiction of the legislature. However, courts have the ultimate authority in interpreting a statute and determining its constitutionality. When evaluating a legal problem, you should always consider whether a statute applies to the client's situation. When there is an applicable statute, you will need to consider all case law interpreting the statute and may also need to investigate the legislative history of the statute.[2]

In United States law, researchers most frequently encounter state and federal statutes. There are also local — city or county — statutes, usually called *ordinances*. This chapter will discuss state and federal statutes, and then address ordinances. This chapter will also address the laws governing the courts, known as court rules.

II. Session Laws and Codification

Usually, U.S. statutes are published in three basic versions both at the state and federal levels. The first version of a newly enacted statute is a *slip law*. Traditionally, each law was issued by itself on a single sheet or as a pamphlet with separate pagination. Neither state nor federal slip laws are widely distributed in print now, but access is generally available online. Slip laws are primarily useful in research when you need to look at a very recent law, not yet available in other forms.

---

1. Sometimes legislative counsel or interested groups may write the laws.
2. For a more detailed explanation of the structure of the Iowa legislature and for information about researching legislative history, refer to Chapter 7.

Table 6-1. Research Strategy for Statutory Research

1.	Identify keywords or terms relevant to your research using the journalistic or TARPP methods discussed in Chapter 1.
2.	In print, use the index volume(s) for the applicable code (e.g., state or federal) to locate those terms. Online, search the index or the full text for your terms; note that if the index was well prepared, it will often be more efficient to find statutes with an index search rather than a full-text search.
3.	Once you identify a code section you think is relevant, go to that section to read and analyze the statute. To read the statute carefully, pay attention to the statutory scheme; other statutes explicitly referenced in the statutory text; and other related statutes, such as those providing definitions.
4.	Refer to an annotated version of the statute to find citations to cases that interpret or apply the statute.
5.	Read and analyze relevant cases.
6.	Apply the statute to the facts of your client's particular situation.

Next are the *session laws*. Statutes are arranged by date of passage and published in separate volumes for each legislative term. Official session laws are generally published only in bound volumes after a session has ended, but advance session law services provide the texts of new laws either online or in pamphlet form more quickly. Session laws are typically consulted in research if the law has not yet been codified, when you are tracing the history of a statutory provision, and if you need to see a single law in its entirety.

The third publication format is the *statutory compilation* or *code* (codification). Codes collect current statutes and arrange them by subject. Statutes are grouped into broad subject topics, usually called *titles*; within each title, statutes are divided into chapters and then numbered sections. Because of this subject arrangement, codes are often the starting point for statutory research. Their wide variety of finding aids, from indexes to popular name tables, also make codes particularly useful.

III. Iowa Statutory Publications

The session law and codification process discussed above applies to Iowa statutes, whose publication formats are discussed below.

A. Iowa Slip Laws

Iowa slip laws are freely available online through the Iowa General Assembly site.[3] On this site, slip laws are presented as bills. Be careful in using this site because it includes both enacted and pending legislation; only enacted statutes are slip laws. Print versions of the slip laws are cumulated in supplementation to the *Iowa Code Annotated* through the *Iowa Legislative Service.* This West pamphlet service publishes the laws during and immediately after each session of the General Assembly.

B. Iowa Session Laws

Session laws are published as *Acts and Joint Resolutions* by Iowa's Legislative Services Agency.[4] The volumes contain enacted bills and resolutions arranged chronologically, by date enacted, and sequentially, by chapter number assigned upon enactment. One volume is published for each session of the General Assembly.[5] Iowa session laws are freely available online through the Iowa General Assembly site.[6] Bloomberg Law, Lexis and Westlaw also contain Iowa session laws.

C. Iowa Statutes

After the Iowa legislature has enacted statutes, the portions of enacted bills intended as permanent laws are codified into the *Code of Iowa.* The Code consists of sixteen titles, each on a particular subject. The titles are listed in Table 6-2. Each title is then divided into subtitles and then further divided into chapters. For instance, Title IV: Public Health, has three subtitles:

1: Alcoholic Beverages and Controlled Substances
2: Health-Related Activities
3: Health-Related Professions

---

3. Current slip laws can be accessed at https://www.legis.iowa.gov/legislation, using tools such as the "Code & Acts Sections Amended" link and the "Bill Subject Index" link, which then presents separate links for bills introduced and those passed.

4. Researchers can use the *Acts* to help determine legislative intent. The process of researching legislative history is discussed in depth in Chapter 7.

5. "A General Assembly is a legislative period that consists of two regular legislative sessions. The first session of a General Assembly is held in odd-numbered years and lasts for approximately 110 calendar days. The second session is held in even-numbered years and lasts for approximately 100 calendar days." Legal Servs. Div., *Legislative Guide: The Iowa General Assembly* 20 (2006), *available at* https://www.legis.iowa.gov/docs/resources/gaguide.pdf.

6. Session laws are found at https://www.legis.iowa.gov/archives/shelves/actsChapter.

Table 6-2. Titles in the *Code of Iowa*

I.	State Sovereignty and Management	IX.	Local Government
II.	Elections and Official Duties	X.	Financial Resources
III.	Public Services and Regulation	XI.	Natural Resources
IV.	Public Health	XII.	Business Entities
V.	Agriculture	XIII.	Commerce
VI.	Human Services	XIV.	Property
VII.	Education and Cultural Affairs	XV.	Judicial Branch and Judicial Procedures
VIII.	Transportation	XVI.	Criminal Law and Procedure

Each subtitle is broken into chapters: Chapters 123–34 are under Subtitle 1; Chapters 135–46 are under Subtitle 2; and Chapters 147–58 are under Subtitle 3.[7] (Note: In Iowa, the citation includes the chapter and section, for instance § 123.10. Numbers and letters after the decimal point indicate the specific section or subsection of the chapter.)

The official version of the *Code of Iowa* is published by the State of Iowa biennially. It is also freely available through the General Assembly site in both unofficial and official versions.[8] Since 1979, it has been updated each year it is not published (i.e., every other year) with a supplemental volume. The supplement was originally printed, but starting with the 2013 Code, it is only available online, integrated into the PDF version of the code available from the Iowa General Assembly site.

The code is a multi-volume set with a separate index volume. Code sections are consecutively numbered throughout the volumes. In print, the number ranges on the spine of each volume refer to the range of code sections contained within that volume; online an entire volume can be opened, or a specific chapter or section can be brought up using the Iowa Code Quick Search box.[9] The print index volume contains many additional features. Conversion

---

7. Note, however, that some of these chapters have been repealed or transferred.

8. The code on the Iowa General Assembly site is at https://www.legis.iowa.gov/law.

9. The Iowa Code Quick Search box appears in the right menu on many pages on the General Assembly site, including https://www.legis.iowa.gov/law.

Tables of Senate and House Files and Joint Resolutions to Chapters of the *Acts of the General Assembly* for the previous two years can aid you in correlating the original senate or house file with its eventual publication in the acts; Tables of Disposition of Iowa Acts to the Code that identifies where different sections of the acts have been codified; a Table of Code Sections Altered from the Previous Code to the Current Code listing each code section changed from the prior to the current year; and a Table of Corresponding Sections of the Previous Code to the Code Supplement for the Current Code which will tell you if the number of a code section has changed allowing you to trace its history. On the General Assembly site, the features of the index volume are available in two different files: one for the tables and one for the index.

West publishes an unofficial annotated code, *Iowa Code Annotated*, also available on Westlaw. In print, the *Iowa Code Annotated* is updated with annual pocket parts; on Westlaw, the updates are integrated into the code sections, making this version more current than the print version or the official code. In addition, the index to the *Iowa Code Annotated* provides much more detail than that of the official code, making it easier to identify statutes on a specific topic. It also includes a Popular Name Table that allows you to find the citation to a statute when you know its common name and a Legislative Highlights Index listing significant legislation passed the prior session. A known code section can easily be retrieved by typing the citation in the Westlaw search bar at the top of each screen. The annotated code can be an excellent resource as it provides citations to state and federal cases that have interpreted each statute. The *Iowa Code Annotated* also contains historical and statutory notes, cross references to other relevant code sections, and references to law review and journal commentaries. Refer to Figures 6-1 and 6-2 for an example of the differences between content in the unannotated and annotated versions of the Iowa code.

A few additional online sources of the code are also available. Bloomberg Law and Westlaw maintain unannotated versions of the code. Fastcase offers an unannotated version of the code, but it does include a list of cases that cite each code section. Similar to Westlaw, Lexis has a more fully annotated version of the code that provides citing cases along with a brief summary. Known citations can easily be retrieved in all products by browsing or, for all products except Fastcase, entering the citation in the product's main search box. The main Fastcase search box is specific to case law, so here you must click on the "Search Statutes" link, select the "Citation Lookup" button, click the box next to Iowa, enter a specific section number, and then click the search button to retrieve a known code section. See Table 6-3 for online locations of Iowa statutes.

Figure 6-1. *Code of Iowa* Example

600C.1 Grandparent and great-grandparent visitation.

1. The grandparent or great-grandparent of a minor child may petition the court for grandchild or great-grandchild visitation when the parent of the minor child, who is the child of the grandparent or the grandchild of the great-grandparent, is deceased.

[Complete text of code section continues, and the section concludes as shown below.]

13. The court shall not issue an order restricting the movement of the child if such restriction is solely for the purpose of allowing the grandparent or great-grandparent the opportunity to exercise the grandparent's or great-grandparent's visitation under this section.

2007 Acts, ch 218, §206; 2010 Acts, ch 1193, §130; 2011 Acts, ch 34, §134
Referred to in §600.11

Source: Iowa Code §600C.1 (2015).

Figure 6-2. *Iowa Code Annotated* Example

600C.1.   Grandparent and great-grandparent visitation

1.   The grandparent or great-grandparent of a minor child may petition the court for grandchild or great-grandchild visitation when the parent of the minor child, who is the child of the grandparent or the grandchild of the great-grandparent, is deceased.

[Complete text of code section continues, and the section concludes as shown below.]

13.   The court shall not issue an order restricting the movement of the child if such restriction is solely for the purpose of allowing the grandparent or great-grandparent the opportunity to exercise the grandparent's or great-grandparent's visitation under this section.

Added by Acts 2007 (82 G.A.) ch. 218, H.F. 909, § 206. Amended by Acts 2010 (83 G.A.) ch. 1193, H.F. 2531, § 130; Acts 2011 (84 G.A.) ch. 34, S.F. 475, § 134.

Historical and Statutory Notes

2010 Legislation

Acts 2010 (83 G.A.) ch. 1193, H.F. 2531, § 130, rewrote the section, which had read:

"1.   The grandparent or great-grandparent of a minor child may petition the court for grandchild or great-grandchild visitation.

"b.   The parent who is being asked to temporarily relinquish care, custody, and control of the child to provide visitation is unfit to make the decision regarding visitation.

"c.   It is in the best interest of the child to

[Description of changes from 2010 and 2011 legislation continue and the Historical and Statutory Notes section concludes with a history Derivation section.]

order or commenced a proceeding under this section.

"7.   The court shall not enter any temporary order to establish, enforce, or modify visitation under this section.

"8.   An action brought under this section is subject to chapter 598B, and in an action brought to establish, enforce, or modify visitation under this section, each party shall submit in its first pleading or in an attached affidavit all information required by section 598B.209.

"9.   In any action brought to establish, enforce, or modify visitation under this section, the court may award attorney fees to the prevailing party in an amount deemed reasonable by the court.

"10.   If a proceeding to establish or enforce visitation under this section is commenced when a dissolution of marriage proceeding is pending concerning the parents of the affected minor child, the record and evi-

Derivation:

Codes 2007, 2005, 2003, 2001, 1999, § 598.35.

Acts 1998 (77 G.A.) ch. 1104, § 1.

Acts 1997 (77 G.A.) ch. 118, § 1.

Codes 1997, 1995, 1993, 1991, 1989, § 598.35.

Acts 1987 (72 G.A.) ch. 159, § 9.

Codes 1987, 1985, 1983, 1981, 1979, 1977, 1975, § 598.35.

Acts 1974 (65 G.A.) ch. 1253, § 1.

Codes 2007, 2005, 2003, 2001, 1999, § 598.35.

Acts 1998 (77 G.A.) ch. 1104, § 1.

Acts 1997 (77 G.A.) ch. 118, § 1.

Codes 1997, 1995, 1993, 1991, 1989, § 598.35.

Acts 1987 (72 G.A.) ch. 159, § 9.

Codes 1987, 1985, 1983, 1981, 1979, 1977, 1975, § 598.35.

Acts 1974 (65 G.A.) ch. 1253, § 1.

Source: Iowa Code Ann. §600C.1 (West Supp. 2015). Published with permission of West, a Thomson Reuters business.

Figure 6-2. *Iowa Code Annotated* **Example,** *continued*

Cross References

Adoption, notice of adoption hearing to person granted visitation rights pursuant to this section, see § 600.11.

Recovery of attorney fees in paternity, custody, and visitation actions, see § 600B.26.

Law Review and Journal Commentaries

Beyond Troxel: The pragmatic challenges of grandparent visitation continue. Laurence C. Nolan, 50 Drake L.Rev. 267 (2002).

When father (or mother) doesn't know best: Quasi-parents and parental deference

after Troxel v. Granville. Solangel Maldonado, 88 Iowa L.Rev. 865.

Research References

Treatises and Practice Aids

2 Iowa Practice Series § 31:27, Factors in Determining Child Custody and Visitation Provisions.

2 Iowa Practice Series § 31:34, Visitation by Grandparent, Great Grandparent and Others.

10 Iowa Practice Series § 34:33, Petition for Grandparent Visitation.

Notes of Decisions

Contracts 2.5
Modification of order   10.5
State interest, validity   ½
Validity, in general   ½
Violation of order   11.5

―――――――

½. Validity, in general

Challenges to grandparent visitation statute raise questions of substantive due process and liberty interests in the context of statutory interpretation, obliging Supreme Court to review the record de novo, making its own evaluation of the totality of the circumstances. Spiker v. Spiker, 2006, 708 N.W.2d 347. Child Custody ⬄ 919

Statute providing for grandparent visitation when paternity of a child born out of

Section of the grandparent visitation statute permitting a petition for grandparent visitation when the parents of a child are divorced failed on its face to comport with the due process clause; the most critical deficiency in the statute was its failure to require a finding of parental unfitness, statute on its face not only failed to recognize the degree of harm or potential harm to the child needed to support state intervention, but it failed to require a threshold finding of parental unfitness, and statute failed to require the court to consider a parent's objections to allowing visitation, and these provisions had to be a part of any grandparent visitation statute under due process clause. In re Marriage of Howard, 2003, 661 N.W.2d 183. Child Custody ⬄ 4; Constitutional Law ⬄ 4396

[Notes of Decisions continue.]

IV. Iowa Statutory Research

Although all sources of the code offer easy access to retrieve a known citation, you will often need to find the law on a particular issue or topic without benefit of already knowing one or more relevant code sections. In this case, Iowa statutory research follows the process outlined in Table 6-1. This section will more specifically discuss this process for both print and online sources and then explain how to update statutory research.

A. In Print

You should first develop a list of research terms by identifying keywords or terms relevant to your research. Use the journalistic or TARPP methods dis-

Table 6-3. Iowa Legislature General Assembly Online Resources for Iowa Statutes

Publication	Address	Date Range
Slip Laws	https://www.legis.iowa.gov/law/statutory/acts Use Code & Acts Sections Amended or Enrolled Bills link. For enrolled bills, watch out for Governor's action to make sure bill of interest has not been vetoed or at risk thereof.	Current
	https://www.legis.iowa.gov/archives Enrolled bills available back to 1996; Code & Acts Sections Amended available back to 2011.	1996–present
Session Laws	https://www.legis.iowa.gov/archives/shelves /actsChapter	1838–present
Code of Iowa	https://www.legis.iowa.gov/law/statutory /statutory	Current
	https://www.legis.iowa.gov/archives/shelves/code	1839–present

cussed in Chapter 1 or another method of your choice; make sure you have considered the problem thoroughly so that you generate a complete list of terms.

Use the index volume for the code to locate those terms. If you have access to the *Iowa Code Annotated*, use its index, which is much more extensive than the index to the *Code of Iowa*. Main index terms may be divided into multiple smaller concepts that you need to review to find relevant entries; you also may have to check more than one main index term to locate relevant chapters. Even if you find an entry that seems on point, do not stop researching before you have looked for all your keywords. Each entry will have a number, or numbers, after it. These numbers refer to chapters of the Iowa Code.

Using Figure 6-3, look at this process in action. Assume one of the terms you identified was grandparents. Looking that up in the index, you find the main entry "GRANDPARENTS AND GRANDCHILDREN." Under this heading, there are a number of subheadings for smaller aspects of the topic. With reference to the Welch matter, you would identify "Visitation" as a relevant subheading and make a note to check sections 232.102 and 600C.1 in the code. A good index will also provide additional references. It may list no code sections but instead direct you to "See" another index term to find relevant entries, or it may start with a "See, also" reference indicating that in addition to code sections listed under this search term, you can find additional relevant information under the referenced term. For example, Figure 6-3 shows that the heading "GRANTS" has entries under it, but you should also look up the term "Gifts" to ensure you have fully researched all possible headings.

Once you have a list of code sections, go to the volume of the code that contains the relevant chapter; as noted earlier, each volume has printed on its spine the chapters that are included. Then read and analyze the statute. Do not rush through this step. A careful reading of the statute will allow you to determine if it is relevant to your research. Because statutes are often complex and the wording of statutes is so important, you may need to read the statute several times to understand it. You may also need to read the statutes that precede and follow your statute in order to understand your specific provision. For instance, many Code chapters contain a definitions section that pertains to the entire chapter, such as Chapter 256B (Special Education) of which 256B.2 is entitled Definitions — Policies — Funds. The beginning of each chapter includes a list of all the sections it contains; reviewing this table of contents can also help ensure you find all the relevant statutes within the chapter.

After finding and carefully reading relevant statutes, you need to find citations to cases that interpret or apply the statute. If you found the relevant code section in the official, unannotated code, look up that same section in the annotated code to check for relevant case law, secondary sources, and other references that can help you understand the statute. Chapter 9 explains another way to find relevant cases, using a citator.

The Welch Matter

As you recall, the Welch matter, regarding grandparent visitation rights, has been addressed by statute. Careful research in Iowa statutes, e.g., following the relevant *Iowa Code Annotated* index entry shown in Figure 6-3, leads you to Iowa Code § 600C.1. To thoroughly understand the development of this issue in Iowa, you would want to read cases that interpret this statute. In the annotations for § 600C.1, you see references to *Santi v. Santi*, 633 N.W.2d 312 (Iowa 2001), a case decided by the Iowa Supreme Court in which a portion of the prior grandparent's visitation statute, Iowa Code § 598.35(7) (1999), was held unconstitutional. You also see references to *In re Marriage of Howard*, 661 N.W.2d 183 (Iowa 2003), in which another portion of the statute was held unconstitutional. Following *Howard*, § 598.35 was

Figure 6-3. Sample from *Iowa Code Annotated* Index

> **GRANDPARENTS AND**
> **GRANDCHILDREN**
> Abortion,
>   Partial birth, actions and proceed-
>   ings, **707.8A**
>   Pregnant minors, notice, **135L.3**
> Adoption, notice, hearings, **600.11**
> Definitions, pregnant minors, **135L.1**
> Family corporations, real estate
>   transfer tax, **428A.2**
> Inheritance taxes,
>   Exemptions, **450.9, 450.10**
>   Liens and incumbrances, exemp-
>   tions, **450.7**
> Intestate succession, distribution of
>   property, **633.219**
> Support, **252.5**
> Visitation, **232.102, 600C.1**
>
> **GRANTS**
>   See, also, Gifts, generally, this
>   index
> Administrative services department,
>   **8A.108**

Source: Iowa Code Index (2009).

repealed by the 82nd Iowa General Assembly and replaced by Iowa Code § 600C.1. The Iowa legislature replaced the law again in 2010, and made a small correction to it in 2011, which underscores the need to make sure you have the most current law.

Iowa Code § 598.35 is a prime example of how vitally important updating is to legal research. The current code clearly indicates that this section has been repealed. However, if you had started with this statute, e.g., from a reproduction in a secondary source, failed to check to see if this statute was still good law, and based your analysis on § 598.35, your case would fail. In contrast, if your research included an examination of Iowa Code § 598.35, the referenced new Iowa grandparent visitation statute in Iowa Code § 600C.1, and its associated case law, you would likely have a more sophisticated understanding of how this law might apply to the Welch matter.

The final steps are to read and analyze relevant cases you have found[10] and apply the statute to the facts of your client's particular situation.

---

10. Chapter 5 covers case law research.

B. Online

Online, the process of researching statutes varies slightly from the process in print. Even if you are beginning your research online, however, you should review the information in the preceding section as it explains the process in more detail. Regardless of which research medium you choose, the first step, developing a list of research terms, operates the same.

The second step is either reviewing an index for your terms or using the terms to search against the full text of the code. Both are options for the General Assembly site and Westlaw, but Bloomberg Law, Fastcase, and Lexis offer only full-text searching of the code. Statutory language tends to be formal, and in unfamiliar areas of law it can be difficult to guess the terms that lawmakers might have used. A good index will use both legal jargon and common parlance to represent concepts, thus helping you find the relevant sections quickly. Due to the formality of statutory language, full-text searches of annotated codes are more likely to be successful than searches of unannotated codes because the included case headnotes may well employ more accessible language.

At the General Assembly site, you can browse a PDF version of the index[11] to locate your terms, which makes the process similar to print research. You can also use the "Search the Iowa Code" link to open the Legislative Document Research Page.[12] The initial page, "Main Search," provides a simple search box where you can enter your key words. An "Advanced Search" link provides a form-based approach to searching the site or a designated section of the site.[13] Note that if you input a search using the advanced search form, the system will translate that search into a terms-and-connectors search, using the operators the system recognizes.[14] If you already know what these operators are, you can directly input them in the main search box.

From either the main search or advanced search screens, the default search includes all content, i.e., all forms of legislation — bills, acts, and the code —

---

11. The PDF index is linked from https://www.legis.iowa.gov/law/statutory.

12. The direct link to the Legislative Document Research Page is https://www.legis.iowa.gov/publications/search. To search the Legislative Document Research Page as efficiently as possible, you may want to first read the brief documentation, available at https://www.legis.iowa.gov/docs/publications/IHD/680332.pdf, that describes the use of this search engine.

13. The direct link to the advanced search page is https://www.legis.iowa.gov/publications/search/advanced.

14. The Legislative Document Research page is built on the open source SOLR platform, which in turn relies on Lucene for its search functionality.

as well as other publications on the General Assembly site, such as the *Iowa Administrative Code*. The left-hand menu offers a "Search Within" feature that allows you to restrict your search to the code or to one or more particular code titles, subtitles, chapters, or sections. This option also allows you to navigate the code table of contents.

On Westlaw, the index to the code is available from the "Iowa Statutes & Court Rules" page via the "Iowa Statutes Index" link.[15] From the "Iowa Statutes & Court Rules" page, you can also navigate the code's table of contents or search across the entire code, or a subsection of it, using standard Westlaw search functionality.[16] To search the entire code, enter your search in the search box at the top of the screen. To search a subsection of the code, use the table of contents to click on the title, subtitle, or chapter you want to search, and then enter your search terms in the top search box. (Note that this box will now indicate in pale gray words that you are only searching the selected part of the code.)

On Lexis, the source "IA — LexisNexis® Iowa Annotated Statutes" allows you to retrieve code sections by either searching or browsing.[17] By clicking on the "View Table of Contents" link, you can navigate through the code table of contents to bring up particular parts of the code. You can also use the red search box at the top of the page to search the entire code or click on the associated magnifying glass icon in the right column to restrict your search to specific titles, subtitles, or chapters.

On Bloomberg Law, bring up the table of contents for the unannotated code through this path: State Law > Iowa > Iowa Legislative > Iowa Code. You can then navigate the table of contents to bring up certain sections. You can also search within the entire code using the "Keywords" search box on top of the screen, or you can limit your search to a particular part of the code by clicking the associated "Search" box next to the relevant title, subtitle, or chapter.

On Fastcase, click on "Search Statutes," then use the "Select Statutes" menu to select Iowa. Enter your search terms in the search box using either the "Keyword Search (Boolean)" option or the "Natural Language" option. To browse the statutes, click the "Browse" tab on the "Search Statutes" screen, then navigate to the Iowa statutes.

The next step is to find, read, and analyze the statute. As described in Section III.C., this is a relatively straight-forward process in print or on any of

---

15. This page can be found by following this path on Westlaw: Home > State Materials > Iowa > Iowa Statutes & Court Rules.

16. See Chapter 2 for general information about electronic search techniques.

17. Use the Lexis browse sources feature to find Iowa Annotated Statutes.

the noted electronic platforms. Reading a statute is something of an art. Section V. provides information about effectively reading an Iowa statute.

Once you have located and carefully read relevant statutes, you need to find cases that have addressed the statute(s). Annotated codes on Lexis and Westlaw provide references to cases, as do their citator services, which are explained in Chapter 9. The code on Fastcase offers links to some cases that have cited a statute, but this list is unannotated, so it will likely require more time to navigate than a more fully annotated code. If you do not have access to these services, visit a law library to access the annotated code in print or determine whether a public-access version of Westlaw or Lexis is available.

Finally, read and analyze the cases that interpret the statute as explained in Chapter 5 and apply the statute to the facts of your client's particular situation.

C. Updating Your Research

As a final step to any statutory research, remember to update your research to ensure you have the most current text of the statute as well as the most up-to-date list of cases that interpret the statute. If you are researching the code in print, check the pocket parts or supplements for each volume you use. Online, check any site or database for information on when it was last updated.[18]

Whether researching in print or online, always Shepardize or KeyCite statutes[19] to determine if there have been any changes since the source was published and to ensure that the statute has not been declared unconstitutional. If the General Assembly is in session, typically from January to April, you may also want to separately check to see if any pending legislation could affect your statute.[20]

---

18. On Bloomberg Law, currency information appears in the right column. Fastcase notes the edition of the statutes being searched at the top of the screen; do not assume the edition includes laws passed that session of the General Assembly. On Lexis look at the top of the screen for information on currency. On Westlaw, use the "Currentness" link near the top of the statute.

19. These services are explained in Chapter 9.

20. This process is explained in Chapter 7.

V. Interpreting Statutes

As discussed in Section IV., statutory research involves reading and analyzing the text of a statute and any related statutes, analyzing any cases that have applied the statute, and applying the statute to the facts of your client's particular situation. This analytical work can be difficult if the statute is vague or if the application of the statute to the client's situation is not clear. Sometimes ambiguities exist because the statute was badly drafted, other times because of the give and take that is a natural part of the legislative process. A great deal of case law revolves around the meaning of statutes, and you cannot properly evaluate how a statute might apply to your client's facts without examining how it has been interpreted by courts.

The *Code of Iowa* provides guidance on issues related to statutes as well as the construction of statutes. Chapter 3, "Statutes and Related Matters," addresses the forms of bills, bill drafting instructions, and detailed information about the acts, including effective dates. Chapter 4, "Construction of Statutes," includes, among other things, information about terminology, prospective statutes, and interpreting ambiguous statutes.[21] A helpful authoritative treatise on the subject of statutory construction is Norman J. Singer & J.D. Shambie Singer, *Statutes and Statutory Construction* (7th ed. 2007).

In Iowa, statutes are not strictly construed according to the rule of the common law[22] except when the statute is ambiguous.[23] Rather, statutory provisions are liberally construed "with a view to promote its [the statute's] objects and assist the parties in obtaining justice."[24] To determine the statute's purpose, Iowa courts first consider the language of the statute, using definitions provided in the code or the plain meaning of the words.[25] Courts attempt to interpret the statute as a whole, where the language of the provision interpreted should be consistent with the rest of the statute. When the language is ambiguous or conflicting, the court follows the rules of construction established by both Iowa statutes and case law.[26] A *Drake Law Review* article pro-

---

21. Iowa Code § 4.6, addressing the interpretation of ambiguous statutes, is discussed in more detail in Chapter 7.

22. Iowa Code § 4.2.

23. Iowa Code § 4.6(4).

24. Iowa Code § 4.2.

25. *See, e.g., Miller v. Marshall County*, 641 N.W.2d 742 (Iowa 2002).

26. Iowa Code § 4.6, further discussed in Chapter 7, outlines the factors courts should consider in such cases.

vides a more detailed, but still brief, overview of how Iowa courts interpret statutes, as well as questions you can consider when interpreting a statute that may be ambiguous.[27]

VI. Statutes of Other States

Statutory research in other states is similar to that in Iowa. Each state publishes session laws. Many states have both official and unofficial codes. Like the *Code of Iowa*, the majority of official codes are unannotated, but this is not always the case. For example, in Montana the official, state-published code is an annotated version. In any statutory research, you must determine which code is official for citation purposes; it might not be the annotated code used for research. Other states' codes may also be arranged differently than Iowa. Iowa uses numbers to denote code chapters, but other states do not. Several states, such as California and Texas, divide the codified statutes into a number of named codes.[28]

Almost all states now publish their state codes online where they are freely available to the public. Unlike Iowa, though, not all online codes are official versions.[29] Cornell's Legal Information Institute offers a list of links to state codes.[30] Bloomberg Law, Fastcase, Lexis, and Westlaw all contain versions of codes from all fifty states. A good general rule is that the publisher of the print annotated version will provide the most current and up-to-date version electronically as well. In Iowa, this publisher is West (Thomson Reuters), which provides Westlaw.

Sometimes, it is necessary to compare statutes among several states, and there are resources that can make this research easier. In print, the main com-

---

27. Karen L. Wallace, *Does the Past Predict the Future?: An Empirical Analysis of Recent Iowa Supreme Court Use of Legislative History as a Window into Statutory Construction in Iowa*, 63 Drake L. Rev. 239 (2015). The overview of the most important statutory construction rules in Iowa is found at 249–57, and the questions are found at 287–96.

28. For example, you may see code names such as the California Penal Code or the Texas Water Code.

29. The National Conference of State Legislatures conducted a fifty-state survey that indicates whether states' electronic codes were considered official. The report is available at http://www.ncsl.org/documents/lsss/Official_Version_Statutes.pdf. Note, however, that information is only current as of 2011; the fact that it is subject to change is illustrated by the Iowa listing, which indicates the online version is unofficial.

30. Cornell's site is located at https://www.law.cornell.edu/statutes.html.

pilation of state laws is the *National Survey of State Laws* (7th ed. 2015). It digests state law in over fifty areas and is arranged by topic, rather than state. Electronically, it is available on HeinOnline. For a more complete list of sources that contain collections of state statutes, see the bibliography *Subject Compilations of State Laws* (1981–present), which is also available through HeinOnline. Additional sources for finding and comparing state statutes are listed in the Drake Law Library research guide State and Local Law Research.[31]

VII. Federal Statutes

Federal statutes follow the three-tiered publication schedule discussed in Section II. Federal statutes enacted during a session of the U.S. Congress are known as either a *public law* or a *private law*. Public laws are designed to affect the general public, while private laws are passed to meet the needs of an individual or small group. Although both types are passed in the same way and appear in the session laws, only public laws become part of the statutory code.

A. Slip Laws

Public laws are first released as slip laws by the Government Publishing Office.[32] Each public law is cited by the session of Congress and number of the chronological order of enactment. For example, Pub. L. No. 109-11 was the 11th public law of the 109th Congress. All slip laws are only intended to be used on an interim basis until they are replaced by session laws.

After slip laws, the first print publication of federal statutes is in two advance session law services: *United States Code Congressional and Administrative News* (USCCAN) and *United States Code Service Advance* (USCS Advance).[33] Both services issue monthly pamphlets, publishing new federal statutes within a couple of months of enactment. USCCAN is published by West and is also available via Westlaw. The second advance session law service, USCS Advance, is published by LexisNexis and available via Lexis. These

---

31. This guide is freely available at http://libguides.law.drake.edu/stateLaw, although some of the linked sources are not freely available.

32. Slip laws are available online from http://www.gpo.gov and http://www.congress.gov.

33. Both USCCAN and USCS Advance also contain information such as Presidential proclamations and select administrative regulations. In addition, USCCAN publishes excerpts of selective legislative history materials.

pamphlets are intended to be used only until they are replaced by bound volumes of the USCS.

B. Session Laws

The *Statutes at Large* (Stat.) set supersedes slip laws and serves as the permanent official publication for federal laws. A numbered volume is issued for each session of Congress. The volumes arrange the laws chronologically according to their public law numbers and *Statutes at Large* citation. *Statutes at Large* are cited by volume, page number, and year. For instance, Pub. L. No. 109-11 is 119 Stat. 229 (2005) in the *Statutes at Large*. Publication of the *Statutes at Large* is usually delayed by several years. However, slip laws on government sites include the *Statutes at Large* pagination within a few weeks of enactment.

USCCAN serves as an unofficial version of the *Statutes at Large* and is available in print and on Westlaw. Electronically, Lexis and Westlaw contain the full text of statutes from volume one until the present, and HeinOnline provides the full text of statutes starting with volume one to the most recently published volume of the *Statutes at Large*.

Although for research purposes you may gravitate towards the annotated versions of the United States Code, which are discussed in Section VII.C., the *Statutes at Large* play an important role in statutory research. While sections of a public law may be spread among several code titles, the *Statutes at Large* provides the complete text of each act of Congress.

C. Codified Statutes

The *United States Code* (USC) is the final iteration of statutes and is arranged by subject rather than chronologically. Published by the government, the USC is the official codification of federal statutes and the preferred source to cite. It is arranged into more than fifty subject titles, with chapter and section subdivisions.[34] A citation to the USC includes a title and section number, for example, 28 U.S.C. § 1331, where 28 is Title 28, not volume 28.

The USC is not annotated, although it has an extensive index and includes historical notes, cross-references, and parenthetical references following each section that note the public law and *Statutes at Large* references. Other important features of the USC include the Popular Name Table, which lists statutes

---

34. Title numbers range from 1 through 54. Title 34 was repealed, and Title 53 is reserved. Titles 55 and 56 may be added in the near future.

by their commonly used names and provides their official citations, and the Parallel Reference Table, which provides the code section corresponding to the session law number and helps you determine if a law is still in force. Examine Figure 6-4 for an example of the index to the USC and Figure 6-5 for an example from the code itself.

Figure 6-4. Sample of *United States Code* Index

> ## GRANDPARENTS AND GRANDCHILDREN
> Appropriations, housing, demonstration projects or programs, 12 § 1701q note
> Caregiver, grants, 42 § 3030s et seq.
> Census, 13 § 141 note
> Child support, 42 § 666
> Definitions,
> Housing, 12 § 1701q note
> Longshore and harbor worker's compensation, 33 § 902
> Demonstration projects or programs, housing, 12 § 1701q note
> Foster Grandparent Program. National Senior Volunteer Corps, this index
> Generation-Skipping Transfers, generally, this index
> Grants, caregiver, 42 § 3030s et seq.
> Housing, 12 § 1701q note; 42 § 3535
> Housing and Urban Development Department, training, 42 § 3535
> Income tax, controlled corporations, shares and shareholders, 26 § 1563
> Living Equitably: Grandparents Aiding Children and Youth Act of 2003, 12 § 1701q note; 42 § 3535

Source: U.S.C. General Index D-I p. 699–700 (2012).

The USC is published only every six years with cumulative bound supplements issued between editions. Publication usually runs several years behind. To update, check the annual bound supplement for changes. HeinOnline contains the comprehensive full text of the USC. For a list of free websites providing the federal code, see Table 6-4.

There are two unofficial annotated versions of the code. One advantage to these unofficial commercial versions of the code is that they are updated much more frequently. *United States Code Annotated* (USCA) is published by West

Figure 6-5. Sample Entry in *United States Code*

---

§ 3030s. Definitions

(a) In general

In this subpart:

(1) Child

The term "child" means an individual who is not more than 18 years of age or who is an individual with a disability.

(2) Grandparent or older individual who is a relative caregiver

The term "grandparent or older individual who is a relative caregiver" means a grandparent or stepgrandparent of a child, or a relative of a child by blood, marriage, or adoption, who is 55 years of age or older and—

(A) lives with the child;

(B) is the primary caregiver of the child because the biological or adoptive parents are unable or unwilling to serve as the primary caregiver of the child; and

(C) has a legal relationship to the child, as such legal custody or guardianship, or is raising the child informally.

(b) Rule

In providing services under this subpart—

(1) for family caregivers who provide care for individuals with Alzheimer's disease and related disorders with neurological and organic brain dysfunction, the State involved shall give priority to caregivers who provide care for older individuals with such disease or disorder; and

(2) for grandparents or older individuals who are relative caregivers, the State involved shall give priority to caregivers who provide care for children with severe disabilities.

(Pub. L. 89–73, title III, §372, as added Pub. L. 106–501, title III, §316(2), Nov. 13, 2000, 114 Stat. 2254; amended Pub. L. 109–365, title III, §320, Oct. 17, 2006, 120 Stat. 2551.)

AMENDMENTS

2006—Pub. L. 109–365 designated existing provisions as subsec. (a) and inserted heading, inserted "or who is an

---

Table 6-4. Free Online Resources for Federal Statutes

Publication	Source	Address	Date Range
Slip Laws	Government Publishing Office (includes Private Laws)	http://www.gpo.gov/fdsys/ browse/collection. action?collectionCode=PLAW	1995–present
	Congress.Gov	https://www.congress.gov /public-laws	1973–present
Statutes at Large (Stat.)	Government Publishing Office	http://www.gpo.gov/fdsys/ browse/collection.action? collectionCode=STATUTE	1951–present
	Library of Congress	http://memory.loc.gov/ ammem/amlaw/lwsllink.html	1789–1875
United States Code (U.S.C.)	Government Publishing Office	http://www.gpo.gov/fdsys/ browse/collectionUScode. action?collectionCode= USCODE	1994–present
	U.S. House of Representatives Internet Library	http://uscode.house.gov/ search/criteria.shtml	1994–present
	Cornell's Legal Information Institute	http://www.law.cornell.edu/ uscode/text	Current

and available on Westlaw. The print version is updated through annual pocket parts and noncumulative quarterly pamphlets. USCA uses the same title, chapter, and section format as the USC but offers additional information that can aid the researcher, such as annotations for related court decisions and references to secondary sources that may help in interpreting code sections. *United States Code Service* (USCS), which is published by LexisNexis and available on Lexis, is another unofficial annotated code. It contains the same editorial advantages of the USCA, though the information provided in the two is not identical. One difference between the two sets is that the USCA attempts to provide comprehensive coverage of all relevant decisions, while the USCS focuses on the best decisions and tries to weed out obsolete or repetitive information.

Bloomberg Law offers another version of the code. It is kept up-to-date as new public laws are passed, but it is not fully annotated. However, it does offer access to cases that have cited the code section you are viewing through a "Case Analysis" tab. The cases shown can be refined based on date, jurisdiction, depth of discussion and topic using left-hand menu limiters. Fastcase also offers an updated, unannotated version of the code that includes a list of cases that cite each code section.

Researching federal statutes follows the same general principles of Iowa statutory research, as discussed in depth in Section IV. Refer to Table 6-1 for a flowchart of the general statutory research process. Note that in conducting print research, the volume numbers on the spine of each bound book are different from the title numbers that appear in a citation. Thus, a statute in Title 42 of the USC might not be in volume 42 of the USC.

VIII. Court Rules

Court rules govern all stages of litigation, from filing an action through the completion of appeals. Failure to comply with these rules may result in the dismissal of a case, so it is important to know what they are, where they are located, and how to follow them.

A. Iowa Court Rules

"The Iowa Supreme Court is responsible for prescribing all rules of procedure, pleadings, practice, evidence, and the forms of process, writs and notices, for all proceedings in the state courts."[35] Items governed by court rules range from the Rules of Probate Court to Rules for Involuntary Commitment or Treatment for Chronic Substance Abusers.

In print, Iowa court rules are published by the Legislative Service Agency of the Iowa legislature, through commercial publisher West, under the direction of the Iowa Supreme Court. The West print version of the rules is entitled *Iowa Rules of Court: State*, which is published yearly and may also be updated with pocket parts. *Iowa Court Rules* are freely available online through the Iowa legislature's site. They also are accessible through Bloomberg Law, Lexis, and Westlaw.

---

35. Iowa Judicial Branch, "Iowa Court Rules and Forms," http://www.iowacourts .gov/Court_Rules__Forms/Overview/.

Many local courts also have their own rules, which supplement and need to be consistent with the state rules. Check with the individual court to see if there are other rules that need to be applied beyond those at the state level. For example, the Third Judicial District has a rule on the numbering of exhibits in civil and criminal cases. Most courts list the rules on their websites. Table 6-5 lists free online sources of Iowa state and local court rules.

B. Federal Court Rules

Primary federal court rules are the Federal Rules of Civil Procedure, Federal Rules of Criminal Procedure, Federal Rules of Appellate Procedure, Federal Rules of Bankruptcy Procedure, and Federal Rules of Evidence. Unannotated versions are available in the USC and from the United States Courts website.[36] Annotated court rules are also included in the USCA and USCS.

As with local courts, individual federal courts may also have local rules. These are usually available on the court's website; in specialized publications, such as Thomson West's *Federal Local Court Rules*; or on Bloomberg Law, Lexis, or Westlaw.[37] Local rules of the U.S. District Courts for the Northern and Southern Districts of Iowa, rules and procedures for the Eighth Circuit, and more are in *Iowa Rules of Court: Federal*, which is published yearly by West and may also be updated with pocket parts. For local rules of Iowa-related federal courts, see Table 6-5. Always remember to check the currency of your source when consulting court rules.

IX. Local Ordinances

Just as there are statutes at the state and federal levels, so too are there statutes at the county and city, or *municipal*, level, usually called ordinances. Individual ordinances at the local level are similar to slip laws at the state and federal levels. Municipal or county codes are the codification of these ordinances. County and municipal ordinances usually deal with issues such as animal control, building regulations, city land use, emergency services, housing, parking, streets and sidewalks, traffic, and zoning.

---

36. Rules can be downloaded in PDF format from http://www.uscourts.gov /rules-policies/current-rules-practice-procedure.

37. Local federal rules on Bloomberg Law are available in the Federal Court Rules database; on Lexis, they can be found in the state sources that include "state and federal court rules" in their titles; on Westlaw, they are available on the Federal Local Court Rules page.

Table 6-5. Free Online Resources for Iowa Court Rules and Iowa-Related Federal Courts

Court/Document	Address
Iowa Court Rules	Iowa Legislature https://www.legis.iowa.gov/law/courtRules
Iowa First Judicial District Local Rules	http://www.iowacourts.gov/About_the_Courts/District_Courts/District_One/Local_Rules/
Iowa Second Judicial District Local Rules	http://www.iowacourts.gov/About_the_Courts/District_Courts/District_Two/Local_Rules/
Iowa Third Judicial District Local Rules	http://www.iowacourts.gov/About_the_Courts/District_Courts/District_Three/Local_Rules/
Iowa Fifth Judicial District Local Rules	http://www.iowacourts.gov/About_the_Courts/District_Courts/District_Five/Local_Rules/
Iowa Sixth Judicial District Local Rules	http://www.iowacourts.gov/About_the_Courts/District_Courts/District_Six/Local_Rules/
Iowa Seventh Judicial District Local Rules	http://www.iowacourts.gov/About_the_Courts/District_Courts/District_Seven/Local_Rules/
Iowa Eighth Judicial District Local Rules	http://www.iowacourts.gov/About_the_Courts/District_Courts/District_Eight/Local_Rules/
U.S. District Court Southern District of Iowa	http://www.iasd.uscourts.gov/?q=court-info/local-rules-and-orders
U.S. District Court Northern District of Iowa	http://www.iand.uscourts.gov/e-web/home.nsf/home (Clerk of Court > Local and Federal Rules)
Eighth Circuit	http://media.ca8.uscourts.gov/newrules/coa/localrules.pdf

A. Finding Local Ordinances

Local ordinances can be some of the hardest statutes to locate. Even with the enormous amount of information available on the web, many counties and cities are simply too small (or understaffed) to be able to maintain their ordinances online. Some county and city governments do, however, put both their codes of ordinances and zoning ordinances on the web. Others post only specific ordinances, such as those requiring clearing the sidewalks after snow. Some cities publish new or revised ordinances in the local newspaper. The Drake Law Library maintains a regularly updated list of links to Iowa municipal codes and county ordinances.[38]

If a county or city does not make its ordinances available online, contact the county or city government directly. If you can go to the offices, you can simply ask to see the ordinances. If you cannot go in person, however, ask to have a copy of the ordinance in question sent to you. Local ordinances can be quite long, so it may not be feasible for the entire document to be sent to you. It is always better to have an ordinance number on hand in case you are able to request only a limited number of pages. Websites of the Iowa League of Cities and Iowa State Association of Counties contain much useful information about local government.[39]

B. Updating Ordinances

As with all legal research, it is critically important to ensure you are citing to the most current version of an ordinance. Even if the ordinance is available online, it is good practice to contact the city or county directly to verify that you have the most up-to-date material.

---

38. Drake Law Library's list of municipal and county ordinances is at http://libguides.law.drake.edu/IowaLocalCodes.

39. Iowa League of Cities is at iowaleague.org and Iowa State Association of Counties is at http://www.iowacounties.org.

Chapter 7

Legislative History

I. Introduction

In addition to researching Iowa laws as codified in the *Code of Iowa*, you will sometimes need to look to the law-making process to determine how a statute might apply to your client's situation. When a statute's meaning is ambiguous and has not already been clarified by earlier court decisions, you will investigate its legislative history to try to persuade the court that the statutory intent favors your client. You may also need to track current legislation to see if proposed or recently enacted bills might affect one of your clients. Both instances require a basic knowledge of the legislative process in Iowa, and this chapter begins with that introduction. The chapter then builds on this understanding to discuss the specific research tools and strategies involved in locating legislative history or tracking current legislation.[1]

II. Iowa Legislative Process

The state legislative body in Iowa is called the General Assembly (G.A.). It is composed of two chambers: the House of Representatives, whose members serve two-year terms, and the Senate, whose members serve four-year terms. Each G.A. is numbered consecutively and consists of two *regular sessions*, together spanning two years. The first session is held at the beginning[2] of the odd-numbered year. The second is held at the beginning of the even-numbered year. For instance, the 86th G.A. began in 2015 (first session) and ended in

---

1. Thanks to Cory Quist and Mandy Easter of the Iowa State Law Library, Meaghan McCarthy and Jeffrey Dawson of the Iowa State Archives, and Valerie Hansen and Jonetta Douglas of the Legislative Services Agency for their guidance in researching this chapter for the first edition.

2. Sessions typically run from January into April.

2016 (second session). Some General Assemblies may have additional sessions, called *extraordinary sessions*.

The two general forms of Iowa legislation are bills and resolutions. Most proposals of law take the form of a *bill*. A special kind of bill, called a *study bill*, is sponsored by a committee, the governor, or a state agency. The objective of a study bill is to get a sense of how the legislature will respond to the proposal. If a study bill earns committee approval, it will then be introduced as a regular bill. The second form of Iowa legislation, a *resolution*, is often used to address rules of legislative operation or ceremonial matters, such as issuing a congratulatory message. Resolutions may also be passed to issue a temporary law.

Iowa legislation must be sponsored by one or more legislators or by a legislative committee. The legislative sponsor submits a bill request form to the Legal Services Division of the nonpartisan Legislative Services Agency (LSA).[3] Consulting with the sponsor as needed, an LSA drafter will then write a bill that, if passed and not vetoed, would enact the proposal. The sponsor reviews the bill draft and may send it back to the LSA for further revision. The sponsor may choose to introduce the legislation by filing the bill with the chamber's chief administrative officer, either the Secretary of the Senate or the Chief Clerk of the House. Typically, the draft is assigned a bill number beginning with SF for Senate file or HF for House file. In the case of a study bill, the draft is assigned a number beginning with SSB for Senate study bill, or HSB for House study bill.

The remainder of the legislative process is similar to that of most states and the federal government. See Figure 7-1, Iowa Legislative Process Flowchart, for a flowchart representation. Proposed legislation is debated and amended in committee. If the bill is approved by the committee, it will be debated and amended on the floor of the chamber that introduced it. If approved in that chamber, the bill then goes to the other chamber and follows the same process. If the second chamber amends the bill, the amendments are considered by the first chamber. If the two chambers cannot pass an identical bill, a conference committee will meet to try to resolve the differences. After both the House and Senate have passed the same version of a bill, it is *engrossed*, a process that incorporates all the approved amendments into the bill text. Then the bill is certified by the chief administrative officer of the chamber in which

---

3. The Legislative Services Bureau performed legislative drafting until a reorganization, effective April 14, 2003, created the new Legislative Services Agency. *See* 2003 Iowa Acts 44.

Figure 7-1. Iowa Legislative Process Flowchart

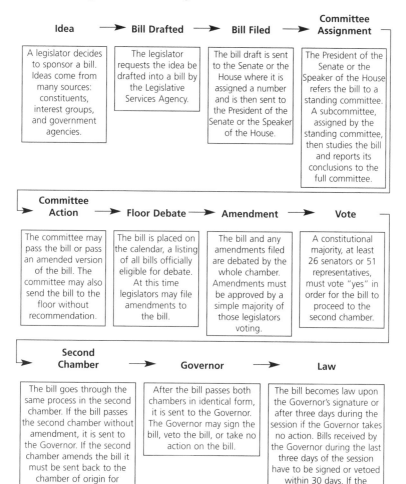

Source: Flowchart derived from Iowa Legislature General Assembly website: http://www.legis.iowa.gov/Docs/ Resources/HowAnIdeaBecomesALaw.pdf.

it originated. The certified, engrossed bill is sent to the governor, who can sign it, veto it, or take no action on it.

If the governor signs the bill, it becomes law. Unless otherwise specified in the bill, the effective date is July 1 or August 15, if signed by the governor after July 1. If the governor vetoes the bill, it is sent back to the legislature if it is still in session; the veto can be overridden with at least two-thirds of the members of each chamber voting for it. A bill with an overridden veto also becomes law, effective July 1 of that year unless otherwise specified in the bill. If the governor takes no action on a bill received before the last three days of the session, it will become law after the passage of three days. If the governor does not take action for thirty days on a bill received during the last three days, it fails to become law, a result known as a *pocket veto*.

III. Iowa Legislative History Research

A. Introduction to Iowa Legislative History Research

As discussed in Chapter 6, an attorney must read a statute carefully to understand its meaning. In fact, a meticulous reading of the words of the statute and surrounding sections, such as definitions, is the first step in determining legislative intent. However, when a statute can be construed in more than one way, courts may look beyond the language of a statute to try to determine the legislature's intent in enacting it. The tools a court may consider are outlined in Iowa Code § 4.6, shown in Figure 7-2.

If court cases have already interpreted the statute, you will want to read these opinions to better understand its application. If the courts have not already interpreted the part of the statute related to your legal issue, or considered its legislative history, you will want to look at the statute's history to learn more about its purpose. You will identify the bills that enacted and amended the statute, analyze how these proposals changed the law, and assess the objectives of these changes.

Iowa, like many states, has available only a limited amount of documented legislative history.[4] Be aware when you begin your research that you will not

---

4. For a guide to legislative history sources in other states, see *State Legislative History Research Guides Inventory*, compiled by Jennifer Bryan Morgan, Documents Librarian, Indiana University School of Law Library — Bloomington at http://law. indiana.libguides.com/state-legislative-history-guides.

Figure 7-2. Iowa Code § 4.6

If a statute is ambiguous, the court, in determining the intention of the legislature, may consider among other matters

1. The object sought to be attained

2. The circumstances under which the statute was enacted

3. The legislative history

4. The common law or former statutory provisions, including laws upon the same or similar subjects

5. The consequences of a particular construction

6. The administrative construction of the statute

7. The preamble or statement of policy

Source: Code of Iowa 2015. Des Moines: Legislative Services Agency, General Assembly of Iowa, 2014.

likely find vast quantities of information. However, if you search systematically, as outlined in Table 7-1 and explained in Section III.B., you will find the available information and, possibly, something useful. A 2015 empirical analysis of the Iowa Supreme Court's use of legislative history in construing ambiguous statutes found that the Court cited some type of Iowa legislative history in almost 11% of the cases studied.[5]

B. Sources of Iowa Legislative History

1. Overview

To follow the legislative history process outlined in Table 7-1, you will consult several sources. Some of these sources will allow you to complete several steps, while others may only allow you to complete part of a single step. The rest of this section presents these key sources in the order in which you should consult them when following the research process.

---

5. Karen L. Wallace, *Does the Past Predict the Future?: An Empirical Analysis of Recent Iowa Supreme Court Use of Legislative History as a Window into Statutory Construction in Iowa*, 63 Drake L. Rev. 239, 266 (2015). Note, too, that other historical examinations, such as tracing the evolution of a code section without necessarily also looking at the legislative consideration of a particular bill, informed even more decisions; in total, the court engaged in some type of historical analysis in 37% of the decisions in the data set.

Table 7-1. General Process for Researching Iowa Legislative History

1. Determine whether a legislative history analysis already exists for the code section.

2. If there is no compiled analysis, read the history information below the code section to note the acts that created and changed the section.

3. Examine each act to ascertain what changes were made and whether the changes are relevant to your issue.

4. If the act is relevant, note the *file number* at the top of the act.

5. Consult the *bill book* to determine how the bill changed from introduction to enrollment. If it was originally a study bill, also consult that file.

6. Examine the explanation at the end of the introduced bill and, if relevant, at the end of the study bill.

7. If the bill is neither a Ways and Means nor Appropriations measure but has a significant effect on the state's finances, determine whether a fiscal note is attached to the bill.

   * *At this point, you have likely already found most of what will be influential to the courts in determining intent. However, you can continue searching to be completely thorough and to obtain additional background or other contextual information.*

8. Determine whether there is a compiled bill history to review what actions each chamber took on the bill. If a compilation does not already exist, compile your own, using the House and Senate *journals*.

9. Check *committee minutes*.

10. Determine whether any relevant *reports* have been filed.

11. Examine the original *bill drafting file*.

12. Search for newspaper articles discussing the legislation.

2. Compiled Legislative History: Annotated Codes and Index to Legal Periodicals

An efficient first step in legislative history research is to determine whether others have already examined the legislative history of your statute in a published article or book. Relatively few Iowa legislative histories have been published, so you often will not find anything relevant. However, if an analysis of the history of your code section does exist, you will save a great deal of time by beginning your research with this source. Moreover, such analyses may be persuasive to a court, so you will want to review one if it exists.[6]

Published legislative histories for a particular statute should be cited in an annotated code. You can also check for one using the tools for searching by subject for treatises and law review articles, described in Chapter 3. If you use an index, be aware that the term "legislative history" will probably not appear in the subject field and may well not be in the title, either. You will want to search by the act or code name. In addition, the *Index to Legal Periodicals* database[7] allows searching by the field statute. This method allows you to enter the Iowa code citation to see if any journal articles have examined it.

3. Code Section History

If you do not find a published legislative history analysis for your code section, you will want to examine the legislative history references (or credits) as well as historical and statutory notes found in the *Iowa Code Annotated*, published by West.[8] See Figure 7-A in the chapter appendix for an example of these notes. The references list the acts that created and changed the code section and any prior section numbers where the law was previously codified. The historical and statutory notes briefly explain the changes made by each act. The notes can help you determine whether the change was relevant to your situation and which session laws you need to consult. Similar notes appear in the annotated code versions available through Lexis and Westlaw, more thoroughly described in Chapter 6.

If you do not have access to an annotated code, you can find the legislative history citations at the end of the code section in the *Code of Iowa* in print or online as well as in Bloomberg Law. The way this information was presented changed between 1982 and 1984. The older history notes are provided in

---

6. In one Iowa decision, the court established legislative history by referencing two law review articles. *See Richardson v. City of Jefferson*, 134 N.W.2d 528 (Iowa 1965). In *Richardson*, when the court turned to legislative history, it noted, "For legislative history see "'Home Rule' For Iowa Cities and Towns?" 13 Drake Law Review 53; and "Municipal Home Rule in Iowa: House File 380," 49 Iowa Law Review 826." *Id.* at 532.

7. *See* https://www.ebscohost.com/academic/index-to-legal-periodicals-and-books -full-text.

8. The LexisNexis "Iowa Annotated Statutes" database provides most of this information as well. However, it does not give the session law references for the acts that created and changed the code section; it provides only references to the years the code section changed.

Figure 7-3. Excerpt from *Code of Iowa* History with Explanation

275.41 Alternative method for director elections — temporary appointments.

[Statutory text omitted]

[C62, 66, 71, 73, 75, 77, §275.25; C79, 81, §275.41]
83 Acts, ch 53, §5; 85 Acts, ch 221, §9; 93 Acts, ch 160, §12, 13; 2005 Acts, ch 3, §58; 2008 Acts, ch 1115, §17, 21; 2009 Acts, ch 41, §248
Referred to in §275.1

Explanation of code history:
1. Bracketed information provides earlier versions of code where material appeared. In the 1962-77 codes it was at §275.25; in the 1979 and 1981 codes, it was at its current placement, §275.41
2. Information outside the brackets provides references for session laws that added or modified the section. This section was modified in 1983, 1993, 2005, 2008 and 2009.
3. Beyond the history, there is another note indicating that §275.1 references §275.25.

Source: Code of Iowa § 275.41 (2015). Explanation added by authors.

brackets and simply reference earlier versions of the code that covered the topic along with the section number where it appeared. The newer version, listed outside of the brackets, only indicates changes to the section. Notes with a code reference indicate that the section was moved; Acts references indicate the section was created or amended. Figure 7-3 provides an example of the *Code of Iowa* history for §275.41 with an added explanation of those history references.

These unannotated sources also do not provide references to court cases that have interpreted the statute, secondary sources that have commented on it, or notes on how new laws may have changed the statute. See Chapter 9 for an explanation of how to find these references using citators. Fastcase provides an approach in the middle. It lists the code history references as they appear in the *Code of Iowa*. If there are secondary sources available through HeinOnline (which is linked to Fastcase) that discuss the statute, these references will appear in a "Suggested Results" box to the left of the search results. Once the code section is opened, an unannotated list of cases citing the statute appears at the bottom of the screen.

In the empirical analysis of Iowa Supreme Court cases discussed in Section III.A., an analysis of code section history occurred in almost 29% of cases in the data set. This number includes times when the court notes that the legislature had amended a code section in response to an earlier decision it thought the court got wrong (5%) or had opted not to amend, apparently acquiescing to the court's interpretation (5%).[9] Not only does looking at the code section history form the basis for further investigation of legislative history, it is also fairly frequently considered by the court when construing ambiguous statutes.

4. Session Laws

Both the *Iowa Code Annotated* and the *Code of Iowa* reference individual acts that have affected a code section by providing their session law citations in this form: [year] Acts [chapter and section number]. For instance, 2009 Acts 52 refers to the act with the heading Chapter 52 in the 2009 Iowa session laws. As noted in Chapter 6, Iowa session laws are published in the *Acts and Joint Resolutions of the General Assembly* and are also available through several online sources.

Acts in the session laws are printed in order by chapter number. When reviewing your referenced act, you will see a heading that includes chapter number, title, and legislation number (probably SF or HF for Senate file or House file).[10] This heading is followed by a brief summary that describes the act. Courts have occasionally referenced this summary in interpreting intent.[11] Next, examine the text of the act to note any changes made to the code, shown via special formatting known as redlining. <u>Underlining</u> indicates new text; ~~strikeouts~~ indicate deleted text. If entirely new sections are being added, only the words New Section or New Subsection will be underlined. Note that some acts include a section entitled "LEGISLATIVE INTENT," indicating what the legislature wants to accomplish in enacting the law. The court has cited the act text when interpreting a statute.[12] Also record the legislation

---

9. Wallace, *supra* note 5, at 266.

10. Wallace notes that, between 2004 and 2013, the court once referenced the act title when interpreting an ambiguous statute. Wallace, *supra* note 5, at 307. The case, *State v. Lathrop*, 781 N.W.2d 288, 295 (Iowa 2010), referenced an act with a long title and indicated it summarized the legislation.

11. *See, e.g., State v. Lathrop*, 781 N.W.2d 288 (Iowa 2010). The *Lathrop* court cited the specific language of the summary to determine the legislative intent in enacting a special sentence of lifetime parole for sex offenders. Wallace, *supra* note 5, at 307 (noting that, between 2004 and 2013, the court referenced the act summary five times when interpreting an ambiguous statute).

12. Wallace, *supra* note 5, at 307 (noting that, between 2004 and 2013, the court referenced a bill amendment that passed eight times and an amendment that failed once when interpreting an ambiguous statute). *See, e.g., In re Det. of Johnson*, 805 N.W.2d 750 (Iowa 2011). In *Johnson*, the court examined the act to evaluate the legislation as whole, noting that the new requirement that a final hearing on civil

number from the heading of the act, the G.A. number, and the session year, in case you decide to delve deeper into the bill's history. See Figure 7-B in the chapter appendix for an example of an act published in the session laws. Note that for the session law depicted in that figure, the legislation number, S.F. 500, is listed under the chapter number and brief title. The G.A. and session number, in this case 65-2 (the second session of the 65th G.A.), and the session year, 1974, are all visible from the volume spine. The title page includes the G.A. number and session year; you could determine the session number easily by remembering that, starting in 1969, the first year of an Iowa G.A. is odd, and the second is even.

5. Bill Books

a. Bill Versions

Bill books include the introduced bill with all its amendments. Print sources use a color-coded system, as seen in Table 7-2.

Tracking the changes made to a piece of legislation from introduction to enrollment can provide insight into legislative intent and has occasionally been considered by the courts.[13] If a bill started out as a study bill, that number will be indicated near the top of the original bill. You will want to look back at the study bill, too, to see how the legislation evolved.[14] Finally, note the bill title because it might shed light on the statute's interpretation.[15]

---

commitment be set within sixty days of the decision to have such a hearing was added "as part of a comprehensive amendment to chapter 229A in 2002 which increased the procedural protections given to civilly committed." *Id.* at 754. Wallace, *supra* note 5, at 307 (noting that, between 2004 and 2013, the court referenced the act text twelve times when interpreting an ambiguous statute).

13. *See, e.g., Chelsea Theater Corp. v. City of Burlington*, 258 N.W.2d 372 (Iowa 1977). In *Chelsea*, the court noted that a Senate amendment struck the phrase "to minors" from the version originally passed by the House. The court explained, "The deletion of the phrase 'to minors' by both the House and Senate before enactment of § 725.9 lends support to our conclusion that the statute prohibits local governments from regulating the availability of obscene materials generally, and not just with respect to minors." *Id.* at 374.

14. Wallace, *supra* note 5, at 307 (noting that, between 2004 and 2013, the court twice referenced prior bills when interpreting an ambiguous statute). *See, e.g., Iowa Right To Life Comm., Inc. v. Tooker*, 808 N.W.2d 417, 430 (Iowa 2011). In *Iowa Right To Life*, the court referenced both a study bill and another prior version of the law being construed to note that these bills, too, relied on the same regulatory scheme as the statute being interpreted. *Id.*

15. Wallace notes that between 2004 and 2013, the court once referenced the act title when interpreting an ambiguous statute. Wallace, *supra* note 5, at 307. The case,

Table 7-2. Iowa Bill Book Color Coding

White.................Bill as introduced	
Blue ....Senate amendment	
Yellow...............House amendment	
Pink...................Bill with amendments passed by originating chamber	
Green................Senate study bill	
Salmon.............House study bill	

b. Bill Explanations

As noted earlier, the Legislative Services Agency drafts Iowa bills in response to a request from a legislator or legislative committee. Starting with the 49th G.A. (1941), House rules require an explanation to accompany most bills.[16] The Senate adopted a similar rule starting with the 63rd G.A. (1969).[17] Written by the drafter, the bill explanation is based on information conveyed by the legislator to the drafter. This information may have been written on the bill request form or provided through conversation with the drafter. Some explanations are lengthy, but many are brief. Iowa courts have used these explanations fairly frequently in interpreting legislative history.[18] Within the bill book, the explanation is found at the end of the original version of the bill and preceded by the heading EXPLANATION. See Figure 7-C in the chapter

---

Sallee v. Stewart, 827 N.W.2d 128, 141 (Iowa 2013), cites the title of the Iowa bill, illustrating it shared its name with the model legislation on which it was based, although the Iowa version then deviated from that model legislation.

16. For the current iteration, see Rule 27 in the House Rules: https://www.legis .iowa.gov/DOCS/ChamberRules/HouseRules.pdf.

17. For the current iteration, see Rule 29 in the Senate Rules: https://www.legis .iowa.gov/DOCS/ChamberRules/SenateRules.pdf.

18. *See, e.g., City of Waterloo v. Bainbridge*, 749 N.W.2d 245, 248 (Iowa 2008) (directly quoting from and citing to the bill explanation in noting why the legislature enacted the statute). Wallace notes that, between 2004 and 2013, the court referenced the bill explanation twenty-one times when interpreting an ambiguous statute. Wallace, *supra* note 5, at 307. In the study, this was the most cited source of Iowa legislative history; however, starting in 2014, bill explanations are now prefaced by a disclaimer that they are not endorsed by the General Assembly. *Id.* at 303–05. This change may make the court less likely to cite bill explanations in its opinions.

appendix for an example of an original bill with explanation from the bill book.

c. Fiscal Notes

If legislation other than Appropriations or Ways and Means measures will have a significant financial effect on the state's revenues, expenditures, or fiscal liability, the Fiscal Services Division of LSA attaches an explanatory fiscal note.[19] This note indicates how the bill will affect the state's finances, specifies the projected dollar amount of this effect over the law's first five years, and details how resources will be allocated. Fiscal notes are included in the bill book. They are also available on the Iowa legislature's site back to 2002, on Westlaw back to 2007, and on Lexis back to 2005.[20] Iowa courts have sometimes looked at fiscal notes in determining legislative intent.[21]

d. Sources of Bill Books and Older Bill Text

In print, Iowa's State Law Library offers bill books from 1937 to the present and bill text for 1868–1980. Bills are in their original, unamended form, and include an explanation if one is available. They are arranged chronologically and then alphabetically by broad topic. The top of the first page of each bill has a note indicating what happened to it.

---

19. *See* Joint Rules of the Senate and House, Rule 17, which notes how it is determined whether a bill will require a fiscal note. The rules can be found online at https://www.legis.iowa.gov/DOCS/ChamberRules/JointRules.pdf.

20. The direct link to the most recent fiscal notes on the G.A. website is https://www.legis.iowa.gov/publications/information/fiscalNotes. Use the green arrow in the bar with the G.A. number to select an earlier G.A. On Westlaw, the easiest way to access fiscal notes is by following this path: Home > Legislative History > Iowa > Bill Analysis & Other Reports. On Lexis, you can use the red search box to select the source "Iowa Legislative Bill History," or run the search and then limit your results, choosing to view "Statutes and Legislation," then limiting to "Iowa" as the jurisdiction and "Legislative Histories" as the category. Both Westlaw and Lexis include more than just fiscal notes.

21. *See, e.g., State v. Dohlman,* 725 N.W.2d 428 (Iowa 2006). In *Dohlman,* the court considered evidentiary requirements to establish wrongful imprisonment. The court noted first that, on its face, the statutory language requires "clear and convincing evidence." *Id.* at 432. The court further assessed the plaintiff's evidentiary burden as fairly strict in quoting one of the assumptions of the fiscal note indicating that cases that meet the bill's requirements would occur less than once a year. *Id.* at 432. Wallace notes that between 2004 and 2013, the court referenced a fiscal note four times when interpreting an ambiguous statute. Wallace, *supra* note 5, at 307.

The materials are also available online in one of three locations, depending on the time period covered:

- 12th–81st G.A., 1868–2006 (coverage has gaps): in the General Assembly Archives.[22]
- 80th G.A., 2003, to last G.A.: in the "Legislation" section of the General Assembly website.[23]
- 12th–Current G.A., 1868–present (coverage has gaps): in the Legislative Document Research Page.[24]

The first two options work if you are looking for a known citation. This should be the case when you are tracing a code provision; the code history references would have led you to the correct Act, which would have provided the relevant House or Senate file number. If you are looking for bills by topic, you can either search the Legislative Document Research Page or use a subject index to bills to guide your search.[25]

e. Navigating Bill Books

Each online bill book source works a bit differently. Tips on successfully using each follow.

General Assembly Archives

1. Use the down arrow in the empty box to the right of the content area you want to select the desired G.A. session. In the case of "Billbooks," the only option will be "All," and once you select this, it will bring up a new screen.

2. In the new screen that opens, entitled "BillBooks," use the drop-down menu at the top of the screen to select the G.A. session you want. Click on the file number you want.

3. To find the explanation, look at the end of the introduced bill.

---

22. The General Assembly archives are available at https://www.legis.iowa.gov /archives. Under the heading "Legislation," there is a section called "Billbooks."

23. The Legislation section of the General Assembly site is at https://www.legis .iowa.gov/legislation. Under the heading "Legislation," there is a section called "Billbooks."

24. The Legislative Document Research Page is the search tool for the General Assembly site. It is available at https://www.legis.iowa.gov/publications/search.

25. In the General Assembly Archives, available at https://www.legis.iowa.gov /archives, you can access a "Subject Index of Legislation" that dates back to the 80th G.A. (2003).

General Assembly Legislation page: BillBook

1. Click on the "BillBook" link near the top of the page.
2. The default that opens is the current (or most recent) G.A. To select a different G.A., use the drop-down arrow at the top of the left-hand column.
3. Select the bill you want to examine by entering the file number and type under "Quick Find," then click on the "Go" button. You can also browse by clicking on "Display Bill Lists" and then by using the drop-down menus that appear next to "Senate Bills" and "House Bills."
4. Once you have brought up the desired bill, you will see it in the main viewing area on the screen. If multiple versions of the bill are available (which will be the case for all legislation that passed, even if it was not amended), there will be a "Bill Versions" box on the left. Select "Introduced" to bring up that version in the center viewing area. Scroll to the end of the introduced bill to see the explanation.

Legislative Document Research Page[26]

1. Select a search type.

This search tool is designed to search all available content, including legislation, the code, the administrative code, and more. If you only want to search one or more specific content types, you will want to apply those limits before executing your search. However, you will need to reapply the limits if you change search types, so first decide which type of search you want to run. The choices appear in the blue bar directly above the left menu (the navigation pane) and the main part of the screen (the document viewing area):

- "Main Search" is a single search box where you can enter a single keyword or enter a more complex search using the connectors, special characters, and field limiters listed under the "Search Tools" link. The "Main Search" feature also provides check boxes so you can quickly limit your search to current materials or exclude reserved chapters. You also can use the feature to browse different content areas, further described in the next step.
- "Advanced Search" uses a search form to help guide you through the process of creating a more nuanced search. The page includes a chart

---

26. Addition information on this search feature can be found by clicking on the "Documentation" link at the top of the Legislative Document Research Page. The direct link to the documentation is https://www.legis.iowa.gov/docs/publications /IHD/680332.pdf.

with the same special characters and connectors found under the "Search Tools" link, but it does not list the field limiters.

- "Topics" lets you explore all content under particular topics. This type of search is designed for browsing, and the content type cannot be limited. The "A-Z" option presents an alphabetical list of subjects. Click on the one you want to see documents from across the General Assembly site that address that topic. The "Tree" options presents a list of subjects in folders. Click on the folder itself to reveal documents associated with that subject, or select a narrower subject by clicking on the arrow to the left of the folder to open it and reveal the subtopics it contains.

2. Limit the content you are viewing or searching.

Find the "Search Within" feature on the left. In the bill book context, you want to click the arrow to the left of "Legislation" to open that menu. If you are unsure which General Assembly session you want, you can select all that are available by clicking the box to the left of "Legislation." Otherwise, you can select one or more specific assemblies by clicking on the corresponding box for that G.A. Note, too, you can click the arrow to the left of the G.A. to open that menu and then select from among the available options, which may include three different bill versions (introduced, reprinted, and enrolled) as well as introduced amendments.

With "Main Search," you can also use this content selection feature to browse all documents that fit the criteria you have selected. As you check boxes, a list of documents appears in the document viewing area. These can be sorted by year or name. In the gray bar at the bottom of the screen you will see the number of results available.

3. Enter your search, and revise as necessary.

If you do not want to browse to find content, input your search terms. When you are ready to execute the search, click "Go" from the "Main Search" feature or "Search" from the "Advanced Search." You can edit your search in the search box or boxes. In "Main Search" the content limits you set will remain until you clear them or change search types. However, in "Advanced Search," you will not keep those limits if you revise your search without selecting them again.

6. General Assembly Actions: House and Senate Journals

The *House Journal* and the *Senate Journal* record actions taken in the specified chamber. They include information like motions made and how legislators voted. Typically, they provide little to no detail about debate on bills or amendments. Using the journals to outline the path of a piece of legislation through the G.A. may provide additional context for your understanding of a bill.

Journals can be accessed online from the G.A. website. For journals published during or after 2004 (House) or 2005 (Senate), select the "Legislation" tab and then the "Senate & House Journals" link on the left for a variety of access options. The "Archives" tab offers access to older journals, dating back to 1840. All journals can also be found in print in any one of Iowa's three major law libraries.[27]

For bills from 1995 or later, you should be able to find a compiled list of relevant journal entries by bringing up the bill on the G.A. website. Use the "Archives" tab for any year back to 1995. You can also use the "Bill History" link on the "Legislation" tab for bills from 2003 or later. Although the interface has changed somewhat over the years, all bills on the website will include a link called either "Current Bill History" or "Complete History." (If you access the bill through the "Bill History" link, it will open to the history.) The information at this link includes the name of the sponsor, a brief description of the bill, and a list of all the actions taken on it with links to the pages of the House or Senate journal that document each action. One of the last actions taken on some bills is that the governor issues a message to accompany its signing or veto. This message might provide context to help better understand the circumstances surrounding the enactment of the law. These messages are published in the journals and linked under the bill history sources described earlier in this paragraph.

Lexis and Westlaw also offer databases with limited compiled Iowa legislative history. On Lexis, actions taken on Iowa legislation are listed without House or Senate journal references; selective coverage dates back to 1989, with more complete coverage starting in 1995.[28] Lexis also offers selective coverage of governor's messages back to 2002.[29] On Westlaw, bill histories extend back to 2000 and include unlinked journal citations.[30] Westlaw also offers the full

---

27. Iowa's three major law libraries, described further in Chapter 2, are Drake University Law Library, the State Law Library of Iowa, and the University of Iowa Law Library.

28. After running a search, view results in the "Statutes and Legislation" content area, then limit to "Iowa" under "Jurisdiction" and "Bill Tracking" under "Category."

29. Governor's messages on Lexis are found in the source "Iowa Legislative Bill History."

30. Follow this path in Westlaw to limit your search just to the Iowa legislative history materials that include bill histories: Home > Legislative History > Iowa > Bill Analysis & Other Reports. When you find the desired legislation, click on the "Bill Tracking" tab to see the history.

text of the House and Senate journals back to 2000[31] and governors' messages back to 2004.[32]

You can also find journal entries by searching the print *Index to House and Senate Journals*. This title includes a Senate-House companion bill table and brief histories of bills, with references to the journals. Indexes back to 2004 or 2005 are also available via the G.A. site.[33]

7. Committee Minutes

Legislative committee minutes are available, but they also tend to be very limited in their coverage. They note who attended the meeting and what bills were considered. They record votes, but do not typically document the points made in discussion. The minutes might mention if someone spoke or distributed materials to committee members.

The G.A. website includes committee minutes back to 2008. From the committees page, click on the committee you want and then on the "Meetings" link.[34] Available minutes for the current session of the G.A. will be available as PDF documents in the column labeled "Minutes." To search an earlier G.A. session, choose that session using the drop-down menu in the blue bar that indicates which G.A. you are viewing. Committee minutes can also be accessed in hard copy by contacting the chief clerk of the House or secretary of the Senate.[35]

8. Reports

Reports associated with legislation or with a governmental body might also be available. *Interim Study Committees* meet between sessions to study issues on which legislation may be enacted. Each committee releases final reports with its recommendations, which may provide valuable insights into the motivations for a piece of legislation. Reports are available through the State Law

---

31. To search just this collection of Iowa journals, follow this path in Westlaw: Home > Legislative History > Iowa Legislative History > Iowa Legislative History: Journals.

32. To access governor's messages on Westlaw follow this path: Home > Legislative History > Iowa > Governor Messages.

33. For the Senate, the index extends back to 2005; for the House the index extends back to 2004. Links to both can be found at https://www.legis.iowa.gov/chambers/journals.

34. The committees page is at https://www.legis.iowa.gov/committees.

35. Contact information for the House is available at https://www.legis.iowa.gov/agencies/house/chiefClerksOffice; contact information for the Senate is available at https://www.legis.iowa.gov/agencies/senate/secretaryOfSenateOffice.

Library, 1965–current; the State Archives, 1955–current;[36] and the G.A. website, 1956–current.[37] These reports are not currently indexed, so to see if there is a relevant report to your legislation, you have to search by topic. A good general rule is to check the committees for the four years preceding the introduction of your legislation.

In addition, the Legislative Services Agency prepares Legislative Guides and Legal Background Briefings. Both provide information on a particular topic; the guides survey the relevant law and the briefings provide background information. These are available from the G.A. website back to 2009.[38] The Legislative Services Agency also maintains a list of documents that state agencies have filed with the General Assembly. These reports can provide a wealth of data that may have influenced future legislation. Entries date back to 2003.[39]

Other types of reports related to legislation may be available from bar committees or other groups who helped shape the proposals that led to the legislation. Unfortunately, there is not a direct mechanism that connects legislation to these reports, so they can be more difficult to find. Such reports might be referenced in the bill explanation, the bill drafting file (described in the next section), or a law review article found when checking for compiled legislative history, as described in Section III.B.2.[40] Another approach to searching for

---

36. The State Archives are open to anyone, and the materials can be used on site during reading room hours. *See* http://www.iowahistory.org/archives/public-refe rence-services/index.html.

37. Visit https://www.legis.iowa.gov/archives/shelves/isc and select the G.A. you want using the drop-down menu next to the box called "Year."

38. The guides are available at https://www.legis.iowa.gov/publications/legal Pubs/legisGuides. The background briefings are available at https://www.legis.iowa .gov/publications/legalPubs/legalBriefings. Both can also be searched using the Legislative Document Research Page at https://www.legis.iowa.gov/publications/search. To limit content to just the guides, choose the following menu options: "Publications and Reports," then "Legal Services," and finally either "Legislative Guides" or "Legal Background Briefings."

39. These reports are available at https://www.legis.iowa.gov/publications/other Resources/reportsFiled.

40. Wallace notes that between 2004 and 2013, the court twice referenced such a report when interpreting an ambiguous statute. Wallace, *supra* note 5, at 307. In one case, the court looked to the drafter's comments for the 1963 Iowa Probate Code, which was crafted by an Iowa State Bar Association committee. *See In re Estate of Sampson*, 838 N.W.2d 663, 667, 670 (Iowa 2013). In the other case, the court looked at a report to the government of Iowa and the Iowa State Bar Association related to re-

these reports involves looking at other sources of contemporaneous circumstances, such as Iowa State Bar Association proceedings around the time of the legislation[41] or newspaper articles, as described in Section III.B.10.

9. Bill Drafting Files

The Legislative Services Agency maintains confidential bill drafting files for the current General Assembly plus the prior General Assembly.[42] Older files are sent to the State Archives, where they become publicly accessible. A file sent to the archives must include the request form for the LSA to draft the bill and the version of the bill as introduced. At the drafter's discretion, additional materials may be included, such as earlier bill drafts, notes, written comments from legislators, or model legislation from other states. However, it is uncommon for these additional materials to be maintained in the files. It is possible that notes written on or accompanying the request form might provide additional information about legislative intent.

The archives extend back to 1967 and include files for all Iowa bills, both those that were enacted and those that were not enacted. At a minimum, you will need to know the House or Senate file number and the number of the General Assembly to request a file. If you know the sponsor or LSA/LSB number, that might also be useful. Ask a reference librarian at the archives to find and retrieve the relevant file for you.

10. Newspaper Articles

Although unlikely to be persuasive to a court, newspaper articles from the time when the legislation was introduced and debated may provide context about the legislation. Articles from the *Des Moines Register*, which is the largest newspaper in the state and located in the capital city, can be found through news databases on Lexis and Westlaw. Your institution or a local public library may also offer access to *Register* stories through other newspaper article indexes, such as ProQuest.

---

vision of the Iowa Administrative Procedure Act. *See Sierra Club Iowa Chapter v. Iowa Dep't of Transp.*, 832 N.W.2d 636, 647 (Iowa 2013).

41. The annual meeting proceedings are published and can be accessed through one of Iowa's law libraries, described in Chapter 2.

42. Confidentiality can be waived with permission from the bill sponsor.

The Welch Matter

In the hypothetical grandparents' visitation rights scenario, you would not likely research legislative history beyond looking at the prior version of the current statute, as described in Chapter 6. Remember that the courts look to legislative intent only when the statute's meaning is unclear.

However, for purposes of illustration, we will look at the major steps of the process considering the original statute, Iowa Code § 598.35.

Because this statute was repealed in 2007, imagine you have returned to 2002, when the district court in the *Howard* case held this statute unconstitutional.

First, look at the then current (2002) *Iowa Code Annotated* to see the legislative credits and other references. Figure 7-A in the chapter appendix shows that information on Westlaw.

The information under CREDITS gives you the list of statutes creating and affecting the code section. When the section was current, there would have been information under the heading LAW REVIEW AND JOURNAL REFERENCES and LIBRARY REFERENCES that led to interpretative materials. If you decided you wanted to see the statute as it was originally introduced, you would follow up on the first line of the credits, indicating it was added by Acts 1974 (65th G.A.) ch. 1253, § 1.

Next, you obtain the referenced volume of the *Acts and Joint Resolutions of the General Assembly*. You could obtain it from a law library in hard copy or as a PDF on the G.A. site. See Figure 7-B in the chapter appendix. From the top of the act you find the bill number, SF 500.

With the bill number, you can go to the bill book to see the original bill with explanation and the bill's progress through the legislative process. The G.A. Archives offer the bill book for 1974 (the 65th G.A.); search that G.A. and then click on the link for SF 0500.pdf.

This brings up the original bill, with explanation and its amendments, as shown in Figure 7-C in the chapter appendix. (Note: If your clients were grandparents but not blood relatives, the adopted Senate amendment striking the term "by consanguinity" could be relevant to your argument.)

IV. Iowa Bill Tracking

Proposed legislation may affect a client's situation and, therefore, the way you advise that client. The General Assembly website's "Legislation" page offers a variety of options for following legislative proposals during and after the session.[43] You can also get a jump on the session with links to "Prefiled Bills" listing legislation submitted before the session begins and "Bill Request Logs," which let you ascertain what legislation the LSA has been asked to draft for the current session, excluding any confidential requests.

A. Alert Services

The General Assembly site provides several no-fee services that will alert you to legislative actions without the need to visit the home page. You can subscribe to an RSS feed that lists newly filed legislation or amendments with the bill number and a brief description. Alternatively, you can sign up for email notification of the release of a new issue of a legislative publication, including such choices as "Daily Legislation" or committee subscriptions.[44] You can also follow the LSA on Twitter to learn of the publication of a variety of reports.[45]

From the legislation tab on the General Assembly site, you can also register for a no-fee service called Bill & Code Watch, listed under the link name "Proposed Legislation Tracking." This service allows you to set up customized lists to track the legislation of a specific committee, selected bills, or any legislation that would affect a specific Iowa code chapter or section. For each list you create, you can choose from among several options to have legislative actions emailed to you or available upon your login.

B. Search Options

The General Assembly "Find Legislation" page provides several ways to search for information about proposed legislation.[46] You may search for bills by bill number, subject, sponsor, and committee and for amendments by amendment number, bill number, sponsor, or date filed. You can also create a list of all filed amendments or bring up all legislation that has reached a certain stage in the legislative process, such as "Passed by Both Chambers" or "Vetoed by Governor."

---

43. The page is available at https://www.legis.iowa.gov/legislation.
44. All options are listed at https://www.legis.iowa.gov/subscribe/subscriptions and linked pages.
45. Follow at http://twitter.com/IowaLSA. More information on the account is available at https://www.legis.iowa.gov/subscribe/twitter.
46. This page is available at https://www.legis.iowa.gov/legislation/findLegislation.

C. Post-Session Publications

Two LSA publications, both linked from the "Iowa Law & Rules" page under the "Iowa Acts and Passed Legislation" link, are particularly useful in reviewing the developments of a legislative session.[47] "Enrolled Bills" provides the file number with linked text, the bill title, and the dates the legislation passed, was signed by the governor, and will take effect. A separate "Code & Acts Sections Amended" list has one list organized by code section followed by a second organized by Acts reference. It lists the action taken, the file number with linked text, the relevant part of the bill, and the date when the law becomes effective, the date it first practically applies (as specifically noted in the bill), and any action taken by the governor on the bill and the date of that action.

V. Federal Legislative Research

A. Federal Legislative Process

The federal legislative process is very similar to the Iowa process described above, with legislation arising in one chamber, going to committee before possibly being considered on the chamber floor, and, if passed, being sent to the other chamber for consideration.[48] At the federal level, however, a bill may be drafted by others besides the chamber's legislative counsel. A federal bill does not need to include an explanation.

As in Iowa, federal bills are consecutively numbered and generally preceded by an S. if they originate in the Senate or H.R. if they originate in the House of Representatives. Once a bill passes both houses in identical form, it is sent to the president. The legislation becomes law if the president either signs it or takes no action on it for ten days while Congress is in session. If the president takes no action for ten days during which time Congress adjourns, the bill doesn't become law. Upon enactment, the statute is given a public law number indicating the Congressional session in which it passed and assigning it a chronological number. For instance, Pub. L. No. 111-148 was the 148th bill passed by the 111th Congress: the Patient Protection and Affordable Care Act.

---

47. This page can be accessed at https://www.legis.iowa.gov/law/statutory/acts.

48. For a detailed consideration of the federal legislative process, see John V. Sullivan, *How Our Laws are Made* 2007, available at http://www.gpo.gov/fdsys/pkg /CDOC-110hdoc49/pdf/CDOC-110hdoc49.pdf.

B. Federal Legislative History

1. Federal Legislative Documents and Their Uses

The federal legislative process is much better documented than the Iowa process, which means there are more solid sources of legislative history information to consult. A brief description of some of the more important sources follows.

Bill versions. Many bills are amended multiple times before they pass. Comparing bill versions may help determine legislative intent.

Committee reports. If a committee recommends passage of a bill, it will often introduce the bill with an accompanying written committee report that includes a statement of the bill's purpose and the reasons why the committee supports it. The report may also include opinions from dissenting committee members. Conference committee reports are presented as joint explanatory statements from the floor managers of both chambers as they iron out differences in bill versions passed by each chamber. This analysis of the bill makes reports, particularly conference committee reports, some of the most important sources for determining legislative intent.

Committee hearings. Congressional committees hold public hearings on significant issues. Published transcripts, available for most hearings, record the views expressed by the people invited to testify. Transcripts may also include introductory remarks or commentary from the committee members.

Congressional debates. Since 1873, the *Congressional Record* has served as the official record of U.S. Congressional proceedings and debates. Although it documents the actions taken and speeches given in Congress, it does not provide an exact transcript. Business conducted in an abbreviated form will be reported in full, and members have the opportunity to edit their remarks. Note that the *Congressional Record* is published first as a daily version and later in a permanent, bound edition with new page numbers.

Other sources. Additional sources, such as *committee prints* and *signing statements*, may also be referenced in a legislative history. However, these are generally considered less important and will not be discussed in this chapter.

2. Compiled Legislative History

Before attempting to build your own list of a bill's legislative documents and then locate them all, it is wise to try to find a history that has already been compiled. There are several ways to search for a compiled history.

First, check a law library online catalog for relevant works. See Chapter 2 for suggested catalogs and how to use them. Search under the broad subject heading "Legislative histories — United States — Bibliography" to locate finding aids like *Federal Legislative Histories: An Annotated Bibliography and Index to Officially Published Sources* by Bernard Reams or the looseleaf *Sources of Compiled Legislative Histories: A Bibliography of Government Documents, Periodical Articles, and Books, 1st Congress–94th Congress* by Nancy P. Johnson, which is also available electronically via HeinOnline.[49] Search for the name of the law to find works specifically about that act, such as *Congress and Sports Agents: A Legislative History of the Sports Agent Responsibility and Trust Act (SPARTA)* by Edmund P. Edmonds.

Second, search a major legal database. Lexis, Westlaw, and HeinOnline all offer collections of compiled legislative history materials. In addition, Pro-Quest Congressional, a separate database that you might find in general academic libraries, as well as law school libraries, provides options for locating compiled histories as well as compiling your own.

Next, search for law review articles. Using the periodical sources described in Chapter 3, search for articles that provide an act's legislative history. Try searching for the name of the act and the term "legislative history."

Fourth, check *United States Code Congressional and Administrative News* (USCCAN), which reprints the text of laws passed by Congress in each session as well as selected legislative history documents. USCCAN is available as a Westlaw database and in print. When using it in print, be aware that the set is divided into two main parts. Volumes labeled "Laws" reprint the acts, and volumes labeled "Legislative History" reprint select reports and statements. In addition, a separate section reprints Presidential signing statements. All of these sections are organized by public law number. USCCAN also includes a helpful legislative history table that lists the public law number, *Statutes at Large* reference, bill number, House and Senate report numbers and reporting committees, and dates of passage.

Finally, examine an annotated federal code, such as USCA or USCS, both described in Chapter 6. As with ICA, an annotated version of a federal code will provide you a rudimentary compilation of acts that have affected a code section and references to other materials of interest.

---

49. More information about this and other HeinOnline holdings can be found at http://home.heinonline.org/content/list-of-libraries/ under the "U.S. Federal Legislative History Library" heading.

3. Finding Legislative Documents

Particularly on the web, many sources offer access to multiple types of legislative documents. Key sources include Congress.gov, the Government Publishing Office, the U.S. Congressional Serial Set, Lexis, Westlaw, and HeinOnline. Each is described briefly below.

- **Congress.gov.** This is the official site for U.S. federal legislative information and the successor to THOMAS.[50] It includes a wealth of documents, such as the text, summary, and status information for bills and resolutions; roll call votes; *Congressional Record* text; and committee reports. The full text of most of the documents on Congress.gov can be searched. Some coverage dates back to 1973, with the site becoming more robust for recent years. Most information is available from 1995 to the present.[51]
- **Government Publishing Office (GPO).** GPO disseminates federal information for all three branches of government. It has a wealth of legislative materials available through its Federal Digital System (FDsys).[52] GPO's new govinfo.gov will eventually replace FDsys.[53] Materials may also be issued in print and available through federal government document depository libraries throughout the U.S.[54]
- **U.S. Congressional Serial Set.** Since 1817, this government title has published Congressional reports and documents, assigning each a sequential number. Select materials from 1833 to 1917 are freely available online; others may be available through a subscription database or library collection.[55]
- **ProQuest Congressional.** This platform provides indexing or full-text access to a broad range of legislative materials. The basic database begins its coverage in 1970, while historical databases extend coverage

---

50. THOMAS will remain available until all its data has been transferred to Congress.gov. THOMAS can be accessed at http://thomas.loc.gov/home/thomas.php.

51. The site offers a "Coverage Dates for Legislative Information" chart at https://www.congress.gov/about/coverage-dates.

52. FDsys is available at http://www.gpo.gov/fdsys.

53. The beta version of govinfo.gov was released as this book was being finalized. Govinfo.gov will include everything in FDsys but with a new interface and features to facilitate use.

54. *See* http://www.gpo.gov/libraries/ for more information about the depository program, including library locations.

55. *See* http://memory.loc.gov/ammem/amlaw/lwss.html for the documents freely available online.

back to 1789. The print counterpart, the *CIS Annual*, offers an index to Congressional publications dating back to 1970.

- **Bloomberg Law.** Its U.S. Congress database includes several types of legislative information, including committee reports back to 2007. Coverage dates for other legislative information vary.
- **Lexis.** This legal research system provides access to many legislative materials, particularly from 1990 forward.[56]
- **Westlaw.** This legal research system also offers broad access to legislative materials, beginning with the late 1980s and early 1990s.[57] In addition, the West title *United States Code Congressional and Administrative News* (USCCAN) offers laws and selected reports starting with the 78th Congress, 2nd Session (1944). Coverage on the parallel Westlaw database, "USCCAN," extends to 1948.
- **HeinOnline.** In addition to its U.S. Federal Legislative History Library that includes compiled legislative histories, HeinOnline offers the U.S. Congressional Document Library. For federal legislative history, this collection most notably provides access to the *Congressional Record* and its predecessors and the *Statutes at Large*.

For additional guidance, consult a more detailed federal legislative history research guide, such as the Law Librarians' Society of Washington D.C. *Federal Legislative History Research: A Practitioner's Guide to Compiling the Documents and Sifting for Legislative Intent.*[58]

C. Federal Bill Tracking

The web provides an abundance of aids to track federal legislation. Congress.gov, discussed in Section V.B.3., provides up-to-date information about Congressional activities. You can also get updates via RSS feed, email, Facebook, and Twitter. GovTrack provides similar information but offers additional search capabilities and the ability to set up customized trackers.[59] Additional news and analysis can be found at sites like the Congress.org

---

56. To see available Lexis content, follow this path: Browse > Sources > By Category > Statutes and Legislation. Then apply the "U.S. Federal" jurisdiction limit.

57. Navigate to specific U.S. federal legislative sources to view content and coverage details by following this path in Westlaw: Home > Legislative History.

58. This guide is linked at http://www.llsdc.org/sourcebook under the heading "Research Guides and Explanations."

59. GovTrack is available at https://www.govtrack.us.

news site and *Roll Call*, a nonpartisan Congressional newspaper.[60] Through a library, you may be able to access other print and electronic current awareness sources, such as those created by Congressional Quarterly, Inc., a publisher specializing in coverage of the U.S. Congress.

Appendix: Iowa Legislative History Excerpts

The following exhibits illustrate the Iowa legislative history example provided in the sidebar.

Figure 7-A. Screenshot of Old Version of Iowa Code § 598.35 on Westlaw

Source: Westlaw. Published with permission of West, a Thomson Reuters business.

---

60. The site is http://www.rollcall.com.

Figure 7-B. Sample *Acts and Joint Resolutions of the General Assembly*

CHAPTER 1253

VISITATION RIGHTS OF GRANDPARENTS

S. F. 500

AN ACT relating to visitation rights.

Be It Enacted by the General Assembly of the State of Iowa:

1   SECTION 1. NEW SECTION. The grandparents of a child may peti-
2 tion the district court for grandchild visitation rights when:
3   1. The parents of the child are divorced, or
4   2. A petition for dissolution of marriage has been filed by one of the
5˜ parents of the child, or
6   3. The parent of the child, who is the child of the grandparents, has
7 died, or
8   4. The child has been placed in a foster home.
9   A petition for grandchild visitation rights shall be granted only
10 upon a finding that the visitation is in the best interests of the child.

Approved April 25, 1974

Source: 1974 volume of *Acts of Joint Resolutions of the General Assembly.* Des Moines: General Assembly of Iowa.

Figure 7-C. Screenshots Excerpting S.F. 500 (65 G.A.)

Source: Iowa Legislature Archives, Bill Book for the 65th G.A. Available: https://www.legis.iowa.gov/docs/shelves/billbooks/65GA/SF%20500.pdf.

Figure 7-C. Screenshots Excerpting S.F. 500 (65 G.A.), *continued*

```
15                        EXPLANATION
16    This bill provides that grandparents, by blood, may peti-
17 tion for child visitation rights in certain instances.  The
18 visitation rights may be granted only upon a finding that
19 it is in the best interests of the child.
20
21
22
23
24
25
                                              LSB 1639
                                              dh/mg/5
```

```
S—2020
1   Amend Senate File 500, page 1, lines 3 and 4 by striking the
2   words",by consanguinity".

S—2020 Filed and adopted          By HEYING
January 18, 1974
```

```
H—2429
1      Amend Senate File 500, as passed by the Senate,
2   page 1, by striking lines 9 and 10.

H—2429 Filed-Withdrawn 4/5 (541)  By NIELSEN of Polk
March 11, 1974
```

Chapter 8

Administrative Law

I. Introduction

The area of administrative law consists of rules, regulations, orders, licenses, advisory opinions, and decisions that are promulgated by agencies. The Iowa General Assembly or United States Congress may pass a statute to delegate to an agency the authority to formulate rules or regulations. Alternatively, the Governor of Iowa or the President of the United States may delegate administrative rulemaking authority through an executive order. Primarily, agencies have two types of actions: rulemaking and adjudication.

While statutes and many agency rules are relatively easy to access, some policies, regulations, guidelines, and decisions may be more difficult to locate. In fact, some information is never published.[1]

This chapter will cover general information about administrative agencies and rules, then move into specific information about Iowa rules followed by federal regulations. The chapter concludes with information about other documents from the executive branch, encompassing Iowa and federal agency decisions as well as executive orders and proclamations. For additional information, you may want to consult a research guide on administrative law developed by an academic law library.[2]

---

1. For example, federal agencies may have policy statements or manuals that do not require publication in the *Federal Register*. However, these documents can help the researcher determine how an agency perceives its mandate. Some agencies provide handbooks, policies, and the like on their websites. For example, the Bureau of Prisons offers a complete policy library, available by visiting http://www.bop.gov/re sources and then clicking on the "BOP Policies" link. Other agencies may not make information easily accessible or, in some instances, even available.

2. *E.g.*, Drake Law Library's Administrative Law Research Guide is at http:// libguides.law.drake.edu/adminlaw.

II. Administrative Agencies

Although agencies are administered by the executive branch, they are generally established through enabling statutes enacted by the legislature. An *enabling statute*[3] is a law that confers powers on an executive agency to carry out delegated tasks. It dictates what the agency is permitted or forbidden to do. Agencies are created to administer and oversee government programs and to monitor and regulate certain industries. In order to perform their job, agencies promulgate *rules* or *regulations*,[4] which articulate how the laws are to be administered.

III. Administrative Rules

Administrative agencies promulgate rules. In operation, rules resemble statutes and are written in a format similar to statutes. Like statutes and judicial opinions, these rules and regulations are primary authority and have the force of law.

Administrative rules exist in part because, when a legislature passes a law, the statute may not specify all the details necessary to explain clearly how to comply with the law. The Iowa General Assembly and the U.S. Congress cannot legislate the detailed requirements of complex activities. Also, agencies have more subject-specific expertise to oversee the rules. For instance, when the U.S. Congress passed the Truth in Caller ID Act,[5] enforcement of the law was left to the Federal Communications Commission (FCC). It was within the FCC's authority to develop the rules for complying with the law, which prohibited the provision of inaccurate caller identification.[6]

Although both rules and statutes are primary authority, rules are subordinate to statutes. If there is any inconsistency between a rule and a statute, the statute is the prevailing authority. Also, if a statute is declared unconstitutional, a rule cannot be promulgated to remedy the deficiency in the statute.

---

3. Sometimes enabling statutes are also referred to as enabling acts.

4. Both terms refer to rules originating from administrative agencies and are often used interchangeably. In Iowa, they are usually referred to as rules, while at the federal level they are normally called regulations.

5. Pub. L. No. 111-331, 124 Stat. 3572 (2010).

6. The FCC issued a final rule to implement the act in 76 Fed. Reg. 43196 (July 20, 2011). The key provisions are codified in 47 C.F.R. § 64.1604.

IV. Iowa Administrative Rules

Iowa agencies are established through enabling statutes.[7] Except when otherwise expressly provided by statute, all agency rules are subject to the provisions of the Iowa Administrative Procedure Act (IAPA)[8] and the Uniform Rules on Agency Procedure.[9] The IAPA imposes a set of minimum requirements on each agency regarding access to its laws and policies. To have the force of law, agency rules must be published in the *Iowa Administrative Bulletin* and *Iowa Administrative Code*[10] unless they fall within a few specified exceptions.[11]

When beginning administrative research, it is helpful to have an idea of which agency is responsible for your area of research because codified regulations are categorized by agency, as further discussed in Section IV.A.1. A complete list of Iowa agencies is available online[12] with links to official sites.

A. Finding Iowa Rules

Iowa agencies are required to file a "Notice of Intended Action" with the governor's administrative rules coordinator, who assigns each rulemaking document an ARC number.[13] This notice, labeled with its associated ARC number, is also published in the *Iowa Administrative Bulletin*. The public has a chance to comment on the proposed rule, a process that has become easier with the creation of an administrative rules website that provides easy access to proposed rules and associated web-based forms for submitting comments.[14] If adopted, the rule is again submitted to the administrative rules

---

7. Iowa Code § 17A.23 (2015). The agency departments and their primary responsibilities are set forth in Iowa Code § 7E.5 (2015).

8. Iowa Code § 17A (2015).

9. The *Uniform Rules on Agency Procedure* can be found at the Iowa legislature site https://www.legis.iowa.gov/law/administrativeRules/ruleWriterInfo.

10. See Sections A.1. and A.2. below for locations and more detail on using these sources.

11. These exceptions are specified in Iowa Code § 17A.2(11)(a–l) (2015).

12. State of Iowa Department Listing is available at http://phonebook.iowa.gov/agency.aspx.

13. Iowa Code § 17A.4(1)(a) (2015). Much more information about the rulemaking process, including general principles and practices and deviations for emergency rulemaking, is available at https://rules.iowa.gov/info/rules-overview. ARC is a reference to the Administrative Rules Coordinator.

14. The Iowa Administrative Rules Website is at https://rules.iowa.gov.

coordinator, who assigns another ARC number,[15] and the "Adopted and Filed" version is published in the *Iowa Administrative Bulletin*. At the same time, the rule will be added to the *Iowa Administrative Code*, which provides all adopted Iowa rules, organized by agency.[16]

At the end of each chapter in the *Iowa Administrative Code*, bracketed information references the history of the rule changes. Up until approximately 2009, the information included dates of the different stages in the rulemaking process. More detailed information can be found in the *Iowa Administrative Bulletin* for these dates. Starting around 2010, both dates and ARC numbers are now published in the code history.

1. *Iowa Administrative Code*

Typically, you will begin your search for Iowa regulations in the *Iowa Administrative Code* (IAC). Its arrangement of rules by agency and the fact that it only contains adopted rules generally make it more conducive to topical research than the chronologically arranged *Iowa Administrative Bulletin*. The table of contents for each agency section of the *Iowa Administrative Code* provides references to the Iowa Code in parentheses after each rule number; see Table 8-1 for an example. These references indicate the statute that the rule implements.[17] The Iowa legislature's website also contains a Table of Rules Implementing Statutes,[18] as well as information about the fiscal impact of administrative rules.[19]

Iowa Administrative Code citations found in Iowa legal documents often follow this structure: [agency number] IAC [chapter and rule]. For example, 11 IAC 4.3 tells you that 11 is the agency, in this case the Administrative Services Department; 4 is the chapter, Public Records and Fair Information Practices; and .3 is the rule, Requests for access to records. If you have the citation to an IAC section, you can easily retrieve it through the IAC "Quick Search"

---

15. Iowa Code § 17A.5(1) (2015).

16. More information about how Iowa rules are published is available at https://rules.iowa.gov/info/rules-publication.

17. These references are provided in accordance with Iowa Code § 2B.5A(2) (2015).

18. The Table of Rules Implementing Statutes is found at https://www.legis.iowa .gov/law/administrativeRules/additionalInfo.

19. Iowa Code § 17A.4(4) (2015) requires the Legislative Services Agency (LSA) to analyze the fiscal impact of all administrative rules with an annual impact of $100,000 or more or an impact of $500,000 or more within five years and provide a summary of the impact to the Administrative Rules Review Committee (ARRC).

Table 8-1. Example from the Table of Contents of the
Iowa Administrative Code

ADMINISTRATIVE SERVICES DEPARTMENT[11]
[Created by 2003 Iowa Acts, House File 534, section 2]
TITLE I
GENERAL DEPARTMENTAL PROCEDURES
CHAPTER 1
DEPARTMENT ORGANIZATION

1.1(8A) Creation and mission

1.2(8A) Location

1.3(8A) Director

1.4(8A) Administration of the department

CHAPTERS 2 and 3
Reserved
CHAPTER 4
PUBLIC RECORDS AND FAIR INFORMATION PRACTICES

4.1(8A,22) Definitions

4.2(8A,17A,22) Statement of policy, purpose and scope

4.3(8A,22) Requests for access to records

4.4(8A,17A,22) Access to confidential records

4.5(8A,17A,22) Requests for treatment of a record as a confidential record and its withholding from examination

4.6(8A,22) Procedure by which a person who is the subject of a record may have additions, dissents, or objections entered into a record

4.7(8A,17A,22) Consent to disclosure by the subject of a confidential record

4.8(8A,17A,22) Notice to suppliers of information

4.9(8A,22) Disclosures without the consent of the subject

4.10(8A,22) Routine use

4.11(8A,22) Consensual disclosure of confidential records

4.12(8A,22) Release to subject

4.13(8A,22) Availability of records

4.14(8A,22) Personally identifiable information

4.15(8A,22) Other groups of records

4.16(8A,22) Data processing systems

4.17(8A,22) Applicability

4.18(8A) Agency records

Source: Iowa Admin. Code Administrative Services Dept. Table of Contents p. 1 (2016), https://www.legis.iowa .gov/law/administrativeRules/agencies.

box on the legislature's site.[20] When citing according to the *Bluebook* or *ALWD Guide*, note that the format is Iowa Admin. Code r. 11-4.3 (2016).

While libraries may have back issues of the code, it is no longer generally available in print. The IAC is available from 1998 to the present via the Iowa legislature's website.[21] Lexis contains the current IAC and select older versions, which, for some sections date back to 2004.[22] Westlaw contains the code from 2002 to the present.[23] Current codes also are accessible on Bloomberg Law[24] and Fastcase.[25]

2. Iowa Administrative Bulletin

The *Iowa Administrative Bulletin* contains rules and proposed rules of administrative agencies and is published biweekly.[26] Issued chronologically, the *Administrative Bulletin* "is the official notice of all proposed and adopted changes to the rules in the Iowa Administrative Code (IAC); documents that pertain to the business of the Administrative Rules Review Committee (ARRC); Executive Orders; and other documents as prescribed by statute."[27]

Within the bulletin, <u>underscored text</u> indicates new material that has been added to existing rules while ~~strike through~~ designates deleted material. The

---

20. The *Iowa Administrative Code* Quick Search box appears in the right menu on many pages on the Iowa legislature site, including https://www.legis.iowa.gov/law.

21. The *Iowa Administrative Code* is available at https://www.legis.iowa.gov/law/administrativeRules.

22. On Lexis, you can bring up the current IAC by entering *Iowa Administrative Code* in either the "Browse Sources" feature or the red search box. From a current IAC section, any older versions available will be linked in the right margin as "Archived code versions." Alternatively, from the "Archives" box on the Lexis homepage, click "Archived Codes Search," then limit your search to "Administrative Codes" and "Iowa."

23. Access the current IAC on Westlaw through this path: Home > Regulations > Iowa. From this page, use the "Iowa Historical Regulations" link in the right column to access annual editions of the IAC back to 2002.

24. On Bloomberg Law, follow this path to access the current IAC: Home > State Law > Iowa > Iowa Regulatory & Administrative > Iowa Administrative Code.

25. From the Fastcase homepage, click on "Search Regulations." Then click the plus symbol to the left of "Iowa" to open that menu. Any available versions of the IAC will be listed; as of the time of this writing, the only content available is the current IAC. Check to search this material using the search box and options at the top of the screen.

26. The content of what is published as well as the publication schedule is set pursuant to Iowa Code chapters 2B and 17A.

27. Iowa Legislature, *Iowa Administrative Bulletin (IAB) & IAC Supplement*, https://www.legis.iowa.gov/law/administrativeRules/bulletinSupplementListings.

Iowa Administrative Bulletin also contains other valuable information, such as a schedule for rulemaking and information about public hearings for proposed rules.

Libraries may have back issues of the bulletin, but it is no longer available in print. Issues of the bulletin from September 24, 1997, to the present are available through the Iowa legislature's website.[28] Although the site does not provide a "Quick Search" box for the IAB, it does provide one by ARC number from each of the Iowa Administrative Rules pages.[29] Lexis contains the bulletins from June 19, 1996, to the present. Westlaw has databases entitled "Iowa Proposed & Adopted Regulations." You can limit your search to the past two years by selecting the "-Current" database or you can search back to 2006 by selecting the "-All" database.[30] Bloomberg Law's coverage goes back to 2011.[31]

B. Researching Iowa Rules

Depending on your research starting point and the information you are trying to obtain, you may choose from among a variety of techniques to research Iowa regulations. The three most common approaches are described below.

1. Starting with a Code of Iowa Section

If you already have a relevant code section, you can use that information to search for related regulations. You could look up the section in an annotated code, using one of the sources described in Section III.C. of Chapter 6, to determine if its notes reference applicable regulations. In the hypothetical grandparent visitation scenario, there are no rules referenced in the annotated code for the current relevant statute, § 600C.1. However, as noted in the Welch matter text box, there are some regulations that may be relevant. The Welch matter demonstrates why you cannot simply rely on references in the annotated code for all regulations applicable to a particular statute.

---

28. The *Iowa Administrative Bulletin* can be found at https://www.legis.iowa .gov/law/administrativeRules/bulletinSupplementListings.

29. A Quick Search box labeled "Rule-Making Document" is found on the main Iowa Administrative Rules page and all those rule subpages linked within it. https:// www.legis.iowa.gov/law/administrativeRules.

30. Westlaw's "Iowa Regulation Tracking" database gives a summary of the notices of intended action indicating which provisions would be amended by the regulation.

31. On Bloomberg Law follow this path to access the IAB: Home > State Law > Iowa > Iowa Regulatory & Administrative > Iowa Rulemaking.

You could also access the Iowa legislature site for the annually updated Table of Rules Implementing Statutes to determine which rules are promulgated under a particular code section.[32] The table begins with a list of code chapters and specific sections and then provides the associated IAC references. More than one entry may apply. For instance, with a starting code reference of 8.57(5)(c), you would want to review that specific entry as well as the broader one for 8.57. Because each administrative rule has to state the applicable code section, as indicated in parentheses following the rule number,[33] you could use your *Code of Iowa* reference as part of an electronic search of the full text of the IAC. For instance, on Westlaw, you could search the Iowa Administrative Code for *"iowa code" /6 8.57.*[34] This search would specify that you wanted results where the phrase Iowa Code appears within six words of your section number. In this case, *8.57* is a smarter search term than *8.57(5)(c)* to retrieve anything that refers to the broader section and also to avoid potential problems with differences in how the subsection is represented, such as subsection 5(c) of section 8.57.

2. Electronically Searching the IAC or IAB Full Text

This approach is similar to statutory research. Begin by generating a list of terms, using the TARPP or journalist techniques discussed in Chapter 1. Then, search for these keywords on a source allowing full-text electronic access to the IAC and IAB. Because the *Iowa Administrative Code* is organized by agency rather than subject, your topic may appear under multiple chapters and agencies.

At the Iowa legislature site, you can use the "Search Administrative Rules" link to open the Legislative Document Research Page.[35] The initial page, "Main Search," provides a simple search box where you can enter your keywords. An "Advanced Search" link provides a form-based approach to

---

32. From the Iowa Law & Rules pages, the table is under Additional Information & Resources at https://www.legis.iowa.gov/law/administrativeRules/additionalInfo. The table also includes information on regulations associated with particular US Code cites, state and federal session laws, CFR cites, and executive orders.

33. This requirement is explained in Section IV.A.1. of this chapter.

34. On Westlaw, the code database is called "Iowa Regulations."

35. The direct link to the Legislative Document Research Page is https://www.legis.iowa.gov/publications/search. To search the Legislative Document Research Page as efficiently as possible, you may want to first read the brief explanation of the search engine, available at https://www.legis.iowa.gov/docs/publications/IHD/680332.pdf.

searching the site or a designated section of the site.[36] Note that if you input a search using the advanced search form, the system will translate that search into a terms-and-connectors search, using the operators the system recognizes.[37] If you already know what these operators are, you can directly input them in the main search box.[38]

From either the main search or advanced search screens, the default search includes all content, i.e., all available administrative materials, all forms of legislation, and other publications on the Iowa legislature site, such as fiscal reports. The left-hand menu offers a "Search Within" feature that allows you to restrict your search to one or more subsets of materials available. Administrative options are the administrative code, administrative bulletin, or administrative rulemaking documents. You can also open any of these sub-menus to further limit your search to one or more agencies within the IAC, to a specific IAB, or to an ARC year back to 2008.[39] You can also search the full text of the IAC in Bloomberg Law, Fastcase, Lexis, and Westlaw.[40] The sidebar on the Welch matter and Figures 8-1 through 8-3 demonstrate this approach on the legislature's website.

The Welch Matter

Regarding the grandparent visitation scenario, if you wanted to expand your research to include regulations, you could do so following the steps outlined in Section IV.B. Figures 8-1 through 8-3 illustrate this procedure.

Assume there is a question as to how financial support for the minor might be affected by a change in visitation. Even though the father is dead, you would likely want to investigate whether an adjustment of visitation rights might give rise to a financial obligation.

Using the "Advanced Search" tab on the legislative website, check the box to "Search Within" the Iowa Administrative Code, found under the Iowa Law and

---

36. The direct link to the advanced search page is https://www.legis.iowa.gov /publications/search/advanced. It also is accessible by clicking the magnifying glass in the upper-right corner found on the rules pages.

37. The Legislative Document Research page is built on the open source SOLR platform, which in turn relies on Lucene for its search functionality. *See* https://www .legis.iowa.gov/publications/search/help.

38. For additional information, see the "Search Tools" tab from the Legislative Document Research Page at https://www.legis.iowa.gov/publications/search.

39. ARC numbers are described in Section IV.A.

40. Information on accessing the IAC on each of these platforms is available in Section IV.A.1.

Figure 8-1. Advanced Search Form in the *Iowa Administrative Code*

Source: Iowa Legislative Document Research Page, https://www.legis.iowa.gov/publications/ search.

Rules menu. In the box for "Containing **all** these words" you could enter *visitation adjustment* and in the box "and containing this **exact phrase**" you could type *child support*. See Figure 8-1. Note that the grayed out search terms are default examples; they will not actually be searched. When you click the search button, the system populates the Main Search box with your query, using the proper operators: *(+visitation +adjustment) AND ("child support")*. You can also see your results in the main viewing window: IAC Rule 441.99.4 and 441.99.69. See Figure 8-2. The display indicates these rules are from the Human Services Department. The first number, 441, represents that department. The subsequent numbers indicate first that the rules appear in chapter 99 and are followed by the specific rule number, in one case 4 and in the other 69. Links to the IAC rules and to the enabling statutes in the Iowa Code allow you to easily read those sources.

You would check both rules to see if they apply to your case. Rule 99.4(5), shown in Figure 8-3, addresses "extraordinary visitation adjustment" and may be relevant.

Figure 8-2. Advanced Search Results in the *Iowa Administrative Code*

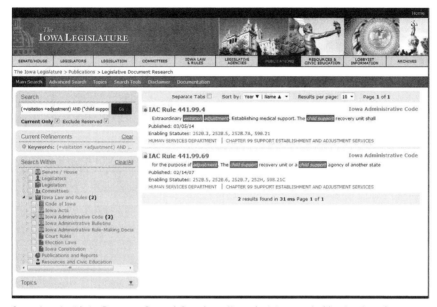

Source: Iowa Legislative Document Research Page, https://www.legis.iowa.gov/publications/ search.

Figure 8-3. Example from the *Iowa Administrative Code*

99.4(5) *Extraordinary visitation adjustment.* The extraordinary visitation adjustment is a credit as specified in the supreme court guidelines. The credit shall not reduce the child support below the amount required by the supreme court guidelines.

The extraordinary visitation adjustment credit shall be given if all of the following apply:

a. There is an existing order for the noncustodial parent that meets the criteria for extraordinary visitation in excess of 127 overnights per year on an annual basis for the child for whom support is sought. The order granting visitation can be a different order than the child support order. If a controlling order is determined pursuant to Iowa Code chapter 252K and that controlling support order does not meet the criteria for extraordinary visitation, there is another order that meets the criteria.

b. The noncustodial parent has provided CSRU with a file-stamped or certified copy of the order.

c. The court has not ordered equally shared physical care.

99.4(6) *Establishing medical support.* The child support recovery unit shall calculate medical support as required by Iowa Code chapter 252E and the Iowa Supreme Court guidelines. The cost of the health insurance premium for the child is added to the basic support obligation and prorated between the parents as provided in the Iowa Supreme Court guidelines, and the parent ordered to provide health insurance must provide verification of this expense or anticipated expense.

[ARC 1357C, IAB 3/5/14, effective 5/1/14]

Source: Iowa Admin. Code r. 441-99.4(5) (2016), https://www.legis.iowa.gov/docs/iac/chapter/ 441.99.pdf.

3. Using the *Iowa Administrative Code* Index

The State of Iowa produces an index to the *Iowa Administrative Code*, available on its website.[41] The listed IAC sections are all hyperlinked, making it easy to access them, but there are no descriptions for the linked sections. For example, the heading "Opticians" references two specific IAC sections:

OPTICIANS, 441 — 77.7, 78.7

Although it is easy to check just a couple of sections in this case, the lack of descriptive subheadings makes the index less useful when many sections are listed. For instance, the heading "Professional Licensure" refers to hundreds of chapters from twenty-seven different agencies, with no additional explanation of what you will find at any of these references, just scores of numbers. Another limitation of this index is that it is not comprehensive. Searching the Legislative Document Research Page for *optician* leads to eight IAC sections. Although the index might still be a viable way to begin searching the IAC, it should be used with caution.

C. Currentness of Iowa Rules

Once you have found a relevant regulation, you need to make sure you have the most recent changes. On the *Iowa Administrative Code* page[42] the date of the last update will be listed at the top of the screen.[43] Then, check the *Iowa Administrative Bulletin* to make sure there have been no updates since the last IAC update. You also will want to check the Iowa Code chapter (shown in parentheses following the administrative code section) to make sure there have been no legislative changes in the enabling statute. That can be easily done with the "Quick Search" box for the Iowa Code on the legislature's website.[44] If you retrieved the

---

41. The index is linked from the main Iowa Administrative Rules page at https://www.legis.iowa.gov/law/administrativeRules.

42. The address is https://www.legis.iowa.gov/law/administrativeRules/agencies.

43. This information can also be found on vendor platforms. When a specific IAC section is open, on Bloomberg Law, look in the right column under the heading "Currency"; on Lexis, look for a statement of currency under the "Copy Citation" button near the top of the viewing box; and on Westlaw, use the "Currentness" link in the box that shows your place in the source. On Fastcase, find the last update information before opening the source through the "info" link to the right of the "Iowa Administrative Code" link (follow the path Home > Search Regulations > Iowa > Iowa Administrative Code).

44. The "Quick Search" box is found several places on the legislature's site, including https://www.legis.iowa.gov/law.

regulation using the legislative website's main search function, the enabling statutes are provided as hot links on the initial display. The site also provides a "Rule Tracker" that enables you to track the progress of each rulemaking document and one that links to "Emergency Rule-Making Documents."[45]

V. Iowa Attorney General Opinions

As the state's chief legal officer, the attorney general has responsibility for the state's legal business.[46] The office issues a formal opinion to answer "legal questions of a public nature that relate to a public official's duties.... [It] is similar to a legal precedent and stands until a court or later opinion overrules it or new legislation is enacted to change the statute in question." Questions often arise "about inconsistent statutes or legal principles, confusion in the law itself, the constitutionality of a statute or rule, or legal disputes between two government entities."[47] The attorney general also issues informal opinions, such as when a state agency seeks advice, but these are not binding.

Formal attorney general opinions issued after 1898 and informal letter opinions are available online from the attorney general's website.[48] Westlaw provides coverage from 1898 as well and Lexis has opinions starting in 1977.[49]

VI. Federal Regulations

Federal administrative agencies are formed in much the same way as those in Iowa. As with Iowa, they are established and delegated authority by enabling acts. The scope of the authority of the agency, its internal organizations and procedures, and its rights of judicial review are all governed by

---

45. Both are found under the Iowa Administrative Rules page at https://www.legis.iowa.gov/law/administrativeRules.

46. More information is available at the Iowa Attorney General's webpage at https://www.iowaattorneygeneral.gov.

47. Iowa Dept. of Justice, *Attorney General Opinions*, https://www.iowaattorneygeneral.gov/about-us/attorney-general-opinions.

48. The database of Iowa attorney general opinions is maintained by Westlaw and is freely searchable at https://www.iowaattorneygeneral.gov. From the attorney general's homepage, you can go to About Us > Attorney General Opinions > Search Attorney General Opinions. You can search using terms and connectors or natural language.

49. On Westlaw, go to State Materials > Iowa > Iowa Administrative Decisions & Guidance > Attorney General Opinions. On Lexis, go to Browse > Source > By Jurisdiction > Iowa > IA Attorney General Opinions.

enabling acts. The fundamental piece of legislation that dictates the actions of federal agencies is the Administrative Procedure Act (APA).[50]

Federal regulations can be accessed via the *Code of Federal Regulations* (CFR) and the *Federal Register* (FR), which are discussed in Section VI.A., as well as select websites. The federal government provides a Federal Digital System (FDsys) at the Government Publishing Office (GPO) site,[51] and also maintains Regulations.gov, a U.S. government portal for proposed and final regulations of executive branch agencies. GPO's new govinfo.gov will eventually replace FDsys.[52] Agency websites are also excellent resources for finding regulations. Many agencies' sites provide the text of the enabling statutes under which that agency operates as well as current regulations and information on proposed rules. USA.gov provides links to all U.S. government agencies. The *United States Government Manual*,[53] the official handbook for the federal government, contains comprehensive information on the agencies of the legislative, executive, and judicial branches.[54]

Some unofficial sites also provide access to proposed and final federal regulations. The University of Virginia Library has an excellent topically organized site that links to administrative actions that are outside the scope of the CFR and FR.[55]

A. Finding Federal Regulations

Federal regulations are published in two stages, first daily as the *Federal Register* (FR) and then by subject as the *Code of Federal Regulations* (CFR).

---

50. 5 U.S.C. § 551.

51. The FDsys is at http://www.gpo.gov/fdsys.

52. The beta version of govinfo.gov was released as this book was being finalized. Govinfo.gov will include everything in FDsys but with a new interface and features to facilitate use.

53. The *United States Government Manual* is available at usgovernmentmanual .gov.

54. Examples of legislative and executive agencies are given in section VII.A.2. The United States Sentencing Commission is an example of an independent agency in the judicial branch.

55. The University of Virginia Library guide includes links to many sources of government information at http://guides.lib.virginia.edu/findinggovinfo.

1. Code of Federal Regulations

The *Code of Federal Regulations* (CFR)[56] is the codified form of all final regulations that have already been published in the daily *Federal Register* and that are currently in effect. As such, federal regulation research typically starts with the CFR, rather than the FR. The regulations are contained in fifty subject-specific titles, numbered one through fifty. Most agencies will have all of their rules in the same title. An example of a citation to the CFR is 7 CFR § 412.1 (2015), where 7 refers to the CFR title number covering agriculture[57] and 412.1 is the section number.

The CFR is updated annually, but the updating process occurs throughout the year and not always on schedule. Technically, titles 1–16 are updated January 1; titles 17–27 are updated April 1; titles 28–41 are updated July 1; and titles 42–50 are updated October 1. In print, the color on the paperback binding changes each year, providing a quick way to determine whether a particular volume has been updated yet.

The CFR is available in print or online. (See Figure 8-4 for an example.) Online, the FDsys provides free access to the full text from 1996 to the present.[58] Coverage from 1938 to 1995 is provided by the Library of Congress.[59] While the online text is only updated as frequently as the print version, FDsys is an official version. Another government option is the e-CFR,[60] which is updated daily and, although not an official version, may be the most current of all the resources mentioned here. Bloomberg Law, Fastcase, Lexis, and Westlaw have the full text of the CFR, although their coverage dates vary.[61] HeinOnline contains the full text from 1938 to the present.

---

56. While the *Iowa Administrative Bulletin* is comparable to the *Federal Register*, the *Iowa Administrative Code* is not analogous to the *Code of Federal Regulations* because the latter is arranged by topic or subject, not agency.

57. Note that not all of the fifty subject-specific titles of the CFR are identical to the fifty plus titles in the USC.

58. The CFR is located at http://www.gpo.gov/fdsys or https://govinfo.gov.

59. The CFR coverage on the Library of Congress page is at http://loc.heinonline .org/loc/LOC?index=cfrloc.

60. e-CFR is located at www.ecfr.gov.

61. Lexis covers from 1981 to the present; the CFR is under Browse > Sources > Search for a Source > CFR. Westlaw contains the CFR from 1984 to the present at Regulations > Code of Federal Regulations (CFR). On Fastcase, go to Search > Search Regulations > Code of Federal Regulations with options for the current or archived

Figure 8-4. Example from the *Code of Federal Regulations*

§ 664.32   34 CFR Ch. VI (7-1-15 Edition)

§ 664.32 What priorities may the Secretary establish?

(a) The Secretary may establish for each funding competition one or more of the following priorities:

(1) Categories of projects described in § 664.10.

(2) Specific languages, topics, countries or geographic regions of the world; for example, Chinese and Arabic, Curriculum Development in Multicultural Education and Transitions from Planned Economies to Market Economies, Brazil and Nigeria, Middle East and South Asia.

(3) Levels of education; for example, elementary and secondary, postsecondary, or postgraduate.

(b) The Secretary announces any priorities in the application notice published in the FEDERAL REGISTER.

(Authority: 22 U.S.C. 2452(b)(6), 2456(a)(2))

§ 664.33 What costs does the Secretary pay?

(a) The Secretary pays only part of the cost of a project funded under this part. Other than travel costs, the Secretary does not pay any of the costs for project-related expenses within the United States.

(b) The Secretary pays the cost of the following—

(1) A maintenance stipend related to the cost of living in the host country or countries;

(2) Round-trip international travel;

(3) A local travel allowance for necessary project-related transportation within the country of study, exclusive of the purchase of transportation equipment;

(4) Purchase of project-related artifacts, books, and other teaching materials in the country of study;

(5) Rent for instructional facilities in the country of study;

(6) Clerical and professional services performed by resident instructional personnel in the country of study; and

(7) Other expenses in the country of study, if necessary for the project's success and approved in advance by the Secretary.

(c) The Secretary may pay—

(1) Emergency medical expenses not covered by a participant's health and accident insurance; and

(2) The costs of preparing and transporting the remains of a participant who dies during the term of a project to his or her former home.

(Authority: 22 U.S.C. 2452(b)(6), 2454(e)(1))

Subpart D—What Conditions Must Be Met by a Grantee?

§ 664.40 Can participation in a Fulbright-Hays Group Projects Abroad be terminated?

(a) Participation may be terminated only by the J. William Fulbright Foreign Scholarship Board upon the recommendation of the Secretary.

(b) The Secretary may recommend a termination of participation on the basis of failure by the grantee to ensure that participants adhere to the standards of conduct adopted by the J. William Fulbright Foreign Scholarship Board.

(Authority: 22 U.S.C. 2452(b)(6), 2456, and Policy Statements of the J. William Fulbright Foreign Scholarship Board, 1990)

PART 668—STUDENT ASSISTANCE GENERAL PROVISIONS

Subpart A—General

Sec.
668.1   Scope.
668.2   General definitions.
668.3   Academic year.
668.4   Payment period.
668.5   Written arrangements to provide educational programs.
668.6   Reporting and disclosure requirements for programs that prepare students for gainful employment in a recognized occupation.
668.7   [Reserved]
668.8   Eligible program.
668.9   Relationship between clock hours and semester, trimester, or quarter hours in calculating Title IV, HEA program assistance.
668.10   Direct assessment programs.

Subpart B—Standards for Participation in Title IV, HEA Programs

668.11   Scope.
668.12   [Reserved]
668.13   Certification procedures.
668.14   Program participation agreement.
668.15   Factors of financial responsibility.
668.16   Standards of administrative capability.
668.17   [Reserved]

432

Source: 34 C.F.R. § 664.40 (2015).

There are several finding aids for the CFR. Like the rest of the set, the volume entitled "Index and Finding Aids" is revised annually. This volume contains a subject index as well as parallel tables of authorities, including citations to the USC, the *Statutes at Large*, public laws, and presidential documents. Another essential aid is the *List of CFR Sections Affected* (LSA), which is issued monthly and cumulates throughout the year. Available online and in print, the LSA must be checked to ensure that your CFR section has not changed since being published. The LSA is explained in Part C below.

2. Federal Register

The *Federal Register*[62] is published each weekday and includes regulations, proposed rules, notices, presidential proclamations, and executive orders. It has a continuous page count for the entire year, and regulations are printed as they are promulgated. It contains extensive background information about regulation changes that is not available in the CFR, making the *Federal Register* an invaluable resource in understanding regulations and the policies behind them.

The *Federal Register* is available online and in print. Online, FDsys provides free access from 1994 to the present[63] and the Library of Congress provides coverage from the first issue in 1936 to 1993.[64] The FederalRegister.gov site covers from 1994 to the present in an easy-to-use web newspaper format with the ability to search agencies, topics, and citations and set up RSS or email feeds. Bloomberg Law, Lexis, and Westlaw also provide access to the *Federal Register* although their coverage dates vary.[65] HeinOnline provides full-text access from 1936 to the present.

B. Researching Federal Regulations

As with Iowa regulatory research, federal regulation research operates somewhat like statutory research. Before you begin your research, it is helpful

---

editions back to 2011. Bloomberg Law has the current CFR under Federal Law > Federal Regulatory & Administrative > Code of Federal Regulations (CFR).

62. The *Iowa Administrative Bulletin* is comparable to the *Federal Register*.

63. The *Federal Register* is located at http://www.gpo.gov/fdsys or https://govinfo.gov.

64. The *Federal Register* coverage on the Library of Congress page is at https://www.loc.gov/collections/federal-register/.

65. Bloomberg Law provides *Federal Register* coverage from 1999 to present by going to Federal Law > Federal Regulatory & Administrative > Federal Register (FR). Lexis covers from 1980 to the present under Browse > Sources > Search for a Source > Federal Register. Westlaw offers the *Federal Register* from 1936 to the present under Federal Materials > Federal Register — All.

Table 8-2. Researching Federal Regulations

1. Search the CFR to locate keywords on your topic.
2. Search for cases and other authorities that have examined the regulation.
3. Search an annotated code for statutes related to your regulation.
4. If you feel you need more information, look for law review articles and treatises that have addressed the regulation.

to have an idea of what agency would have jurisdiction over your issue as well as the structure of the agency, both of which can be found by reviewing information on the agency on USA.gov or in the *United States Government Manual*.[66] This information can aid in interpreting the regulation.

As noted in Table 8-2, the first step is to search the CFR to locate keywords on your topic. Online, you can search for your keywords in any source (see Section V.A.1.) that contains the CFR.

The next step in administrative research is to search for cases, law review articles, or other texts that have examined a regulation. One of the most convenient ways to find court decisions is to use one of the commercial versions of the CFR. On Westlaw, the CFR is annotated, like the USCA, and includes notes, decisions, references to relevant agency decisions, and links to statutes and secondary sources using KeyCite.[67] The CFR on Lexis includes case annotations, and the Shepard's link provides additional citations to decisions, law reviews, and treatises that have examined your regulation.[68] Bloomberg Law provides a "Case Analysis" tab to show cases citing the regulation.

In addition to law review articles, other secondary sources might provide more information on the regulation you are researching. Treatises, such as Pierce's *Administrative Law Treatise*,[69] are excellent research options. *American Law Report*'s volume "Table of Laws, Rules and Regulations" provides a table listing CFR sections and the ALR annotations that cite them. Looseleaf services[70] collect and reprint agency regulations in a particular subject area.

---

66. The *United States Government Manual* is available at usgovernmentmanual .gov.

67. On Westlaw, go to Regulations > Code of Federal Regulations (CFR).

68. See Chapter 9 for more detailed information on using citators.

69. Richard J. Pierce, *Administrative Law Treatise* (5th ed. 2010). Lexis and Westlaw provide access to administrative law treatises by various authors.

70. Refer to Chapter 3 for more detailed information about looseleaf services.

These topical looseleaf services focus on the work of one of the major agencies and provide up-to-date, annotated texts of federal regulations in their subject areas. To locate a looseleaf in a particular subject area, check the catalog of your local law library or ask a librarian.

Searching an annotated code for laws related to your topic may also be helpful. Because regulations are used to implement statutes, annotated codes frequently include references to applicable regulations. As detailed in Chapter 6, two major annotated versions of the U.S. Code are available online and in print. Of these, the *United States Code Service* (USCS) contains more extensive regulatory annotations than the *United States Code Annotated* (USCA). The USCS also has a table volume that provides citations for related statutes and regulations. References to the relevant sections of the CFR follow the text of the section in both the USCA and USCA.[71]

C. Updating Federal Regulations

Agencies can act at any time during the year, so updating your CFR research is essential. Although it is more common to update online, the process for print is also discussed.

1. Online

The fastest and easiest way to update regulations is to use the FDsys site.[72] The quarterly publication schedule is the same in print and online with FDsys providing free online access. To update regulations via the FDsys site, follow the steps outlined in Table 8-3.[73] Although the Electronic Code of Federal Regulations (e-CFR) is a helpful source for finding current regulations, it remains an unofficial source until technical and performances issues are resolved.[74]

If you are accessing the CFR on Bloomberg Law, Lexis, or Westlaw, the currentness is noted with the section where it lists the date of the most recent *Federal Register* issue that was checked and incorporated in the CFR.

---

71. See Chapter 6 for more detailed information on statutes.

72. FDsys is at http://www.gpo.gov/fdsys until it is replaced by https://govinfo.gov.

73. This updating process is covered in detail in: Patrick Charles, *How Do You Update the Code of Federal Regulations Using FDsys?*, 20 Perspectives 128 (2012), *available at* http://info.legalsolutions.thomsonreuters.com/pdf/perspec/2012-winter-spring/2012-winter-spring-9.pdf.

74. The e-CFR is at http://www.ecfr.gov.

Table 8-3. Updating a CFR Citation Using FDsys

---

1. Find your regulation by citation and note the date the section was last revised (which is normally the first of January, April, July, or October).

2. At the main FDsys page, click "Browse All" and then click "List of CFR Sections Affected."

3. Click the "Monthly LSA" for the most recent year and open the latest month to see if your section is listed. If there has been a change, the LSA will refer you to the page in the *Federal Register* where the change was published.[75]

4. Go back to the "List of CFR Sections Affected" page and check the link "Browse CFR Parts Affected from the Federal Register" for your citation from the date of the last LSA you checked. (Note this step may not be necessary if the most recent month LSA listed in step 3 is very current.)

---

2. In Print

Begin by locating the desired regulation in the most recently revised edition of the CFR. Then consult the most recent monthly edition of the *List of CFR Sections Affected* (LSA). Because the LSA is cumulative, you only need to check the most recent issue to determine whether any changes to a regulation have taken place since the last CFR was published.

Then go to the most recent issue of the *Federal Register* for each month not covered by the LSA. At the back of each issue is a cumulative list called "CFR Parts Affected During [month]." This listing updates the most recent edition of the LSA. You can also update your research using the LSA online at the FDsys site.[76]

If the CFR section is not listed in any of these places, there are several steps you can follow to ensure you have the most up-to-date information:

- Look in the LSA to see if it has been redesignated, i.e., given a new number.
- Look in the back of the appropriate CFR volume for a Redesignation Table.
- Look in the back of the appropriate CFR volume for an LSA table by year. This will reflect any changes that have occurred since 1986.

---

75. The FDsys home page at https://www.gpo.gov/fdsys provides a "Retrieve by Citation" link, which makes it easy to find *Federal Register* pages. Govinfo.gov provides a "Citation" tab with search boxes to find those pages.

76. From the FDsys page at https://www.gpo.gov/fdsys, click "Browse All" and select "List of Sections Affected."

Table 8-4. Partial List of Iowa Agency Decisions Available on the Web

Agency	Address	Available Dates
Iowa Department of Education	https://www.edinfo.state.ia.us/web/appeals.asp	1975–present
Iowa Public Employment Relations Board	https://iowaperb.iowa.gov/content/decisions	1975–present
Iowa Public Employment Relations Iowa Unemployment Insurance Decisions	http://decisions.iowaworkforce.org/ui	2001–present
Iowa Workers' Compensation Decisions	http://decisions.iowaworkforce.org/worker-scomp	2000–present

However, because the FDsys site provides free, easy, official online access that is the recommended route.

VII. Other Documents from the Executive Branch

A. Decisions of Agencies

1. Iowa

As stated at the beginning of the chapter, one of the primary actions of agencies is adjudication. Some Iowa agencies hold hearings to resolve disputes arising from their regulations. Some of these decisions are available online, as exemplified by Table 8-4.[77]

2. Federal

As in Iowa, federal agencies hold hearings to resolve disputes. While some decisions are published in agency-specific reporters, others are available via agency websites. In print, Appendix 7 of the *ALWD Guide to Legal Citation* contains a list of major official agency publications. In addition, Washburn

---

77. Drake Law Library's Iowa Legal Research Guide provides a detailed list of up-to-date information on Iowa agency resources. Visit http://libguides.law.drake.edu/IowaBasic and click on the "Administrative" tab.

University School of Law maintains a list of agency sites with links to their opinions.[78] Bloomberg Law, Lexis, and Westlaw contain databases that include the decisions of some agencies.[79] HeinOnline also has a library of U.S. Federal Agency Documents, Decisions, and Appeals, which includes opinions and reports from scores of administrative bodies, such as the Atomic Energy Commission, the Comptroller General of the United States, the Federal Communications Commission, the Federal Trade Commission, and the Securities and Exchange Commission.[80]

B. Executive Orders and Proclamations

1. Iowa

Executive orders and proclamations from the governor have the force of law. *Executive orders* address issues such as creating task forces and committees, budgetary matters, and state resources. These executive documents are numbered in the order in which they are issued, beginning with number one. The numbering restarts for each governor.

Executive orders of Iowa governors going back to 1854 are available on the State Law Library of Iowa's website.[81] More general information is available at the governor's official site.[82]

Executive proclamations include things such as the proclamation of a state of emergency after a severe weather event, for example, the hundred-year floods of 2008, or the proclamation that a special event will be held. Current proclamations are available via the news archive on the governor's site.[83]

2. Federal

At the federal level, executive orders and proclamations have basically the same legal effect as similar documents in Iowa, but are usually used for different purposes. Executive orders are issued by the president to help manage the operations of the federal government, and proclamations communicate

---

78. The Washburn site is available at http://www.washlaw.edu/doclaw/executive5m.html.

79. On Bloomberg Law go to Federal Law > U.S. Government Departments & Agencies, on Lexis go to Browse > Sources > Administrative Law, and on Westlaw go to Administrative Decisions & Guidance (which includes an index).

80. HeinOnline is available at http://heinonline.org.

81 The State Law Library of Iowa list of executive orders of Iowa governors is at http://www.statelibraryofiowa.org/services/collections/law-library/govexecorders.

82. The Governor of Iowa's site is https://governor.iowa.gov.

83. Press releases are located at https://governor.iowa.gov/category/newsroom.

ceremonial or broad policy statements. Both are numbered, in separate series, in order of issuance. Numbering does not restart with each new president. Presidential documents are published in the *Federal Register* and codified in title 3 of the *Code of Federal Regulations*. However, a better source is the *Compilation of Presidential Documents*,[84] as it includes press releases and signing statements as well as executive orders and proclamations.[85]

---

84. The *Compilation of Presidential Documents* is available from the FDsys page at https://www.gpo.gov/fdsys going back to 1993. Since 2009 the weekly and daily compilations have been combined. The papers also are at https://govinfo.gov.

85. For links to some excellent, non-governmental sources see the Administrative Law: Presidential Materials Research Guide at http://libguides.law.drake.edu/c.php?g=150997&p=992569.

Chapter 9

Updating with Citators

I. Introduction

The law is not static. Legal authorities change as they are interpreted by courts and modified by the legislature. As courts continue to decide cases in a particular area of law, determining which case to rely upon becomes increasingly difficult. Thus, a legal researcher must be able to locate all authorities applicable to an issue in order to evaluate cases and statutes in the context of developing law. As cases are questioned, reversed, or overruled and statutes are modified, the researcher must also be able to determine the status of a legal authority and whether it remains "good law."

The process of examining how a legal authority has been interpreted or changed subsequent to its issuance is known as *updating*. Updating is often referred to as "Shepardizing" because the first major updating tool, or citator, was *Shepard's Citations*. Shepard's is available online through Lexis and in print. Although print versions are still being published, many libraries no longer carry them and instead provide online access. Westlaw also has an online citator known as KeyCite. More limited research citators are available on Bloomberg Law (BCite), Fastcase (Authority Check), and Google Scholar ("Cited by" feature). This chapter focuses on online updating, which provides the most current information and is easier and more efficient to use than print citators. The Lexis website provides information on updating in print Shepard's.[1]

II. Purposes of Updating

As a legal researcher, you must update all authorities you intend to rely upon for two important reasons. The first reason is to fulfill ethical and pro-

---

1. *See, e.g., How to Shepardize* at https://www.lexisnexis.com/shepards-citations /printsupport/shepardize_print.pdf.

fessional obligations to cite the most current and applicable sources. In this situation, updating is done for validity purposes. The second reason is more strategic and practical; locating all applicable sources of law helps provide the most effective representation. In this situation, updating is done for research purposes. Using a citator to verify that you are relying on good law is a requirement of law practice. Using a citator as a research finding tool is an optional approach; there are many other ways to locate relevant authority.

A. Ethical and Professional Considerations

The *Iowa Rules of Professional Conduct* require that a lawyer provide competent representation, which "requires the legal knowledge, skill, thoroughness, and preparation reasonably necessary for the representation."[2] Moreover, lawyers are prohibited from "fail[ing] to disclose to the tribunal legal authority in the controlling jurisdiction known to the lawyer to be directly adverse to the position of the client and not disclosed by opposing counsel."[3] Comments to the rules explain that a "lawyer is not required to make a disinterested exposition of the law, but must recognize the existence of pertinent legal authorities . . . . The underlying concept is that legal argument is a discussion seeking to determine the legal premises properly applicable to the case."[4] Updating for both validity and research helps the lawyer ensure that she is presenting the court with the most relevant legal authority.

In addition to honoring clear ethical obligations to find and cite relevant authority, highlighting applicable authority for the court helps protect a lawyer's professional reputation. Courts are not hesitant to publicly criticize a lawyer's failure to locate and identify applicable authority.[5]

---

2. Iowa R. Prof. Conduct 32:1.1.
3. Iowa R. Prof. Conduct 32:3.3.
4. *Id.* at cmt. 4.
5. *United States v. Barnes*, 912 F. Supp. 1187 (N.D. Iowa 1996). In *Barnes*, the court noted:

> The government's brief was most unsatisfactory, indeed misleading, in that it failed to cite the decision of the Sixth Circuit Court of Appeals in *United States v. Brown*, 988 F.2d 658 (6th Cir.1993), which is not so recent as to excuse the government's failure to find and discuss it. The *Brown* decision is critical to disposition of any motion for a preliminary injunction under 18 U.S.C. § 1345, because of its discussion of the appropriate standards and burdens of proof for issuance of such an injunction as well as such an injunction's proper scope. Thus, the government's brief is an example of the kind of gross oversight that can result from failure to update a "canned"

B. Practical Considerations

Updating is a sensible, as well as ethical, practice. Using citators is an efficient and effective way to conduct legal research. Once you have located a single applicable source for a client problem, you can use certain citators to locate all of the other legal sources that have cited that source. As a result, the citator will lead you to a number of additional, potentially relevant and useful authorities.

III. Updating: An Overview

As noted, this chapter will focus on using online citators—Shepard's (available on Lexis), KeyCite (available on Westlaw), BCite (available on Bloomberg Law), Authority Check (available on Fastcase), and the Google Scholar "Cited by" feature. You should note that Shepard's and KeyCite can be used for many types of legal sources, while BCite, Authority Check, and Google Scholar are limited to updating judicial opinions. Moreover, BCite, Authority Check, and Google Scholar differ from Shepard's and KeyCite in terms of the information provided.

Using a citator requires an understanding of some basic terminology. The source that you are updating is referred to as the *cited source*. The authorities listed in the citator that refer to your cited source are known as *citing sources*, *citing decisions*, or *citing references*.[6] Your cited source may be a judicial opinion, constitutional provision, statute, rule, regulation, or agency decision. As explained in Chapter 1, you might ground your legal argument in any of these primary sources. Because they may have been overturned or otherwise modified by a later primary source, you need to determine whether they are still current. You can also use certain citators to update certain secondary authorities, such as a law review article or ALR annotation. In this instance, your objective would likely be to identify additional authorities, rather than

---

brief, however repetitive a specialized practice may become. Merely "Shepardizing" the cases cited in the government's brief would have revealed the *Brown* decision. At worst, the government knew of the case, and intentionally failed to cite it; at best, the government was negligent in failing to find and discuss applicable case law.

Id. at 1189.

6. For ease of reading, citing sources/decisions/references will be referred to as citing references throughout.

to verify that the source is good law, because you rarely rely upon a secondary authority in a legal argument.

The process for using online citators is generally the same for both Shepard's and KeyCite. You will either perform a citator search, described more fully below, or you may retrieve a document and then launch the citator. With BCite, Authority Check, and Google Scholar, you must first conduct a case search to access these citation tools. Each platform provides some options with regard to how you view and sort the results.

A. Using Shepard's on Lexis

1. Accessing the Citator

The first step in using Shepard's on Lexis is to access the citator. If you are already logged on to Lexis, you can perform a citator search by typing *shep* followed by a colon and your citation in the text box. You will then launch the search (e.g., *shep: 661 N.W.2d 183*). Alternatively, you can retrieve a document by typing the citation in the search box and, once the cited source is retrieved, either click the "Shepardize® this document" link or any of the Shepard's hot links to citing references above that link.

On Lexis, you can Shepardize case law, statutes, rules and regulations, a variety of federal and state agency decisions, patents, law reviews, restatements, and more. A searchable list of materials Shepardizable online is available by accessing the online help materials. From the "Support" box links on the home page, you can click "Browse" to find Shepard's Citation Formats and Alphabetical List of Editorial Phrases.

2. Selecting a Citation Category

Once you Shepardize a source, you will have up to four categories of citations displayed, depending on the source. The categories for decisions include Appellate History, Citing Decisions, Other Citing Sources (such as law reviews and treatises), and Table of Authorities. The default results for a Shepard's search is the Appellate History for the cited source. Figure 9-1 illustrates a Shepard's search for *Santi v. Santi*, 633 N.W.2d 312 (Iowa 2001). You can see from the figure that the case has no subsequent appellate history. In instances in which a cited source, such as a case, has subsequent appellate history, the history can be presented in a list or map format. The list format presents an outline with indentations demonstrating the relationship between listed cases, and the map presents appellate history in a graphical view. Figure 9-2, adapted

Figure 9-1. *Shepard's®* Appellate History Result for *Santi v. Santi*

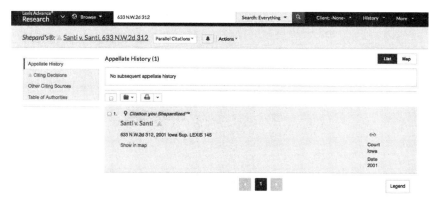

Figure 9-2. *Shepard's®* Appellate History Results for *Cuno v. DaimlerChrysler, Inc.*

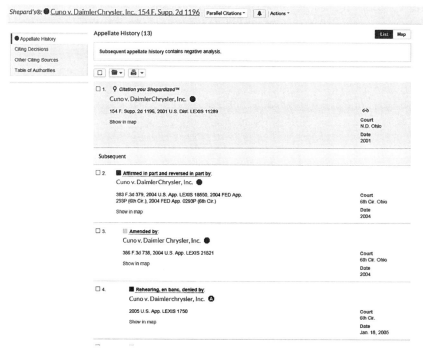

Figure 9-3. *Shepard's®* Citing Decisions Results for *Santi v. Santi*

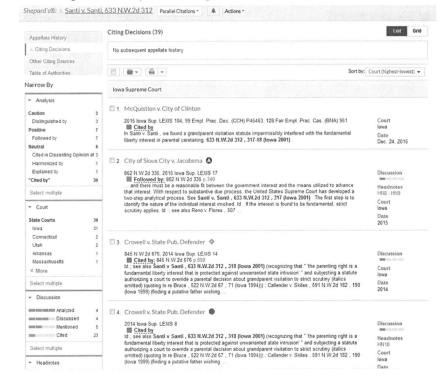

from the Lexis online help section for Shepard's, illustrates the Appellate History for *Cuno v. DaimlerChrysler, Inc.,* 154 F. Supp. 2d 1196 (N.D. Ohio 2001).

In order to view how the source has been treated in other court opinions, select the "Citing Decisions" link. Figure 9-3 illustrates the Citing Decisions results for *Santi v. Santi,* 633 N.W.2d 312 (Iowa 2001), an Iowa case in which a portion of the grandparent's visitation statute, Iowa Code § 598.35(7) (1999), was declared unconstitutional. Note that the results are organized in terms of the hierarchy of citing decisions, beginning with the highest court that has referenced the cited source. You can also sort the results by analysis, discussion, or date using the drop-down menu on the upper-right side of the report. You are also able to limit displayed results by using the "Narrow By" menu on the left side of the report. You can narrow by analysis, court, discussion, headnote, or date, or you have the options of searching within the results.

Figure 9-4. *Shepard's®* Citing Decisions Results Narrowed by "Unconstitutional by"

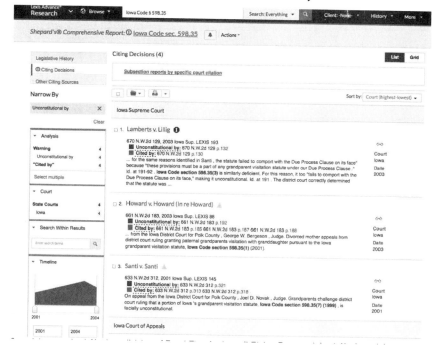

Source: Shepard's® Screenshot. Copyright 2016 LexisNexis, a division of RELX Inc. All Rights Reserved. LexisNexis, *Shepard's, Shepardize*, and the Knowledge Burst logo are registered trademarks of Reed Elsevier Properties Inc. and are used with the permission of LexisNexis.

Shepard's can also be used to update statutes. Figure 9-4 illustrates the results for a Shepard's Citing Decisions result, narrowed by Analysis > Unconstitutional for Iowa Code § 598.35 (1999). Note that the Iowa statute was deemed unconstitutional in its entirety in *In re Howard*, 661 N.W.2d 183 (Iowa 2003).

You may also choose to view other sources under the "Other Citing Sources" link, which contains references to the cited source in law reviews, treatises, and other court documents. Finally, you can choose the "Table of Authorities" link that lists the authorities on which the court relied in making its decision.

3. Analyzing the Citing Symbols and Sorting the Search Results

One of the first ways Shepard's notifies you that an authority has been affected by later authorities is with symbols next to the cited document's citation. The Shepard's Signal Indicator shows whether the cited source is still respected authority. To determine what a particular symbol means, simply rest your cursor over the symbol.[7] Your first step in Shepardizing a case is to review the Appellate History to determine whether there is any negative analysis, such as when a case has been reversed or amended as shown in Figure 9-2. If there is no negative history, you can turn your attention to the citing decisions.

Recognize that you cannot rely entirely on the symbol indicator for your cited source to determine whether your case is valid for the point of law in which you are interested. Most cases contain more than one legal issue, and a symbol indicator on a source may be related to an issue that has nothing to do with your interest in the source. For example, your case may have a signal indicating strong negative treatment, but for an issue unrelated to your research. Your cited source may still be good law for the issue related to your research, notwithstanding the signal. It is your responsibility, therefore, to read the citing references and to determine for yourself how they affect the validity of your cited source.

Another graphical feature for "Citing Decisions" is the bar under the heading "Discussion." This feature indicates the depth of discussion of the cited case in the citing opinion on a scale of one bar (cited) to four bars (analyzed). A "Sort By" drop-down box lets you sort results by type of analysis, level of discussion, court, or date.

The "Narrow By" feature provides additional options for sorting and reviewing citing decisions or other authorities. Note that under the "Analysis" heading, there is an indication of how other cases have treated the cited source. You also have the option of viewing the citing decisions results in grid format by selecting "Grid" in the Shepard's results for Citing Decisions. The Grid option provides a more graphical way to analyze treatment by other courts or by date.

Finally, note the alert option in Lexis. After running the Shepard's report, you can create an alert by clicking the bell icon to the right of the cited source citation at the top of the screen. The alert feature provides several choices for monitoring the status of your cited source and automatically receiving updates at the frequency you specify.

---

7. When in Shepard's, a full list of the symbols is available by going to the right of the search box to More > Help > The Shepard's Signal™ Indicators.

4. Reading and Analyzing the Citing References

Note that simply processing a request for a cited source on a citator is not sufficient to validate a source. As noted, you must analyze the results that the citator retrieves. The symbols are a good, preliminary indication of how a citing reference may affect the validity of your cited source, but remember that the citing reference may challenge the validity of a point of law in your cited source that is not relevant to your research. In this respect, limiting the results by headnote can focus your evaluation of search results to cases likely to be on point. Even with a more limited list, however, you must actually review citing references to determine for yourself the effect the citing reference may have on the cited source. You should typically focus first on citing references that include negative treatment, determining whether the cited source has been overruled, reversed, or modified in some manner. It is also generally good practice to focus on cases from your jurisdiction.

B. Using KeyCite on Westlaw

KeyCite is similar in many respects to Shepard's, but is only available online on Westlaw and not in print.

1. Accessing the Citator

There are several ways to access KeyCite once you are logged on to Westlaw. First, when you see a document with a KeyCite flag, you can click the flag to view KeyCite results. Also, when a document is displayed, you can click on any of the tabs across the top: Negative Treatment, History, Citing References, or Table of Authorities. Finally, you can run a KeyCite search by typing *keycite* or *kc* followed by a citation in the search box. In contrast with Shepard's on Lexis, no colon is necessary. Launching this search opens the Negative Treatment results for the cited source.

2. Selecting a Citation Category

You can display your KeyCite results in a number of ways. The default option when you enter a citation in KeyCite is the Negative Treatment results. This results list first provides Negative Direct History, which shows how the case has been negatively impacted by decisions in the same litigation. Below Negative Direct History is Negative Citing References that typically list cases in the order of the degree of negative treatment.

You can view a more extensive list of citing references by selecting the "Citing References" tab. That tab typically will include a drop-down menu that is

Figure 9-5. KeyCite Citing References for *Santi v. Santi*

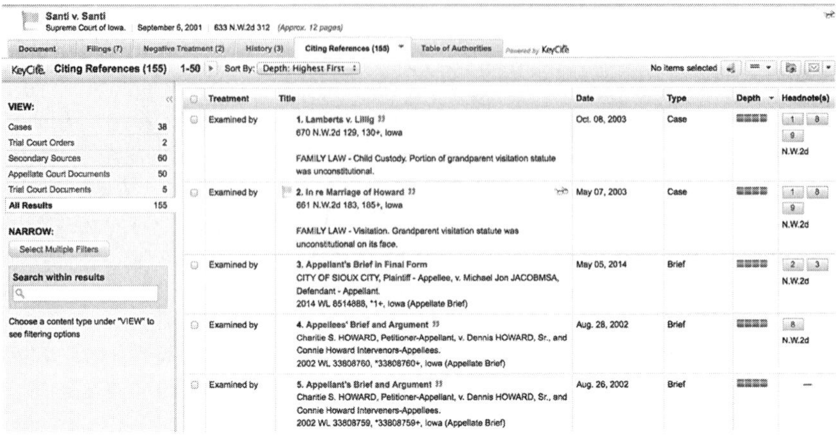

Source: Published with permission of West, a Thomson Reuters business.

broken down by type, such as cases, trial court orders, secondary authorities, and other categories. If you click on "Citing References," those links will be displayed on the left side of the screen. Figure 9-5 illustrates this option for *Santi*. As you can see, the default depth option first displays the citing references that have treated your cited source negatively. You have the option of reorganizing the Citing References list by date using the drop-down menu at the top of the screen. You have the option of selecting the type of content to review and you can also Search within Results. Once you choose a content type to view, such as cases, additional filters are available for your use, such as jurisdiction, date, depth of treatment, headnote topics, treatment status, and reported status.

You can also use KeyCite for statutes. Figure 9-6 illustrates the History Results for Iowa Code § 598.35 (1999). Under the History tab you have the option of viewing in a variety of ways, including graphically, or by Negative Treatment, Prior Versions, Legislative History Notes, Bill Drafts, and Reports and Related Materials. Note that the Iowa statute was deemed unconstitutional in *In re Howard*, 661 N.W.2d 183 (Iowa 2003), the first case that appears in the Held Unconstitutional By list.

3. Analyzing the Citing Symbols and Sorting the Search Results

As with Shepard's, KeyCite uses symbols, known as Status Flags, to designate how a citing reference has treated the cited source. The Status Flag ap-

Figure 9-6. KeyCite History Results for Iowa Code § 598.35 (1999)

598.35. Repealed by Acts 2007 (82 G.A.) ch. 218, H.F. 909, § 208
Iowa Code Annotated   Title XV. Judicial Branch and Judicial Procedures [Chs. 595-686]   Effective: July 1, 2007   *(Approx. 1 page)*

Document   Notes of Decisions (0)   History (13)   Citing References (208)   Context & Analysis (2)   Powered by KeyCite

KeyCite   **Validity (6)**

Select all items   No items selected

☐ 598.35. Repealed by Acts 2007 (82 G.A.) ch. 218, H.F. 909, § 208

Case Treatment (5)

Held Unconstitutional by
☐ In re Marriage of Howard
   661 N.W.2d 183, 183+, (Iowa May 07, 2003), (NO. 02-0211)

☐ Santi v. Santi
   633 N.W.2d 312, 312+, (Iowa Sep. 06, 2001), (NO. 00-0181)

Recognized as Unconstitutional by
☐ Spiker v. Spiker
   708 N.W.2d 347, 348+, (Iowa Jan. 20, 2006), (NO. 04-1182)

Prior Version Held Unconstitutional by
☐ Wurpts v. Iowa Dist. Court, Sioux County
   687 N.W.2d 286, 286+, (Iowa App. May 26, 2004), (NO. 03-0970)

☐ Lamberts v. Lillig
   670 N.W.2d 129, 129+, (Iowa Oct. 08, 2003), (NO. 02-0435)

Source: Published with permission of West, a Thomson Reuters business.

pears to the left of the citation for both cited sources and citing references. The Status Flag can be used as a quick reference to help you determine whether the source is good law but, as with updating in Lexis, you will want to thoroughly consider citing references to determine the specific treatment of the cited source. Again, if your cited source is supported by cases that have received negative treatment because of similar analysis, then you might not want to base your argument on that analysis.

You can sort KeyCite search results to focus on the authorities that are most relevant to your research. Both the "Negative Treatment" and "Citing References" tabs offer a depth indicator that illustrates the degree to which the citing reference addresses the cited source, on a scale of one bar (least discussion) to four bars (most discussion). The "Citing References" tab offers more extensive sorting and filtering features. You can sort this list by depth of treatment or by date using the drop-down menu at the top of the screen. You can also "Search within Results" using the search box in the left column or view citing references by type of source. Once you select a type of content to view, such as cases, you can filter results by headnote by reviewing the relevant headnote topics in the left column. By clicking on "Specify" you can see what the headnote coverage is and select relevant ones to view additional cases on that point of law. You also can hover over the headnote number in the far right column of the citing decisions to see what a headnote covers. Sorting by headnote al-

Figure 9-7. Headnote KeyCite Option in Document View

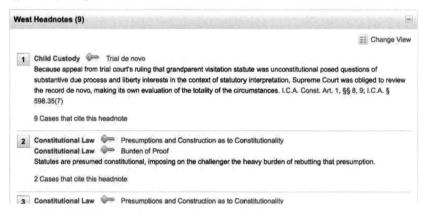

Source: Published with permission of West, a Thomson Reuters business.

lows you to focus your citation results on cases that are applicable to a specific issue. You can also access this sorting strategy in the "Document tab" by clicking the "x Cases that cite this headnote" link under each headnote in the document. Figure 9-7 illustrates this option.

4. Reading and Analyzing the Citing References

As noted, you cannot effectively validate a source by simply running a search on KeyCite. You must also read and evaluate the citing references. Using the citator features, focus your review on cases involving your issue of law, preferably by headnote. Evaluate authorities with negative treatment first, focusing on the most recent cases from your jurisdiction. You can also select "Create KeyCite Alert Entry" by clicking the bell icon in the upper right

Figure 9-8. BCite Case Analysis for *Santi v. Santi*, 633 N.W.2d 312 (Iowa 2001)

Source: Bloomberg Law screenshot. Reproduced with permission from Bloomberg Law. Copyright 2016 by The Bureau of National Affairs, Inc. (800-372-1033) http://www.bna.com.

corner of a document display result. The alert monitors the status of your case or statute and automatically sends you updates at the frequency you specify.

C. Using BCite on Bloomberg Law

In contrast with Shepard's or KeyCite, BCite is only available for cases. You can access BCite whenever you have a case opened in Bloomberg Law. To view citing references, click on one of the following tabs at the top of the result screen: "Direct History," "Case Analysis," or "Citing Documents." You can also use the links under "BCite Analysis" at the right side of the screen. Under

Figure 9-9. BCite Citing Documents for *Santi v. Santi*, 633 N.W.2d 312 (Iowa 2001)

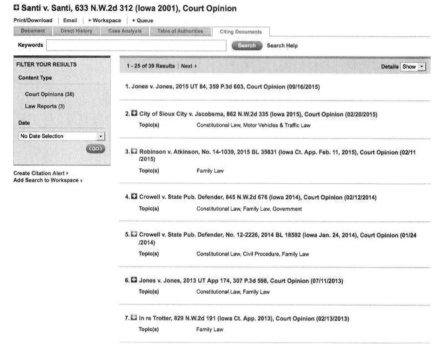

Source: Bloomberg Law screenshot. Reproduced with permission from Bloomberg Law. Copyright 2016 by The Bureau of National Affairs, Inc. (800-372-1033) http://www.bna.com.

the "Case Analysis" tab you can sort results by Citing Case Analysis, Citing Case Status, Citation Frequency, Court, Judge, or Date. Figure 9-8 illustrates this view for *Santi*. Under the Citing Documents tab, you can sort by content or date. Figure 9-9 illustrates this view for *Santi*.

Similar to Shepard's and KeyCite, BCite uses symbols to indicate the treatment of a cited source by citing sources. Figure 9-10 illustrates the Case Analysis and Table of Authorities indicators for BCite.

BCite also has a bar that indicates the extent to which the citing case discussed the cited case. Unlike Shepard's and KeyCite, the BCite bar does not represent the depth of the discussion but the number of times the case was cited, from one bar (cited once or twice) to five bars (cited ten or more times), as shown in Figure 9-8.

Figure 9-10. Case Analysis and Table of Authorities Indicators for BCite

Case Analysis and Table of Authorities		
The Case Analysis summarizes the analysis of the main opinion by cases that subsequently cite the opinion. The Table of Authorities summarizes the analysis by the main opinion of the cases cited within that opinion.		
Analysis	**Definition**	**Indicator**
Cited	Court positively cites this opinion as legal precedent.	⊞
Discussed	Court positively discusses this opinion, providing additional detail about the facts or the law.	⊞
Followed	Court follows this opinion as controlling or persuasive authority.	⊞
Distinguished	Court distinguishes this opinion from another opinion based on differences between their facts or controlling law.	◨
Criticized	Court criticizes the legal reasoning of this opinion without overruling it.	▢
Superseded by Statute	Court states that this opinion has been superseded, displaced or rendered obsolete by an intervening statute, rule or regulation.	▢
Prior Overruling	Court states that this opinion has been overruled in full or in part by a prior decision.	⊟
Overruled in Part	Court overrules a portion of this opinion.	⊟
Overruled	Court overrules this opinion in full.	⊟
Functionality	**Explanation**	**Indicator**
Citation Frequency Indicator	The blue portion of this bar correlates with the number of times the listed case is cited.	■■■■
Expand/Hide Extracts	This functionality displays the portion of the opinion where the case is referenced.	▸ Extracts

Source: Bloomberg Law screenshot. Reproduced with permission from Bloomberg Law. Copyright 2016 by The Bureau of National Affairs, Inc. (800-372-1033) http://www.bna.com.

D. Using Authority Check on Fastcase

Fastcase, a legal research service available to members of the Iowa State Bar Association and other subscribers, includes a citator called Authority Check. Similar to Shepard's and KeyCite, the service provides a linked list of other cases that cite your case. However, Authority Check does not offer the type of editorial services available through Shepard's and KeyCite. Instead, it uses an algorithm to analyze the language of court opinions other than the cited source to determine whether there is potential negative history for the cited source.[8]

From the list of search results, you have an option to click on the Authority Check results for a particular result, limited to other cases that appeared in your search results, or those that appear in the entire database. With a particular case open, you have both of these options, and, if applicable, the option to click on "Negative treatment indicated." Each of these options will open an Authority Check report that displays in a manner unlike any of the other ci-

---

8. This feature is called Bad Law Bot.

tator tools discussed in this chapter. A citation summary, the same no matter which link brought you to the report, indicates the total number of cites to your case, the number of cites from different types of courts, and the date of the decision of the most recent citing case. An Interactive Timeline plots the citing cases on a timeline by either relevance or court level. The color and diameter of the plotted cases indicates the number of times the case was cited in total (gray) and the number of times it was cited for your search terms (gold). Looking for the larger and higher circles provides one way to identify the most authoritative cases, a feature that may appeal to some learners. The report continues with brief case discussions indicating potential negative treatment, a list of citing law reviews, and a list of citing cases. The default sorting order for the law reviews and complete case list is reverse chronological (most recent first), but you may choose to sort the cases by jurisdiction.

Fastcase offers detailed support materials from the "Help and Training" tab at Fastcase.com. Iowa State Bar Association members, including law student members, also can access information about Fastcase and Authority Check by logging in to the Iowa State Bar Association website at http://www.iowabar .org/.[9]

E. Using "Cited By" on Google Scholar

Google Scholar's freely accessible collection of case law includes a "Cited by" feature that lists other cases that have cited your case. This tool does not include the type of helpful, color-coded icons and editorial features of other citators discussed in this chapter and researchers must therefore navigate results by reading through the results. Sorted by the depth of discussion of the cited case, the list starts with those cases with the most discussion.[10] A "How cited" feature shows excerpts of how a sample of citing cases reference the cited case. Google Scholar does not include signals or headnotes, so you cannot filter the list of citing cases in either of these ways. You can, however, filter the list of citing cases by date or court.

Both the "Cited by" and "How cited" links can be accessed from the search results or from the case itself. When you conduct a case law search in Google

---

9. Law students can become student members of the Iowa State Bar Association at no cost. For details go to the ISBA home page > Member Resources > Membership Overview > Join the ISBA.

10. Alex Verstak, *Finding Significant Citations for Legal Opinions*, Google Scholar Blog (Mar. 8, 2012, 1:29 PM), http://googlescholar.blogspot.com/2012/03/finding-sig nificant-citations-for-legal.html.

Scholar, each result ends with a series of links, including "Cited by x" and "How cited." With an individual case open, you will see a "How cited" link near the upper left of the screen. Click on this link to reveal the selected list of excerpts under the heading "How this documents has been cited." On the right of the screen, you can see a "Cited by" list providing citations for the cases at the top of the list and ending with a link to see the complete list of citing cases. To filter search results by date or court, make sure to check the "Search within citing articles" box under the case name, and use the limiters on the left. You can also add keywords to refine the list of citing cases by checking this box and then adding search terms in the Google search box near the top of the screen.

F. Caution: Additional Limitations on the Use of Citators to Update

While updating with a citator is an essential step in legal research, citators do have limitations in terms of ensuring that you are relying upon good law. Citators only identify sources that actually cite to the cited source. A court opinion could change the rule of law relevant to your issue without citing the prior case, statute, or rule you are examining. In this instance, the newer case would not appear in your citator results. However, if you use citators in conjunction with the other legal research sources noted in this book, you should find proper authority for your issue.

Chapter 10

Practice Aids

I. Practice Aids: Types and Use

Lawyers have created a variety of materials, broadly referred to as *practice aids*, to help prepare litigation and drafting documents and to provide additional practical, working guidance within various areas of law. Practice materials are a particularly useful secondary resource. Many contain both background analysis and commentary on specific legal issues and also forms or templates for specific legal documents commonly used in that area of law. In this respect, practice materials enhance efficiency, providing a starting point for drafting a document for a client.

Iowa legal researchers often turn to bar association manuals, form books, continuing legal education (CLE) materials, and other practice aids specifically devoted to Iowa law. Consulting practice aids may enable the researcher to find a relevant answer fairly quickly. However, practice aids have limitations. These materials are crafted for general use, but every client situation is unique. Therefore, the careful lawyer reviews forms and manuals in light of the specific circumstances at hand and adapts these materials accordingly. This chapter will describe techniques to identify relevant practice aids and highlight some resources frequently used in Iowa.

II. Finding Practice Aids

You find relevant practice aids much like you find other secondary sources, as described in Chapter 3. Library catalogs can be searched to identify practice aids, particularly those published as books.[1] Librarians can be consulted to recommend resources. Research guides are another excellent source for locating

---

1. See Chapter 2 for a description of Iowa law libraries and brief instructions on searching a library catalog.

relevant practice aids in all formats. For instance, the Drake Law Library offers separate research guides on practice aids, law-related forms, and legal writing and drafting.[2] These kinds of web guides are often updated regularly, so they will point to the most recent versions of both print and electronic resources. They may also provide brief descriptions of available resources and tips on locating additional resources.

III. Bar Manuals and Practice Guides

A. Introduction to Bar Manuals and Practice Guides

Experts in different areas of law have written books that provide practical guidance to lawyers working in that field. These books typically include narrative descriptions of legal procedures; analysis of issues; references to primary law; and sample forms, letters, or other related documents. Titles addressing the same area of law may differ significantly in terms of depth of treatment, publication format, and frequency of updating.

B. Iowa Manuals and Practice Guides

The Iowa State Bar Association (ISBA) produces manuals in many key areas. Current titles are listed in Table 10-1.

These manuals provide practical information on common issues occurring in each area covered. Most manuals are divided into smaller topics and offer a succinct narrative analysis of each subtopic, with citations to and brief descriptions of relevant cases, statutes, and regulations. All manuals also include sample materials, such as checklists, forms, and letters, which may be incorporated into narrative chapters or included in separate appendixes. Manuals are not indexed, so you will need to consult the table of contents to find a relevant section.

Manuals are typically issued in a looseleaf format. Most are updated periodically, but often infrequently. Therefore, you should always determine the date of the last revision and recognize that, while the manual is a good starting place for research, you will likely need to update the information using other sources. You can access the manuals at either the Drake or University of Iowa law libraries; members of the Iowa State Bar Association may purchase the manuals directly from the association at a reduced price.

---

2. The addresses for the guides are http://libguides.law.drake.edu/PracticeAids, http://libguides.law.drake.edu/Forms, and http://libguides.law.drake.edu/LegalWriting.

Table 10-1. Iowa State Bar Association Manuals

Appellate Practice Manual
Business Law Manual
Civil Jury Instructions
Criminal Jury Instructions
Family Law Manual
Fiduciary Tax Manual
Guide to Electronic Filing in the Iowa Courts
Labor and Employment Law Manual
Probate & Trust Law Manual
Tax Manual
Iowa Land Title Standards*

* Most manual tables of contents may be viewed at https://iowabar.site-ym.com/store/List-Products.aspx?catid=264723&view_type=1. You will have to log in or sign up for a guest account to access this page. Free ISBA membership is available to law students attending Drake or Iowa or Iowa residents attending any ABA-accredited law school.

West's *Iowa Practice Series* is another well-known practice guide that covers many areas of law, listed in Table 10-2. Available in print and on Westlaw, this title provides expert commentary and analysis to help answer questions in specific areas of Iowa law. The series also includes references to primary law and forms. Volumes are revised and reissued annually. To find on-point information, you can consult either the general index volume, which covers the whole series and is found at the end of the set, or the relevant article index, which covers only one particular topic and is included at the back of the last volume of that topic.[3]

In addition to these two series, a variety of other books offer valuable practice resources for the Iowa attorney. One of the best known is the looseleaf George A. LaMarca, *Iowa Pleading, Causes of Action and Defenses* (2000). Replete with forms, the LaMarca book is a helpful source for determining the elements necessary for drafting pleadings in a variety of actions. Other books are subject-specific, such as Lawrence E. Blades & Charles A. Blades, *Iowa Tort Guide* (5th ed. 2000), and Sheldon F. Kurtz, *Kurtz on Iowa Estates* (3d ed. 1995). These guides offer very detailed texts that summarize important issues

---

3. See Chapter 2 for more detail on using an index.

Table 10-2. Topics in West's Iowa Practice Series

Methods of Practice (v. 1–3)

Criminal Law (v. 4)

Criminal Procedure (v. 4A)

Business Organizations (v. 5–6)

Evidence (v. 7)

Civil Litigation Handbook (v. 8)

Civil Procedure Forms (v. 9–10)

Civil and Appellate Procedure (v. 11–12)

Iowa Probate (v. 13–14)

Iowa Workers' Compensation Law and Practice (v. 15)

Lawyer and Judicial Ethics (v. 16)

Iowa Real Estate Law and Practice (v. 17)*

---

* Information on new editions is available at http://legalsolutions.thomsonreuters.com/law-products/.

in the area of law and include references to primary law. They may also include forms. These books tend not to be updated regularly, so you will want to pay particular attention to the copyright date and use additional sources to ensure the currency of your research.

C. Federal and General Practice Guides

An Iowa researcher will often have to research federal law as well as the law in other jurisdictions. Several well-known series cover federal practice, including James William Moore & Danile R. Coquillette, *Moore's Federal Practice* (3d ed. 1997),[4] and Charles Alan Wright, Arthur Raphael Miller & Mary Kay Kane, *Federal Practice and Procedure* (3d ed. 1998 and 4th ed. 2008).[5]

---

4. *Moore's Federal Practice* is also available on Lexis.

5. *Federal Practice and Procedure* is also available on Westlaw. First published in 1969, this title is still often called "Wright and Miller," the names of two of its original authors. Several different authors now contribute to specific volumes. Eventually, the fourth edition will completely replace the third, but now current volumes span both the third and fourth editions.

These highly detailed, multi-volume works cover most issues likely to arise in a federal action.

Many law libraries also have materials devoted to general practice topics. These books can help you identify elements to draft pleadings, understand legal concepts, and prepare for trial. Some examples, updated regularly, include *American Jurisprudence Proof of Facts* (3d ed. 1988), *American Jurisprudence Trials* (1964), and *Causes of Actions* (2d ed. 1993).[6]

IV. Legal Forms and Sample Documents

A. Introduction to Form Books

Because many transactions and court filings occur regularly, there is no need for practitioners to start anew creating related documents each time. Sample forms and documents can be adapted to a particular issue, but care must be taken to ensure that forms adequately address the unique client situation. Consider how each draft provision might affect your particular client and modify as necessary.

Several multi-volume form series contain a broad array of procedural and transactional forms. Other, smaller series of forms may be limited to a particular jurisdiction or type of form. While form books sometimes contain forms with blank lines to fill in, more often they just suggest language and elements to address. Figure 10-1 shows two sample forms illustrating this range of complexity. Both are from West's *Iowa Practice Series*, but the first is taken from Westlaw and the second from the print volume. Note the Westlaw version offers an "Easy Edit" option, providing a version of the form that can be opened and edited in Microsoft Word. Commentary accompanying a form may provide notes on the form's use and reference both primary authorities and other secondary sources that can help the researcher more fully understand the topic and use the source material effectively. As with all materials, references to primary sources need to be updated to ensure that they are still relevant.

Before using a form, do the necessary legal research to ensure you have selected the proper form and are using it correctly. If you do not understand an aspect of the form, you must research to clarify that point. When combining provisions from different forms, be sure to evaluate how those provisions affect your specific situation and whether the provisions you ultimately select are internally consistent in your final document.

---

6. All of these titles can also be accessed on Westlaw.

Figure 10-1. Sample Forms

Source: Westlaw screenshot from *Iowa Practice Series: Civil Practice Forms.* Published with permission of West, a Thomson Reuters business.

B. Iowa-Specific Form Books and Electronic Resources

Relatively few form books are specific to Iowa. In most cases, you will need to adapt a generic form to fit your situation. To find print form books, search the law library catalog, as explained in Chapter 2. Searching for *forms* and *Iowa* in two different keyword fields should return relevant titles. You can also craft a more refined search using subject and/or title searches.

The *Iowa Code Annotated*, the *Code of Iowa*, and the *Iowa Rules of Court* include standard forms prescribed by statute; where applicable, these forms should be used without modification. Other significant sources of Iowa forms include the Iowa State Bar Association (ISBA) manuals and the *Iowa Practice*

Figure 10-1. Sample Forms, *continued*

---

§ 11:24   Statute—Unconstitutionality

Research References
West's Key Number Digest, Constitutional Law ⬤➡46(2); Statutes ⬤➡279
C.J.S., Constitutional Law §§ 86, 88; Statutes §§ 432 to 435

I.C.A. § ____ is unconstitutional and affords Plaintiff no rights
or protection against Defendant because . . ..

[or]

I.C.A. § ____ violates Article _____, § ____, of the Iowa Constitution because . . ..

[or]

§ ____ violates Article _____, § ____, and the _____
Amendment to the Constitution of the United States because
. . ..

NOTES TO FORM
All laws passed by the legislature are presumed to be constitutional.
Therefore, any attack on the constitutionality of a statute must specifically
set forth the grounds on which it is alleged the statute is constitutionally
defective. Cole v. City of Osceola, 179 N.W.2d 524 (Iowa 1970).

Source: Iowa Practice Series: Civil Practice Forms. Published with permission of West, a Thomson Reuters business.

Series, both described in Section III.B. Additionally, ISBA members can subscribe to IOWADOCS®, a collection of sample legal forms produced by the
ISBA, including all forms in the ISBA manuals. This annually updated software allows you to open, modify, and save the form in a word processing program.[7] A print version of these forms can be accessed from the Drake and
Iowa law libraries.

Electronically, Westlaw offers many Iowa forms. Entering *Iowa Form
Finder* in the top search box leads to an index page where you access Iowa-
specific forms, clauses, and checklists by topic or publication, including the
Iowa Practice Series. The entire collection can be searched through terms-
and-connectors or natural-language techniques. Once you open a particular
topical area, you also get a guided search screen to help you narrow your
search. Lexis also offers some Iowa-related forms. On Lexis, you could set a
pre-search filter to restrict your search just to forms. To do this, click on the
"Search: Everything" button in the red search box. This opens a menu where

---

7. *See* http://www.iowadocs.net/ for more information about IOWADOCS®.

you can click on "Category" and then select the checkbox for "Forms." Enter your search terms in the red search box and click the "Search" button. You can then use the filters on the left to further refine your search in a variety of ways, including limiting the jurisdiction to Iowa.

On the web, you can find many law-related forms. However, remember to carefully assess the quality of these forms, as almost anyone can post almost anything on the web. Iowa governmental sites are one good source for reputable forms. The Iowa judicial branch site contains court forms in fourteen categories, including family law, juvenile law, small claims, civil procedure, and probate.[8] Select forms are also available from other agencies, such as business incorporation forms from the Secretary of State's office. The ISBA offers a few free forms, such as a living will. Additional free or low-cost internet sources for Iowa-specific legal forms are listed in Table 10-3.

C. Other Form Books and Electronic Resources

Several series feature forms used in federal practice. These include *Bender's Federal Practice Forms*, also available on Lexis, and *Federal Procedural Forms, Lawyers' Edition*, which is arranged by court rule and also available on Westlaw. Another series, *West's Federal Forms*, is arranged by court and consists of separate volumes covering forms needed in the Supreme Court, Courts of Appeals, District Courts, Bankruptcy Courts and other specialized national courts; it is also available on Westlaw. Additional form books can be found through a search of the library catalog using search terms like "forms" and the specific legal area which you want the forms to cover.

Many situations may not require jurisdiction-specific forms. General form books can provide helpful background information and draft provisions that can be adapted to the client's situation. One of the major legal encyclopedias, *American Jurisprudence 2d*, publishes two helpful form series, both available on Westlaw as well as in print. *American Jurisprudence Legal Forms 2d* includes well over 20,000 forms arranged alphabetically by topic. *American Jurisprudence Pleading and Practice Forms* offers litigation forms with procedural timetables and drafting checklists. Both have indexes that can help you locate the correct form. Another multi-volume series, also available on Westlaw, is *West's Legal Forms*, which is arranged by broad practice areas.

---

8. The website of the judiciary is http://www.iowacourts.gov. Link to forms by clicking on the tab for Court Rules & Forms.

Table 10-3. Selected Internet Sources for Iowa Forms

Source	Web Address
Iowa Department of Human Services	http://dhs.iowa.gov/dhsforms
Iowa Judicial Branch	http://www.iowacourts.gov/Court_Rules__Forms/Overview/
Iowa Secretary of State	http://sos.iowa.gov/business/FormsAndFees.html
Iowa State Bar Association	http://www.iowabar.org/?page=Forms
USLegalForms.com	http://www.uslegalforms.com

Bloomberg Law, Lexis, and Westlaw all contain extensive general forms. Bloomberg Law includes three large form sets: the ALI-ABA Forms Library, PLI Forms & Agreements, and Bloomberg BNA Sample Forms.[9] On Lexis form options can be found by browsing sources by category and selecting "Forms" as the category. On Westlaw, type *"Form Finder"* into the top search box to bring up an index page allowing you to find forms by state, topic, or publication.

Another electronic form database of note is Gale LegalForms. This database contains thousands of state-specific forms that have either been drafted by attorneys and approved for use at one or more law firms, or been designated as official by the state. Many Gale forms are available in Word format, so they can easily be downloaded to your computer and edited. Gale LegalForms is accessible at some academic libraries. Moreover, Gale has actively pursued the public library market, so students and attorneys may also find this resource available to them through their community library.

D. Other Sample Materials

In addition to the sample materials included in form books, lawyers sometimes review actual documents and court filings for guidance.[10] Many law

---

9. All three collections can be accessed by following this path in Bloomberg Law: Home > Transactional Law > Transactional Resources.

10. Form books may also include real-world examples.

firms and legal departments have developed "brief banks" and other collections of sample documents to provide models for other attorneys' work. Institutional collections are only for members' use; however, sample documents can also be found online and in print. For instance, the Drake, Iowa Supreme Court, State of Iowa, and University of Iowa law libraries all maintain collections of briefs from Iowa appellate cases through 2007 when the Iowa Supreme Court stopped distributing them. Later briefs are available from the Iowa Supreme Court and may also be available through Westlaw.[11]

Bloomberg Law contains a large collection of sample documents and clauses in its DealMaker and drafting guidance collections.[12] The University of Missouri-Columbia's Contracting and Organizations Research Institute (CORI) database provides another sample document collection. CORI gathers and categorizes actual contracts, most drawn from filings with the U.S. Securities and Exchange Commission, and makes them available in a searchable database accessible without charge on the web.[13]

As with form books, sample documents provide only a starting point for the lawyer. Sample documents may suggest clear phrasing, persuasive arguments, important points of law to consider, and professional standards of presentation. However, the lawyer's knowledge of the particular client circumstances and requirements of applicable law must provide the basis for crafting any document.

V. Continuing Legal Education (CLE) Publications

A. Introduction to CLE Materials

Iowa court rules mandate that attorneys licensed to practice in the state must undertake a minimum of fifteen hours of accredited continuing legal education (CLE) each calendar year.[14] Many of these CLE classes produce helpful written materials and resources. CLE materials cover a wide variety of topics. The accompanying print publications range from simple outlines that might not be very meaningful for those who did not attend the course to fully developed articles with sample forms or other useful exhibits.

---

11. To inquire about getting briefs from the Iowa Supreme Court contact the clerk's office at 515-281-5911. To check brief coverage on Westlaw, from the home screen follow this path: Briefs > Iowa.

12. Both can be accessed by following this path in Bloomberg Law: Home > Transactional Law > Transactional Resources.

13. The address is http://cori.missouri.edu/pages/ksearch.htm.

14. Iowa Ct. R. 41.3(1).

B. Iowa-Specific CLE Resources

Iowa CLE materials can be located by searching a law library catalog. *CLE* or *"continuing legal education"* may not be very useful search terms. The materials are more likely to be found by searching using subject terms, possibly combined with the additional search term *"practice of law."* CLE materials can also be found by searching by both the legal subject and name of the CLE provider. Iowa's two law schools both provide CLEs, as do many Iowa legal associations. The Iowa State Bar Association's annual Bridge the Gap institutes are specifically designed to provide practical information for new attorneys. In addition, the National Business Institute and Lorman Education Services both provide and publish CLE materials specific to Iowa, as well as to other states and federal practice.[15] Sample titles include *Workers' Compensation Case Preparation Techniques*, *The Probate Process from Start to Finish*, and *Advanced Judgment Enforcement in Iowa*.

C. Other CLE Resources

On a national level, significant providers of CLE materials include the American Law Institute (ALI), American Bar Association (ABA), the National Institute of Trial Advocates (NITA), and the Practising Law Institute (PLI). Many of these materials are published as books and can be found by searching either a law library catalog or the publisher's catalog.[16] Many ALI materials are also available on Westlaw and Lexis, and many ABA and PLI materials are available on Bloomberg Law.

VI. Jury Instructions

A. Introduction to Jury Instructions

Jury instructions provide plain-language explanations of the law intended to ensure members of the jury understand their duties and how to apply the law. The wording should be clear and unbiased, which can make drafting good jury instructions challenging. Consulting a collection of model or pattern instructions can save drafting time and ensure a proposed instruction has been carefully considered.

---

15. You can search the NBI course catalog at http://www.nbi-sems.com/Course-Catalog.aspx and the Lorman site at http://www.lorman.com/.

16. Check the website of the organization publishing the material for a catalog.

Jury instructions may summarize the elements of a crime or cause of action, showing what the attorney must prove. They may also provide references to cases, statutes, and secondary sources. In this respect, jury instructions can help an attorney focus on the most important aspects of a case and serve as a resource in crafting pleadings, analytical and persuasive documents, and opening and closing statements.

B. Iowa-Specific Instructions

The Iowa State Bar Association (ISBA) offers model Iowa jury instructions in a variety of categories. Drafted by the ISBA Committee on Iowa Jury Instructions and approved by the ISBA Board of Governors, instructions are then published in the *Iowa Criminal Jury Instructions* and the *Iowa Civil Jury Instructions*. Both titles are updated periodically and are available on Fastcase, Lexis[17] and, for members, via the association's website.

C. Other Instructions

General practice and form book sets, such as *American Jurisprudence Pleading and Practice, American Jurisprudence Trials,* and *Causes of Action,* may provide jury instructions. Further, many courts provide jury instructions on their websites. For instance, the Eighth Circuit Court of Appeals offers model civil, criminal, and death penalty jury instructions.[18] A variety of books offer instructions specific to a subject or jurisdiction. Search for these in a law library catalog under the subject heading *"Instructions to Juries."* The search can be limited with other relevant search terms.

---

17. On Lexis you can go to Browse > Source > By Jurisdiction > Iowa and see a listing of contents, including jury instructions.

18. *See* http://www.juryinstructions.ca8.uscourts.gov.

Chapter 11

Legal Ethics

I. Introduction to Legal Ethics Research

Iowa attorneys are governed by rules of professional responsibility modeled after the American Bar Association's Model Rules of Professional Conduct (ABA Model Rules). The Iowa rules impose a number of ethical and professional obligations on attorneys, and an attorney's license to practice law in Iowa requires adherence to these rules. Therefore, you need to have a relatively sophisticated understanding of the rules that govern your professional conduct and how those rules have been applied to other practicing attorneys.

Research involving issues of professional responsibility relies upon judicial decisions and statutes as well as the Iowa Rules of Professional Conduct, the ABA Model Rules, and, at times, the ABA's earlier attempt to articulate rules regarding attorney conduct: the ABA Model Code of Professional Responsibility (ABA Model Code).[1] In addition to understanding the rules in Iowa, you may need to determine how courts in other jurisdictions have applied rules modeled after the ABA Model Rules or Model Code. Further, you will need to be familiar with a unique type of advisory opinion, the ethics opinion.[2] Finally, your research in judicial opinions involving lapses in attorney conduct may require inquiry into related substantive areas, such as attorney malpractice, rules of civil and appellate procedure, and criminal appeals.

---

1. The ABA Model Rules and the ABA Model Code, and their relationship to one another, are discussed in Section II.A.1. of this chapter.

2. Ethics opinions are discussed more fully in Section II.A.2. of this chapter.

II. Regulating the Conduct of Attorneys — An Overview

A. Sources of Regulation

1. ABA Model Code and Model Rules

Recognizing how the conduct of lawyers is governed and enforced is essential to understanding the ethical rules themselves. The legal profession is self-regulating; lawyers are subject to rules of ethics by virtue of their admission to the bar in a particular state. The American Law Institute's *Restatement of the Law Governing Lawyers* notes that, "upon admission to the bar of any jurisdiction, a person becomes a lawyer and is subject to applicable law governing such matters as professional discipline, procedure and evidence, civil remedies, and criminal sanctions."[3]

Therefore, lawyers are subject to rules or standards of professional conduct that have been adopted by the state in which they are licensed to practice law. Most states have adopted some form of the various ethical rules promulgated by the ABA. The two main sources are the ABA Model Rules and the ABA Model Code. The term *model* is apt because the ABA is a private organization with no inherent authority to impose rules upon lawyers. The ABA suggests the rules, but only the adoption of the rules by the state bar associations or state court systems gives the rules legal effect.

The ABA's model rules have developed over time. In 1908, the ABA first published a set of ethical rules titled the Canons of Professional Ethics. This set remained in effect until the publication of the ABA Model Code in 1969. The ABA Code was designed to serve as a model for states to follow in adopting legal ethics rules. The ABA Code comprises nine *Canons*, which are described as "axiomatic norms, expressing in general terms the standards of professional conduct expected of lawyers in their relationships with the public, with the legal system, and with the legal profession."[4]

The Canons are further explained by *Ethical Considerations* (ECs) and *Disciplinary Rules* (DRs). The ECs are aspirational and "represent the objectives toward which every member of the profession should strive."[5] DRs, unlike the ECs, are mandatory and "state the minimum level of conduct below which

---

3. Restatement (Third) of the Law Governing Lawyers § 1 (2000).
4. Model Code of Prof. Resp., Preliminary Statement.
5. Model Code of Prof. Resp., Preamble.

no lawyer can fall without being subject to disciplinary action."[6] The ABA Code was designed as a system under which lawyer conduct could be evaluated, and the ABA intended the enforcing agency at the state level to apply the DRs by using "the interpretive guidance in the basic principles embodied in the Canons and in the objectives reflected in the [ECs]."[7] The ABA Code was widely accepted at its inception and within a few years after its initial publication most states had adopted ethical rules modeled after the ABA Code.

Even though the ABA Model Code was extensively adopted, it was criticized for its arguably vague quality. So, the ABA next endeavored to draft a more straightforward set of rules. This attempt resulted in the publication of the Model Rules in 1983. The ABA intended for the Model Rules to replace the Model Code. Indeed, many jurisdictions, including Iowa, ultimately revised their ethics rules to be modeled after the Model Rules, rather than the Model Code. Distinct in approach from the Model Code, the "Scope" section of the ABA Rules describes the rules as "partly obligatory and disciplinary and partly constitutive and descriptive in that they define a lawyer's role."[8] Comments to the Rules are designed as guides to interpretation to explain and illustrate the meaning and purpose of the Rules.[9]

2. Legal Ethics Opinions

The ABA and states issue legal ethics opinions. At the state level, the opinions are often issued by the state bar association. The ABA opinions are authored by the Standing Committee on Ethics and Professional Responsibility. Legal ethics opinions are typically drafted in response to questions posed by attorneys who want to know whether contemplated or past conduct comports with the ethical rules. Some opinions are designated as "formal," which means that the issuing body (e.g., the ABA or state bar association) deems them widely applicable to the practicing bar. These opinions generally provide an in-depth discussion of the issue. In contrast, an "informal" opinion is designed to provide a specific response to the requesting attorney. Even though the ABA has no independent enforcement authority, ABA ethics opinions that interpret the Rules are often cited by courts as they consider the propriety of lawyers' conduct.

---

6. *Id.*
7. *Id.*
8. Model Rules of Prof. Conduct, Scope § 14.
9. *Id.* at Scope § 21.

3. Other Sources of Law Relating to Attorney Ethics

In addition to rules relating specifically to attorney ethics, some substantive and procedural rules impose ethical obligations on attorneys. For example, Federal Rule of Civil Procedure 11 prohibits attorneys from filing frivolous claims. This prohibition therefore implicitly obligates an attorney to conduct effective research, to investigate the matter carefully to ensure that there is a good faith basis in law and fact to support the claim, and to act truthfully. These are also the types of behavior required under ethical rules relating to competence and candor. Additionally, in some jurisdictions, certain claims of attorney malpractice related to ethical failures are addressed by statute or in the context of the common law.[10] In this way, ethics research involves investigation of the application of the ethics rules and can also extend beyond those rules to other substantive areas of law.[11]

B. State Regulation of Attorney Conduct

As noted above, most jurisdictions originally adopted some version of the Model Code. Following the release of the ABA Model Rules, almost all states incorporated material from the Model Rules into their rules of ethics.[12] Further, many states modify the Model Rules before adopting them. Consequently, it is important to be familiar with both the ABA Code and ABA Model Rules, as well as state rules and statutes regarding legal ethics.

In 1971, the Iowa Supreme Court adopted a form of the ABA Model Code. However, in keeping with the transition to the ABA's Model Rules, Iowa

---

10. In Iowa, for example, fraud is a common law matter, but allegations of fraud by an attorney will also likely implicate the duty of loyalty and the duty to avoid conflicts of interest. The latter duties arise in the context of rules of professional conduct. *See, e.g., Iowa Supreme Court Bd. of Prof'l Ethics & Conduct v. D.J.I.,* 545 N.W.2d 866 (Iowa 1996).

11. While an identification of these other, substantive sources of legal ethics are beyond the scope of this book, chapters relating to general research in statutes or cases cover the sources and research strategies associated with locating such authority. This chapter is designed to focus expressly on sources specific to legal ethics research, such as state ethics rules fashioned after the Model Rules and ethics opinions issued for the purpose of communicating advice regarding the propriety of lawyering conduct.

12. According to the Center for Professional Responsibility, California is now the only U.S. state that has not adopted some form of the ABA Model Rules. *See* http://www.americanbar.org/groups/professional_responsibility/publications /model_rules_of_professional_conduct.html.

adopted the Iowa Rules of Professional Conduct in 2005. These have since been amended, but remain similar in many respects to the ABA Model Rules. They are codified in Chapter 32 of the Iowa Court Rules.[13]

In addition to the rules, you will likely want to examine cases that address how the rules apply. In this respect, you will consider judicial opinions that address attorney misconduct, as well as ethics advisory opinions and notices of disciplinary action, described more fully in Section III.C.

C. Regulation of Judicial Conduct

Similar to the rules regulating lawyers, the American Bar Association's Model Code of Judicial Conduct concerns the conduct of judges. This code has been widely adopted in some form by most states. The Iowa Supreme Court adopted the Iowa Code of Judicial Conduct in 1973.[14]

III. The Process of Legal Ethics Research

A. Overview

The number of legal ethics research sources may seem somewhat overwhelming. Methodically consulting these sources can help ensure you find all relevant materials. Table 11-1 provides an overview of the basic research process for legal ethics research.

B. Iowa Rules of Professional Conduct

As noted, the Iowa Rules of Professional Conduct are codified in Chapter 32 of the Iowa Court Rules. Unannotated versions of the rules are available both in print at law libraries and online.[15] You can access an annotated version of the Iowa Rules of Professional Conduct through an annotated version of the Iowa Code, as described in detail in Chapter 6.

---

13. Iowa's rules are explained in Section III.B. of this chapter.

14. Further discussion of judicial regulation is outside the scope of this book. Most law libraries have materials covering the topic, which often is listed in the online catalog under the subject of Judicial Ethics. *See, e.g.,* James J. Alfini, *Judicial Conduct and Ethics* (4th ed. 2007).

15. Online, the rules are available from the website of the Iowa Legislative Branch at https://www.legis.iowa.gov/law/courtRules/courtRulesListings.

Table 11-1. Basic Process for Legal Ethics Research

1.	Identify relevant ethical or procedural rules within your jurisdiction.
2.	Identify cases related to each rule in your jurisdiction, including formal or informal ethics opinions.
3.	Examine the ABA Model Rule counterparts to your rules, any annotations to each rule, and any relevant cases or advisory opinions (formal or informal) issued by the ABA.
4.	Consider whether additional materials, including related ethics rules and opinions from other states or secondary materials, might be helpful and persuasive to your issue.

One good starting point for research in the rules is to familiarize yourself with the topics addressed. The Table of Contents identifies the following subjects:

- Client-Lawyer Relationship
- Counselor
- Advocate
- Transactions with Persons other than Clients
- Law Firms and Associations
- Public Service
- Information about Legal Services
- Maintaining the Integrity of the Profession.

Every category includes a number of related rules. Each individual rule is followed by a series of comments that further explain how the rule should apply. For example, Rule 32:1.3 addresses diligence and provides "a lawyer shall act with reasonable diligence and promptness in representing a client."[16] The second comment to the rule explains "a lawyer's work load must be controlled so that each matter can be handled competently."[17]

The Welch Matter

Consider a question that might arise in the context of this book's hypothetical Welch matter if you are a new attorney, not entirely familiar with the law of domes-

---

16. Iowa R. Prof. Conduct 32:1.3.
17. *Id.* at cmt. 2.

tic relations. To verify that you were competent to represent Mary Welch, you might consult the ethical rule that addresses the attorney's obligation of competent representation. The Iowa rule is logically located under the "Client-Lawyer Relationship" topic, and provides: "A lawyer shall provide competent representation to a client. Competent representation requires the legal knowledge, skill, thoroughness, and preparation reasonably necessary for the representation."[18] Comment 2 to this rule further explains the attorney's obligation:

> A lawyer need not necessarily have special training or prior experience to handle legal problems of a type with which the lawyer is unfamiliar. A newly admitted lawyer can be as competent as a practitioner with long experience. Some important legal skills, such as the analysis of precedent, the evaluation of evidence, and legal drafting, are required in all legal problems. Perhaps the most fundamental legal skill consists of determining what kind of legal problems a situation may involve, a skill that necessarily transcends any particular specialized knowledge. A lawyer can provide adequate representation in a wholly novel field through necessary study. Competent representation can also be provided through the association of a lawyer of established competence in the field in question.[19]

If you were to further review the annotated version of the rule, you would find several cases addressing this issue. In one opinion, the court concluded that an attorney had violated the rule by representing a client in an interstate adoption matter.[20] In another, the court stated that a normally competent attorney may have an obligation to become familiar with a new area of law contemplated by the representation.[21] And in another case, the court explained that in order "to establish incompetence, the board is required to show the attorney (1) 'did not possess the necessary legal knowledge and skill to complete the tasks' or (2) 'had not made a competent analysis of the factual and legal elements of the problem[ ].'"[22] With the case citations, you could easily obtain the full opinions to review in more detail to ensure that you take adequate steps to familiarize yourself with the area of law involved in the Welch matter.

---

18. Iowa R. Prof. Conduct 32:1.1.
19. *Id.* at cmt. 2.
20. *Iowa Supreme Court Bd. of Prof'l Ethics & Conduct v. Hill*, 576 N.W.2d 91 (Iowa 1998).
21. *State v. Schoelerman*, 315 N.W.2d 67 (Iowa 1982).
22. *Iowa Supreme Court Att'y Disciplinary Bd. v. Hauser*, 782 N.W.2d 147, 153 (Iowa 2010) (citing *Iowa Supreme Court Att'y Disciplinary Bd. v. Hoglan*, 781 N.W.2d 279, 285 (Iowa 2010)).

C. Iowa Ethics Opinions

1. Iowa Ethics Opinions[23]

Prior to July 2005, the Board of Professional Ethics and Conduct (Ethics Board) issued Iowa formal ethics opinions. Beginning in July 2005, the Iowa Supreme Court transferred responsibility for ethics opinions to the Iowa State Bar Association. This responsibility now lies with the Ethics and Practice Guidelines Committee. The Iowa Supreme Court issued an order explaining the transfer of responsibility from the Ethics Board to the Committee and the impact on the persuasive effect of the opinions:

> The Iowa State Bar Association has offered to undertake the issuance of advisory opinions and practice guidelines under the Iowa Rules of Professional Conduct in a manner similar to its activities regarding uniform jury instructions. The Iowa Supreme Court welcomes the assistance of the Bar Association to aid Iowa lawyers in their efforts to practice law in accordance with our new rules of professional conduct.

> Advisory opinions and practice guidelines issued by the Iowa State Bar Association do not have the force of law and are not binding on the court, as Iowa law places sole responsibility for the regulation of the practice of law in the supreme court.[24]

---

23. The discussion on the development and force of Iowa ethics opinions is based in large part on Gregory C. Sisk & Mark S. Cady, *Iowa Practice: Lawyer and Judicial Ethics* § 2:12 (2015) (citing Order of the Supreme Court of Iowa dated April 21, 2005).

24. *Id.* note 14. Sisk explains that the practical effect of relying on an ethics opinion is that of a safe harbor. He notes that the Supreme Court has the ultimate responsibility for regulating the conduct of attorneys in Iowa, and it therefore cannot transfer that responsibility and authority to the state bar association. Notwithstanding, Iowa attorneys should be encouraged to seek the opinion of the Ethics and Practice Guidelines Committee. Sisk explains:

> In cases where the court in the context of a disciplinary proceeding effectively rejects the analysis of a pertinent bar association advisory opinion, the respondent lawyer's reasonable reliance upon that opinion should be given considerable weight in evaluating the lawyer's culpability and the appropriate sanction if any. . . . [A] lawyer's careful compliance with the terms of an ethics opinion nonetheless should generally be a safe-harbor against disciplinary sanction.

Id.

Committee opinions are typically reported in the bar association's journal, the *Iowa Lawyer*. Both committee opinions and the opinions previously issued by the Ethics Board are available on the website of the Iowa State Bar Association.[25] To search opinions on the bar association website, simply review the titles of the opinions. There is also a search feature available that allows you to find opinions by keyword, but it has some limitations. Although the site includes the full text of older opinions in html format, the newest opinions are available as linked PDFs. The search feature does not search the full text of these PDFs, so for the newest opinions you are only searching against titles, opinion dates, and opinion numbers.[26]

You can also use the *ABA/BNA Lawyers' Manual on Professional Conduct*, which is available in print, as well as online through Bloomberg Law, to identify relevant Iowa ethics opinions. Although this source only offers summaries of the Iowa ethics opinions, referring you to the ISBA site for the full text, it does include some powerful tools to help you find relevant opinions. First, from the State Ethics Opinions portion of the title, [27] click the plus sign to the left of "Iowa" to open that menu. You can click the "Search" button to use the full search capabilities of Bloomberg Law to search the summaries of the Iowa ethics opinions, or you can open the summaries by opinion title. Second, you can use the ethics opinions index, which includes a section by jurisdiction.[28] Clicking to open the Iowa section reveals a list of topics. Open those of interest to see the titles and numbers of related Iowa ethics opinions.

---

25. The Iowa Bar Association website address is http://iowabar.org. Click on the "Ethics tab" to see recent opinions, or click on the "Ethics opinions" link to search older opinions dating back to 1966.

26. As long as the ISBA keeps these opinions in the current directory, a site-specific search on Google can be used as a work-around to this problem. In the Google search box, input the terms of interest followed by *site:http://205.209.45.153/iabar/ethics.nsf*. The site string limits the search to the section of the ISBA site where ethics opinions are housed and allows for a simple full-text search for a word or phrase within the opinions.

27. On Bloomberg Law follow this path: Search & Browse tab > BNA Manuals > Lawyers' Manual on Professional Conduct > Lawyers' Manual on Professional Conduct: State Ethics Opinions.

28. On Bloomberg Law follow this path: Search & Browse tab > BNA Manuals > Lawyers' Manual on Professional Conduct > Lawyers' Manual on Professional Conduct: Ethics Opinions Index > Ethics Opinions Index by Jurisdiction.

2. Disciplinary Actions[29]

The Iowa Supreme Court has ultimate responsibility for regulating the conduct of attorneys in the state. In terms of disciplinary proceedings, the court has developed procedures for addressing complaints alleging ethical misconduct[30] of attorneys. Complaints against attorneys are initially investigated by the Attorney Disciplinary Board (Disciplinary Board). This is a confidential process. The Disciplinary Board may dismiss the complaint, admonish or reprimand the attorney, or file a complaint before another body, the Grievance Commission. If the Disciplinary Board files a reprimand with the clerk of the Iowa Supreme Court, the attorney has the option to file an exception to the reprimand. If he fails to do so, the reprimand becomes a public document and may be published in the *Iowa Lawyer*.

When the Disciplinary Board files a complaint at the Commission, a hearing is held. This is also a confidential process. At the conclusion of the hearing, the Commission may dismiss the complaint, issue a private admonition, or file a report recommending more serious sanction. Commission reports of recommendations regarding sanctions are filed with the clerk of the Iowa Supreme Court and are therefore public records. The attorney may file an appeal, which is then heard by the Iowa Supreme Court. In the event the Iowa Supreme Court renders an opinion on the matter, the opinion will be available in standard sources for cases as detailed in Chapter 5.

As public records, both reports of the Commission and final decisions on sanctions by the Iowa Supreme Court are available to view. Attorney disability and disciplinary orders are available on the Iowa judicial branch website, but they cannot be searched topically beyond the type of discipline, i.e., suspension, reprimand, etc.[31] Final determinations describing the conduct of the

---

29. Much of the discussion on grievance procedures comes from the Iowa Judicial Branch website, iowacourts.gov, which provides a more detailed explanation at http://www.iowacourts.gov/For_Attorneys/Attorney_Standards__Discipline/Disciplinary_Procedures/.

30. Note that these allegations can involve failings under the Iowa Rules of Professional Conduct or some other law that imposes an obligation on attorney conduct.

31. A database of attorneys licensed in Iowa is available at https://www.iacourtcommissions.org/SearchLawyer.do. Each individual attorney record links to any associated disciplinary orders. In addition, all orders issued within the last sixty days can be viewed through a link on the Office of Professional Regulation homepage at https://www.iacourtcommissions.org. Click on "Recent Disability and Discipline Orders" in the left column or directly access this site: https://www.iacourtcommissions.org/SearchDiscipline.do?action=recentSearch.

attorney and the type of sanction are also published in the *Iowa Lawyer*. Archives of past issues of the *Iowa Lawyer* remain available on the website of the Iowa Bar Association.[32] Unfortunately from a research perspective, the disciplinary reports are published chronologically in the *Iowa Lawyer* and are not separately cataloged for topical searching. Thus, accessing the reports requires a general review of past issues of the bar journal. The wise attorney will therefore review monthly issues of the journal to stay apprised of conduct that results in sanctions.

D. American Bar Association Materials

1. Model Rules of Professional Conduct

The ABA Model Rules of Professional Conduct are available in annotated and unannotated versions, both in print and online. When conducting legal research, an annotated version is valuable because it contains citations to cases that have interpreted the rules. The annotated version is available in print and online on Lexis[33] and Westlaw.[34] To search the rules, you can enter search terms or, on Westlaw, view the table of contents to find the rule(s) applicable to your situation.

The print version of the Annotated Model Rules of Professional Conduct is published by the ABA and includes a subject index, a table of amendments, and a correlation table between the Model Code and Model Rules. These are helpful resources if you are analyzing a topic that was previously considered in your jurisdiction under some version of the Model Code, rather than Model Rules (which were developed more recently).

2. Model Code of Professional Responsibility

Because most jurisdictions now have some form of the ABA Model Rules, it is unlikely that you will need to perform research in the ABA Model Code. However, because the same type of lawyering behavior is covered by both resources (e.g., candor, truthfulness, relationships with clients), you might

---

32. The Iowa Bar Association website is http://iowabar.org. Use the "Publications" link on the homepage to access the *Iowa Lawyer*.

33. To access the annotated Model Rules in Lexis, either use "Browse Sources" or, to add it as a search filter, use the red search box, and begin typing "ABA Model Rules of Professional Conduct."

34. On Westlaw, follow this path: Home > Secondary Sources > Texts & Treatises > Ethics & Professional Responsibility > ABA Annotated Model Rules of Professional Conduct.

consult a topic that had been previously addressed by the ABA Model Code to seek persuasive authority on an issue currently covered by the ABA Model Rules. To that end, the American Bar Foundation publishes an Annotated Code of Professional Responsibility. If your research is directed primarily to an issue involving the ABA Model Rules and you simply want to consult the issue as previously addressed under the ABA Model Code, it is most efficient to use an annotated version of the ABA Model Rules which should contain cross-references to the related ABA Model Code section.

3. ABA Ethics Opinions

The ABA issues both formal and informal advisory ethics opinions in response to questions from attorneys about the propriety of certain conduct under the rules. Again, the formal opinions, issued in response to broadly applicable questions, are more likely to be relevant to you as you examine an ethical issue.

You can search the ABA opinions in the *ABA/BNA Lawyers' Manual on Professional Conduct*, which is available in print, as well as online through Bloomberg Law.[35] Lexis[36] and Westlaw[37] also provide separate databases of ABA ethics opinions. Search online using terms and connectors as described in Chapter 2. You can also review these opinions in print in a number of publications issued by the ABA.[38] In the print volumes, opinions appear in chronological order and can best accessed by using the subject index at the end of the volume. This index is also available on Bloomberg Law. Also, recent opinions are published in the *ABA Journal*.[39]

---

35. On Bloomberg Law, follow this path: Search & Browse tab > BNA Manuals > Lawyers' Manual on Professional Conduct > Lawyers' Manual on Professional Conduct: ABA Ethics Opinions.

36. Lexis offers separate collections of ABA formal and informal ethics opinions. Use "Browse Sources" and begin typing "ABA ethics" (don't enter the quotation marks) to bring a source list that includes both options.

37. On Westlaw, follow this path: Home > Secondary Sources > Texts & Treatises > Ethics & Professional Responsibility > ABA Ethics Materials (under Tools & Resources) > ABA Ethics Opinions.

38. The ABA publishes several compilations of ethics opinions. To access the most recent publications, go the ABA's Center for Professional Responsibility website at http://www.americanbar.org/groups/professional_responsibility.html. From that page, select the "Publications" tab on the left side of the page, and then select "Ethics Opinions."

39. ABAJ can be found at http://www.abajournal.com/magazine/archives.

E. Materials from Other States

To locate materials from other states, including rules on professional conduct and state ethics opinions, a good place to start is the ABA website's Center for Professional Responsibility. The site contains an alphabetical listing of all states with links to bar associations and rules of professional conduct.[40] State court rules typically include rules of professional responsibility. State court rules are available through freely accessible state-specific websites[41] and through paid online research platforms, such as Bloomberg Law,[42] Lexis[43] and Westlaw.[44]

Locating individual state ethics opinions can be tricky because publication differs by state. Most state bar associations publish ethics opinions in their state bar journal or newsletter, but some do not. One good resource is the *ABA/BNA Lawyers' Manual on Professional Conduct*, available in print and on Bloomberg Law, which includes summaries of state ethics opinions.[45] Lexis[46] and Westlaw[47] also include selected state ethics opinions.

F. Secondary Sources for Legal Ethics Research

A variety of secondary resources assist in legal ethics research. The following are good starting points: *ABA/BNA Lawyers' Manual on Professional Con-*

---

40. This list is available at http://www.americanbar.org/groups/professional_re sponsibility/resources/links_of_interest.html.

41. The Drake Law Library's Court Rules research guide contains links to freely accessible sources of state court rules. It is available at http://libguides.law.drake.edu /courtrules.

42. On Bloomberg, access state court rules through this path: Search & Browse tab > State Law > click on state of interest on the map > [State] Court Rules.

43. On Lexis, click on "Browse" then "Sources," and finally "By jurisdiction" to find relevant materials. After selecting the state of interest, use the left-hand filters to limit results. Court rules, including professional responsibility rules, will be in the "Statutes and Legislation" category.

44. On Westlaw click on "State Materials" and then the state of interest. Court rules, including professional responsibility rules, will be under the "Statutes & Court Rules" heading.

45. On Bloomberg Law, access this source through the following path: Search & Browse tab > BNA Manuals > Lawyers' Manual on Professional Conduct > Lawyers' Manual on Professional Conduct: State Ethics Opinions.

46. On Lexis, click on "Browse" then "Sources," and finally "By jurisdiction" to find relevant materials. After selecting the state of interest, use the left-hand filters to limit re- sults. Available ethics opinions will likely be in the "Administrative Materials" category.

47. On Westlaw, click on "State Materials" and then the state of interest. Click on the "[State] Administrative Decisions & Guidance" link to check for ethics opinions.

duct; the *Restatement of the Law Governing Lawyers*;[48] *Understanding Lawyers' Ethics*;[49] *Legal Ethics in a Nutshell*;[50] *Legal Ethics: A Legal Research Guide*;[51] and *The Law of Lawyering*.[52]

There are also a number of law reviews and journals devoted to legal ethics and professional responsibility. These include the following: *Georgetown Journal of Legal Ethics*; *The Journal of Law, Medicine, & Ethics*; *Criminal Justice Ethics*; *Journal of the Legal Profession* (University of Alabama School of Law); *Notre Dame Journal of Law, Ethics and Public Policy*; and the *Professional Lawyer*.

Finally, many resources are available on the internet. The ABA's Center for Professional Responsibility website[53] contains a number of helpful links to material including state-specific resources, national organizations, law school websites, and general legal ethics material.

---

48. Restatement (Third) of the Law Governing Lawyers (2000).
49. Monroe H. Freedman, *Understanding Lawyers' Ethics* (4th ed. 2010).
50. Ronald Rotunda, *Legal Ethics in a Nutshell* (4th ed. 2013).
51. Lee F. Peoples, *Legal Ethics: A Legal Research Guide* (2d ed. 2006).
52. Geoffery C. Hazard & W. William Hodes, *The Law of Lawyering* (4th ed. 2015).
53. From the Center for Professional Responsibility webpage at http://www .americanbar.org/groups/professional_responsibility.html, select the "Resources" link in the left menu and browse sub-menu options. One link of particular note is "Links of Interest," directly accessible at http://www.americanbar.org/groups/profes sional_responsibility/resources/links_of_interest.html.

Chapter 12

Research Strategies[1]

I. Introduction

When a client comes to a lawyer with a problem, the lawyer does not typically have an immediate answer. For most legal issues, the prudent course of action is more deliberate analysis. An effective lawyer listens carefully, hears the client's story, and asks about the client's desired outcome. The lawyer will provide the client with information and recommendations, assessing the feasibility of the desired result and the best means of achieving it, whether through legal action or alternatives, such as mediation or counseling.

As you listen to a story from a client, you will have to determine which facts are legally significant and identify the legal issues. This process may require that you ask questions to elicit facts the client might not have thought to mention. You might also need to review related documents, such as contracts, letters, bills, or public records. You may even need to interview others involved in the client's situation.

The legal issues are not always easily ascertained after the client meeting. A supervising attorney might meet with the client and then turn to junior colleagues to determine the issues or to research specific questions. If the facts involve an area of law in which you have limited experience, some preliminary research into potential legal issues could be required. When you complete the basic research to find the relevant law, you should be able to identify the legal issues that need to be addressed and begin to develop a research strategy. This chapter explains how to formulate that strategy and organize the materials you find.

---

1. Portions of this chapter are based on Elizabeth G. Adelman et al., *New York Legal Research* (3d ed. 2015).

II. Developing and Implementing a Research Strategy

A. Reflect on the Research Process

The research process in Chapter 1 outlines six basic steps: (1) identify the issues, jurisdiction, and scope of the project; (2) gather facts and identify preliminary search terms; (3) identify, prioritize, and consult relevant sources; (4) expand and update your research; (5) make sure your research is responsive to the question(s) being presented; and (6) determine when to stop. These steps provide a basic framework for research; as you become more experienced, you will begin to tailor your strategies to fit the specific project.

Moreover, you will become acutely aware that the research process itself is not necessarily linear. As your research progresses, you may find additional research terms to add to those you initially identified. Later in your research, it may be helpful to review your preliminary work to determine whether you need to broaden your search in those sources. As you begin formulating a written answer to the research question, you might discover gaps, such as issues not originally identified or arguments that require further support, that will lead you to conduct additional research.

B. Getting Started[2]

One of the first steps in an organized research strategy is to make sure you understand the objective of the project you are undertaking. You need to know exactly what the supervising attorney (or client) expects. For example, does your supervisor want you to spend an hour or two finding a handful of applicable cases, or does she expect you to compile a comprehensive review of the case law on the subject, involving many hours of research and writing? Beginning researchers in particular should ask enough questions to fully understand the research task.[3] A related task is to analyze the research problem itself. Considering the following sorts of issues will help you clearly comprehend the purpose and nature of the research project.

What is the time frame for completing this project?

---

2. Section B is adapted from Elizabeth G. Adelman et al., *New York Legal Research* 211–12 (3d ed. 2015), which provides much greater detail on these points.

3. Drake's *Legal Research Starting Points* provides links to articles detailing what those questions should be at http://libguides.law.drake.edu/LRStarting.

If the work must be completed tomorrow as opposed to in a few weeks, the timing will greatly impact your research strategy. With extended time you might be able to consider a more significant review of background materials, such as law review articles. With a short turnaround, you may need to focus on the most important resources rather than additional resources that are more contextual in nature.

Are there budgetary limitations on the research?

Be sure you understand the fiscal resources that can be allocated to the case. The work for a small claims case will be vastly different from that for a multi-million dollar class action. Moreover, you would not want to expend vast resources in online research on a case in which there is little money at stake. Finally, be sure to determine whether there are any budgetary limitations on the project set forth by the client or by the firm.

What research tools are available, and what are the cost and billing considerations?

Finding out what resources are available and their associated costs should be one of your initial inquiries. Many work environments will not offer the unlimited access to online and print resources enjoyed by students using an academic law library. You will want to develop a research strategy that includes determining which tools may be available, how best to use them, and which will be most helpful in light of time and budget limitations.

What kinds of authorities will be most important?

Determining which authorities have the greatest chance of affecting the case will help you narrow your research. If the issue is one where common law governs, you will want to focus on finding relevant cases. In a heavily regulated area of law, such as banking, you will want to locate applicable statutes and regulations. In either type of case, secondary authorities can be great tools in first providing an overview and then guiding you to primary authorities.

What jurisdiction governs the issue(s)?

Normally, it will be clear from the outset whether you are dealing with an issue of federal, state, or local law, although in some instances all will be relevant and in other instances it may be unclear. Make every effort to resolve any ambiguities prior to initiating your research. Consultation with the supervising attorney may be beneficial.

Are there relevant terms of art in this area of law?

As you brainstorm search terms, you will want to be alert for specific words or phrases with specialized meaning in the field. You may be able to identify these by asking the supervising attorney, using a secondary source or basic reference, like a legal dictionary, or reviewing preliminary search results.

What do I already know?

If you are researching an unfamiliar area of law, you may want to begin with a secondary source. However, if you are already familiar with a topic, you could begin with primary sources. For example, in a matter governed by statutory law, such as the grandparents' visitation rights hypothetical used throughout this book, you could proceed directly to an annotated code. In another matter, perhaps you already have a citation to an applicable case. In that instance, you could begin by retrieving the case online and using a citator to make sure it is still good law and to locate related cases that have cited it. Bloomberg Law's BCite, Lexis' Shepard's, and Westlaw's KeyCite provide that information.[4] As described in Chapter 5, you could also identify the most relevant headnote(s) from your starting case and then use the Lexis or Westlaw classification system to find additional cases (or Bloomberg Law if the case includes headnotes). As a final example, imagine you know that the issue is controlled by common law, but you do not have a starting case citation. Researching statutes or constitutions should be unnecessary or require minimal time, and you can focus on finding relevant case law through a keyword search, as described in Chapter 5.

What am I missing?

Marshalling what you currently have may also help you determine what more you may need. Does the firm have a file with documents from a similar case? Do you have all the key dates, facts, and case files? Do you understand the bigger picture, e.g., the desired end product and the relative priority level of this work among other assignments? Remember, assumptions risk bad results; when in doubt, ask.

Some additional questions you might consider include the following:

- How will the research be used? (For example, will you write a client advice letter or draft a motion?)
- What is the scope of the research? (For example, do you only need to provide a brief overview at this point or complete an extensive analysis of the issues?)
- What period of time needs to be researched?
- Is there anything else you need to know?[5]

---

4. Chapter 9 provides details on using citators.

5. Mark E. Wojcik suggests asking this as a final question often yields "surprising answers." *Quick Tip: Ten Questions for New Lawyers to Ask,* at 14 http://www.lwionline.org/publications/seconddraft/dec06.pdf.

Keeping these kinds of questions in mind as you begin the process can help you to formulate an efficient, effective search strategy.

C. Structuring a Plan

With the objective clearly in mind, your first step is to develop your research *strategy*. This is just a list of the different types of legal resources you plan to search and how you plan to search them. By writing out a strategy, you ensure that you check all the relevant sources of law. A written plan can also make a new project seem less daunting since you will have specific steps to follow. Referring to this document often can help keep your research on track and ensure you do not miss a step. As you develop your strategy, you want to stay cognizant of your goal and consider the structure of your research issue.

D. Implementing Your Plan

1. Assess and Update

You should constantly assess your progress and feel free to revise your strategy as you learn more about the issues. For example, you might encounter a case or secondary resource that identifies a related cause of action that you had not previously considered. If that occurs, you will need to adjust your research. Continuing to update your research plan is helpful to memorialize changes and ensure that you are not wasting time. In this process, be sure not to lose sight of your ultimate objective (as noted in step 5 of the research process).

Included in your strategy will be a list of research terms generated from the facts and issues in your problem. Develop an expansive list by brainstorming. As you work in each new resource, refer back to this list. On the list, note which terms were helpful in which resources. As you discover new terms, add them to the list. If you are having difficulty identifying search terms, consider beginning with a secondary resource to give you some context for the project.

2. Organize and Document

Once you begin consulting specific resources, you will want to keep them organized. Lexis, Westlaw, and Bloomberg Law have systems that allow you to save and organize your research. Lexis and Westlaw provide folders, and Bloomberg Law provides a workspace into which documents can be saved. Some researchers find it helpful to have a print copy of the most important authorities while others prefer having everything online. As you work through the sources you locate, you can determine which ones seem most relevant. You may want to be judicious in printing, however, to ensure that you have not accumulated so much paper that it becomes unwieldy. With experience, you will be able to develop a system that works well for you.

Two hallmarks of effective research are good organization and documentation of what you find. Your research needs to be organized in the manner most effective to help you marshal the resources, understand the legal issues, and analyze the problem presented. Most researchers find a computer an efficient means of collecting their research, especially in light of the folders and other tools available in doing online research, but a legal pad, note cards, or an organized folder could also be used.[6] Software that provides fact and issue management, such as CaseMap, can help you organize information about the cases you find as well.[7]

3. Utilize Research Trails

In each step of your research, be aware of the online tools available to save your research trail and enable you to refer back to it. Lexis retains your History for three months, Bloomberg Law's Research Trail is saved for six months, and Westlaw's History is available for one year. You also may want to take some notes as your research progresses. These notes need not be formal, but should be sufficient to indicate what you have done or found. Looking back at your research trail or notes helps you avoid duplication, especially as you start and stop the process to do other work. In addition, your research trail shows you the sources you searched and the ways you searched them to help you assess the effectiveness of your searches. This can save significant time when you review your initial research. For example, noting both successful and unsuccessful terms and searches will help you ensure that you don't repeat those same steps later.

When relying on these trails, make sure you know when they will expire. Some researchers find it helpful to reference the trails available through individual platforms in a single master research trail for the entire project. For example, you could keep a simple chart listing the following: (1) the date you searched, (2) the source consulted, (3) the date the research trail expires, and (4) other notes briefly describing the research, such as "reviewed cases 2005–2015" or "good ALR annotation."

---

6. If you use a laptop, be sure to back up your work to a separate storage device. You don't want to be the subject in the oft-repeated horror story of the researcher whose computer crashed just before a deadline and had nothing backed up.

7. For information about CaseMap go to http://www.lexisnexis.com/litigation /products/case-analysis/casemap. Law students can find further details and download a free copy from http://www.lexisnexis.com/lawschool.

In addition to utilizing your research trail, take analytical notes about the information found. As you review the authorities, don't simply cut and paste the wording of the court. You also should summarize the issues in your own words (noting the pinpoint citations) and state what you learn from them. Such analytical notes should increase your understanding of the legal issues and prove invaluable as you organize and write your document. You should try to strike an appropriate balance. Taking notes that are too extensive or that include inappropriate detail may detract from more important tasks, such as the research itself or analyzing the results. The key is to keep your research organized. Referring to the tools mentioned above can help you do so.

E. Working with Particular Sources

For some issues, it may be beneficial to begin your research with a secondary authority. You will ultimately want to focus your attention on primary authorities, and you will want to ensure that you keep detailed notes as you review these sources.

1. Secondary Authorities

Beginning your research with a secondary authority can help you gain a basic understanding of the relevant area of law and find references to primary authorities. When using a secondary authority, it can be helpful to prepare a short note of what you found and how it applies to your situation. If you discover issues that require more research, note those and consider what the next source to consult might be. Secondary authorities include references to primary authorities, such as cases and statutes. As you find those cites, add them to your primary authority list.

Some inexperienced researchers underestimate the value of secondary authorities in the research process. Although you certainly want to emphasize relevant primary authorities in your legal documents, remember that secondary authorities can help you better understand the law and often enable you to do so more quickly than if you begin by perusing primary authorities. A few minutes with an on-point section of a legal encyclopedia may be more helpful in your initial research than wading through a number of case decisions trying to find the relevant law. After using a secondary authority, you can more effectively turn to your primary authorities.

2. Primary Authorities

Once you are ready to review your list of primary authorities, eliminate any duplicates so you don't check the same source twice. In your initial review, you don't need to read each word of each authority. You may just skim the authority to make sure it is relevant. Later, you can be more deliberate and review it in more detail.

A few tips can help you skim to see if the authority is relevant. For statutes and rules, scan the sections that give definitions or explain the statute's purpose. Look for operative language that establishes duties or proscribes certain conduct. Browse the sections just before and after your code section to see if they are relevant and review the table of contents for the statutory chapter. For cases, begin by reading the synopsis. The headnotes or core concepts follow and can help you zero in on the most relevant parts of the case. Jump from the relevant headnote(s) to the corresponding text of the case and make sure the language of the opinion addresses your issue. That jump enables you to skip unrelated points of law and other parts, such as the procedural history, that perhaps are not germane.

As you initially review sources, make a few notes on your list of authorities. For promising materials, briefly indicate their relevance. Strike through authorities that do not seem applicable. Do not delete them entirely, however, because they might ultimately become useful or relevant, or you may encounter them again and want to ensure you already reviewed them in whole.

After you have selected a set of relevant authorities, develop an organizational schedule for reading them in groups. If there is a constitutional provision, statute, or rule on point, read it carefully, then read cases that interpret the provision. One approach is to read cases in chronological order, so that you see the development of the law over time. However, this approach may be time-consuming for causes of action that have continued for many years. Except for historical research, you should impose an artificial cut-off going back a set number of years so you can focus on more recent cases.[8] Another approach is to begin with the most recent cases. The benefit of reviewing recent cases is that you may be able to avoid reading law in old cases that has been revised or superseded.

After you have assembled this group of relevant authorities, read them with care, especially any areas you skipped initially. For statutory research, be sure to read the definitions section of the relevant statutory provision. In each court

---

8. The cut-off may depend on the substantive issue involved. In an area with dramatic growth and change in law, such as patent infringement, the cut-off would be relatively short. A longer cut-off would be appropriate for an area that develops over time, such as an issue involving constitutional law.

decision, make sure you understand the procedural history, including the standard each court applied. You want to have a thorough understanding of the facts of each case. A time line or chart of party relationships can be helpful. As you read the case, cross out parts that deal with issues not confronting your client so you won't reread those portions the next time you look at the case. If you find a case isn't relevant at all, clearly indicate that on the first page of the case so you don't read it more than once. If you are considering several issues or related claims, you may want to consider them one at a time. Doing so will require separate lists of authorities for each claim being researched.

a. Taking Notes on Statutes

Notes on statutes should include both the actual language of the statute and your analysis or outline of it. Because the exact words of statutes are so critical, you should memorialize that text into your notes. In order to effectively analyze a complex statute, you should outline it. Highlighting is sufficient only if a statute is very short and clear. A statute often includes the elements of the claim or indicates the time limitations for bringing the claim.

The definition sections of statutes are often the most important. If terms are not defined, you will need to make a note to look for judicial definitions. If a relevant statute includes cross-references to other statutes, be sure to read them as well.

b. Taking Notes on Cases

Once you determine that a case is relevant, you should brief it. Doing so does not require any formal style. The brief for each case should be a set of notes highlighting the key aspects of the case that are relevant to your research problem. Create a short summary of the pertinent facts, holding, and reasoning. Each case brief should include the following:

- *Case name and citation.* Having the full citation will make writing easier because you will not have to refer back to the original case.
- *Facts.* Only facts relevant to your problem should be recorded.
- *Holding and reasoning.* Provide a short summary of the court's analysis and include only those issues relevant to your problem. If the case includes a tort claim and a related contract claim, for example, but only the tort claim relates to your problem, then you only should take notes on the tort issues. Skim the contract information just to be sure nothing relevant is buried there and then move on.
- *Pinpoint pages.* When you copy text from an online case, you should be able to automatically capture the pinpoint citation. On Westlaw, when you highlight text you want to copy a pop-up appears that allows

you to "Copy with Reference"; on Lexis the pop-up box offers "Copy (Advanced)"; and on Bloomberg Law the small pop-up is "Copy with Citation." If the case has parallel citations and those will be needed, be sure to set the copying preference to include them.[9]

- *Reflections.* Note your thoughts on the case: How do you expect to use the case in your analysis? Does it resolve certain issues in your problem? Does it raise new questions?

- *Updating information.* Provide a designated space on each brief for updating. Each case you use in your analysis must be updated with a citator such as Shepard's or KeyCite.

F. Updating

Updating, described in detail in Chapter 9, will be helpful at several points in your research. As noted, updating before you begin to rely on an authority is especially important to ensure that the authority remains good law. Using a citator like Shepard's or KeyCite early in the research process will lead you to other relevant authorities.[10] At the end of your research, before you submit the document, you will want to update again to make sure nothing has changed. Checking citing references from a citator is an easy and efficient way to compare new citations with your list of primary authorities.

III. Outlining Your Analysis

Because the most effective research often occurs in conjunction with the analysis of your particular project, try to develop an outline that addresses your client's problem as soon as possible. If you prefer a different framework, consider a chart that organizes all the primary authority into issues or elements, such as in Table 12-1. Either approach will help ensure your research remains focused on the particular issues facing your client, rather than inadvertently wandering into related, but ultimately inapplicable, territory.

Your initial analytical outline or chart could be based on information in a secondary source, the requirements of a statute, or the elements of a common

---

9. For example, to include three pinpoint parallel citations when viewing a U.S. Supreme Court decision on Westlaw, you would choose the "Standard" Copy with Reference and on Lexis Advance you use "Copy (Advanced)." For more details on star pagination using asterisk designations for page breaks, see the discussion and illustrations in Chapter 2.

10. Other online systems also provide citators, such as BCite on Bloomberg Law.

law claim. As you conduct research, your outline will become more detailed. However, you cannot reread every case or statute in its entirety each time you include it in your outline. A better approach would be to refer to your notes and briefs to find the key ideas supporting each step in your analysis.

With an outline or chart, you should be able to synthesize the law, apply the law to your client's problem, and reach a conclusion on the desired outcome. As you apply the law to your client's facts, you may discover other research issues that were not apparent from an abstract review of the law.

Table 12-1 continues on the following page with cases interpreting the statute. For each case you have the general rule of law, the key facts of the case, and the holding or reasoning of the court.

Table 12-1. Sample Analysis Chart— Issue and Statute

Research Question: Is an automobile or truck an "occupied structure" within the meaning of the burglary statute so that breaking into a vehicle is a chargeable crime under that statute?

Controlling Statutes: Burglary is defined under Iowa Code § 713.1 (2009): "Any person, having the intent to commit a felony, assault or theft therein, who, having no right, license or privilege to do so, enters an *occupied structure*, such occupied structure not being open to the public, or who remains therein after it is closed to the public or after the person's right, license or privilege to be there has expired, or any person having such intent who breaks an occupied structure, commits burglary."

Under Iowa Code § 702.12 (2009), "An '*occupied structure*' is any building, structure, appurtenances to buildings and structures, land, water or air vehicle, or similar place adapted for overnight accommodation of persons, or occupied by persons for the purpose of carrying on business or other activity therein, or for the storage or safekeeping of anything of value. Such a structure is an 'occupied structure' whether or not a person is actually present."

Table 12-1. Sample Analysis Chart, *continued* —Cases

Case	General Rule	Facts of the Case	Holding/Reasoning
State v. Williams, 409 N.W.2d 187 (Iowa 1987).	An occupied structure as defined in the Iowa burglary statute includes land vehicles; a topper-enclosed pickup truck that is entered for the purpose of theft falls within that statutory language.	Defendant was observed opening the camper shell door on the back of a pickup, transferring two tires into his vehicle, and then driving away.	The illegal entry into an enclosed camper on a pickup truck is the entry of an occupied structure and may be the basis for a burglary charge under the Iowa statutes.
State v. Sylvester, 331 N.W.2d 130 (Iowa 1983).	Definition of occupied structure under the Iowa Code is very broad. An occupied structure not only includes buildings but extends to vehicles on land, water or air, without regard to whether a person is actually present.	While beer truck driver was making a delivery to a business establishment, the defendants were observed entering the beer truck and removing several cases of beer.	Definition of occupied structure includes any vehicle for the storage or safekeeping of anything of value. Plain meaning includes delivery trucks. Statute does not require the structure to be locked.
State v. Buss, 325 N.W.2d 384 (Iowa 1982).	Consistent with the rules of statutory construction, definition of occupied structure under the Iowa Code encompasses a dwelling and much more, including an automobile.	Defendant was charged with breaking into the cab of a Chevrolet pickup truck.	Although defendant contended that the truck was not an occupied structure because it was not *primarily* used for storage or safekeeping, the Court found that the statute lacked such qualifying language and that an automobile exclusion would eliminate car break-ins as aggravated theft. The Court held that the cab of the pickup was an "occupied structure" within the meaning of the burglary statute and reversed the district court.

IV. When to Stop Researching

Deciding when to stop researching and start writing can be a difficult decision, especially for a novice researcher. If a client, supervisor, or court has set a deadline, this deadline dictates the time that can be spent. Costs to the client will also be a factor.

The most significant misconception in legal research is that you will find a clear answer to the client's issue in some resource if only you look long and hard enough. In reality, things are rarely this straightforward. If you have that "Eureka moment," you can stop researching, but only if you are confident that you have actually located a straightforward answer to your problem. Be sure to carefully question whether a legal source can be distinguished or evaluated in a manner that is inconsistent with your position.

In most instances, there is no such Eureka moment or definitive resource, and you have to determine when to stop your research. Typically, you should feel comfortable stopping when you have come full circle, meaning that you are consistently coming back to the same authorities. When this occurs, you can be confident that you have been thorough. To double-check, you can go through each step of the basic research process to ensure you considered each one. Review your strategy and research trail.

If you work through the research process and find that you are not locating a relevant source, consider the possibility that nothing exists. More than one of the authors of this text was given a research assignment by a senior attorney and spent many fruitless hours without finding a single applicable authority. When those results were reported, the senior attorney responded, "I didn't think there were any. Thanks for confirming that."[11] Finding nothing on point is not unusual. In law practice, that often happens when the area of law is new or rapidly changing, such as in the environmental law field, where there may be no relevant appellate decisions or published trial decisions. However, before you abandon your research, be sure to expand your research terms and look in a few more secondary sources. Also consider whether a persuasive authority from another jurisdiction could be used.

Keep in mind that your ultimate goal is to solve your client's problem and, if that is not possible because legal authority does not support a resolution,

---

11. This was a great relief to the young researchers, who fully expected to be told otherwise. Now more experienced and wiser, both researchers realize this stress could have been avoided by asking more questions about the research task when it was assigned and checking back with the supervisor earlier.

then your goal must be to advise your client accordingly. Sometimes the law will not seem to provide the answer your client wants. In that case you must think creatively. Although you must report to your supervisor what the law is and that your client's desired outcome is in question, be sure to consider if alternative options can be suggested. Finally, keep in mind your ethical obligation of candor, which requires you to deliver disappointing results if that is what your research reveals.

Appendix

Legal Citations

I. Introduction

As explained in Chapter 2, legal citations indicate precisely where material within an authority can be found. Legal arguments normally include references to many authorities and accurate citations are essential so that a judge, opposing counsel, or anyone else viewing the document can locate your supporting authority. Each legal assertion must cite the authority on which it is based. Through citations, the reader can not only locate the authority but also determine the level of support the authority provides.[1] See Table A-1.

Citation rules are much more than technical requirements to which attorneys must adhere. Providing uniform citations ensures that anyone reviewing the document can find the cited sources. Correct citations help a lawyer or judge appreciate that the arguments were well researched and the conclusions supported by authority. Poor citation practices reflect adversely on the writer even if the balance of the document is well drafted. Inaccurate citations can frustrate judges to the point of criticizing the author in an opinion that will be preserved forever.[2]

Depending upon the type of the legal document, references to authority may appear in the text itself, or in footnotes or endnotes. If accurate, citations allow researchers to easily identify relevant authorities that can then be used to find additional relevant sources, as explained in Chapters 5 and 9. As such, keen attention to detail is required in providing citations because a seemingly simple omission or error can misdirect the reader. For example, if a case is in

---

1. ALWD & Coleen M. Barger, *ALWD Guide to Legal Citation* 2–3 (5th ed. 2014) ("*ALWD Guide*").
2. *See, e.g., Bradshaw v. Unity Marine Corp.*, 147 F. Supp. 2d 668 (S.D. Tex. 2001) (criticizing counsel for failing to give correct citations and for not giving pinpoint citations, among other problems).

Table A-1. Purposes of Legal Citation

- Show the reader where to find the cited material in the original case, statute, rule, article, or other authority.

- Indicate the weight and persuasiveness of each authority, for example, by specifying the court that decided the case, the author of a document, and the publication date of the authority.

- Convey the type and degree of support the authority offers, for example, by indicating whether the authority supports your point directly or only implicitly.

- Demonstrate that the analysis in your document is the result of careful research.

Source: ALWD Guide.

the third series of the *Federal Supplement* and the citation is made to "F. Supp." rather than "F. Supp. 3d," the correct case will not be found.

Legal citation practice has developed over many decades to the point that a correctly formatted citation is something that most lawyers understand and recognize. Lawyers and judges expect that new lawyers entering the practice of law know how to construct accurate citations. Most law students start learning those skills during the first year of law school. Two national citation manuals provide citation guidance: *The Bluebook: A Uniform System of Citation*[3] and the *ALWD Guide to Legal Citation.*[4]

Most jurisdictions promulgate citation rules that attorneys filing documents in those jurisdictions must follow and those rules may or may not follow the style of one of the national manuals.[5] Whenever you are preparing a legal document be sure you know who your audience is and what citation rules must be followed.

II. The *Bluebook*

The Bluebook: A Uniform System of Citation was released in its twentieth edition in 2015. The work is compiled by the editors of the Columbia Law Re-

---

3. *The Bluebook: A Uniform System of Citation* (The Columbia Law Review et al. eds., 20th ed. 2015) (*"Bluebook"*). An online version also is available. *See* http://www.legalbluebook.com.

4. ALWD & Coleen M. Barger, *ALWD Guide to Legal Citation* (5th ed. 2014).

5. See Appendix 2 of the *ALWD Guide* for Local Court Citation Rules.

view, the Harvard Law Review, the University of Pennsylvania Law Review, and The Yale Law Journal. A new edition is typically released every five years and, until the *ALWD Guide* was published in 2000, the *Bluebook* was the only national citation system that was widely recognized.[6] As a result, the practice of checking citations in documents to ensure accuracy became known as "Bluebooking."

The *Bluebook* provides citation examples aimed at two different groups: (a) those working with law review articles, and (b) practitioners. The bulk of the book, the "Whitepages," is devoted to the law review audience, and the examples throughout the text show how to prepare citations for law review footnotes.[7] The footnote format requires a different typeface convention than what practitioners use, which sometimes is a bit confusing for first-time *Bluebook* users. For example, large and small caps are required in footnotes for periodical abbreviations, e.g., IOWA L. REV., and book citations, e.g., LAURIE KRATKY DORÉ, IOWA PRACTICE: EVIDENCE. The *Bluebook*'s inside front cover includes a Quick Reference for citing law review footnotes.

The first section contains the "Bluepages," which provides citation guidance for practitioners for court documents and legal memoranda — the format that most lawyers and first-year law students use. The typeface convention is very simple and reminiscent of what can be produced on a typewriter: ordinary Roman type with underlining to show italics. The inside back cover gives a Quick Reference summary of the practitioner rules with examples. Tables in the back show which authority to cite and how to abbreviate properly.

III. *ALWD Guide*

The *ALWD Guide* was created by the Association of Legal Writing Directors to provide a citation manual that is "easy to use, easy to teach from, and easy to learn from."[8] It codifies the most commonly followed rules for legal citation, serving much like a restatement. The *ALWD Guide* is consistent with the *Bluebook* on almost all practices.[9] However, the *ALWD Guide* focuses on the

---

6. The University of Chicago attempted to do so with a *Maroonbook*, but that effort did not attract a following. *The Maroonbook* is available at http://lawreview.uchicago.edu.

7. Bluepages cover the first 56 pages, and Whitepages are from page 57 to 523.

8. *ALWD Guide* Preface xxiii.

9. *See, e.g., ALWD Guide* Preface. A few variations are found in the *ALWD Guide* because it was published in 2014 and *Bluebook* made some rule changes with its 20th

system of citation used in legal memoranda and court documents. The format for law review footnotes is included with each rule with a box highlighting "Academic Footnoting" and a FN designation with the rule number.

IV. Legal Citation in Iowa

A. Introduction

Although some jurisdictions reference a particular citation manual in their rules, Iowa does not. Iowa follows generally accepted citation practices and outlines its rules for citation at Iowa Rule of Appellate Procedure 6.904:[10]

Rule 6.904 References in briefs.

6.904(1) *To the parties.* In briefs counsel should minimize references to parties by such designations as "appellant" and "appellee" and should use the actual names of the parties or descriptive terms such as "the plaintiff," "the defendant," "the employee," "the injured person," "the taxpayer," or "the decedent."

6.904(2) *To legal authorities.*

a. Cases. In citing cases, the names of parties must be given. In citing Iowa cases, reference must be made to the volume and page where the case may be found in the North Western Reporter. If the case is not reported in the North Western Reporter, reference must be made to the volume and page where the case may be found in the Iowa Reports. In citing cases, reference must be made to the court that rendered the opinion and the volume and page where the opinion may be found in the National Reporter System, if reported therein. *E.g.,* _ N.W.2d _ (Iowa 20_); _ N.W.2d _ (Iowa Ct. App. 20_); _ S.W.2d _ (Mo. Ct. App. 20_); _ U.S._, _ S. Ct._, _ L. Ed. 2d _ (20_); _ F.3d_ (_Cir. 20_); _ F. Supp. 2d _ (S.D. Iowa 20_). When quoting from authorities or referring to a particular point within an authority, the specific page or pages quoted or relied upon shall be given in addition to the required page references.

---

edition in 2015. Those differences have been described as "microscopic." *See* Peter W. Martin, *Introduction to Basic Legal Citation* § 1-100, Legal Information Institute (2015), http://www.law.cornell.edu/citation.

10. Iowa Court Rules are available at https://www.legis.iowa.gov/law/court Rules.

b. Iowa Court Rules. When citing the Iowa Court Rules parties shall use the following references:

(1) "Iowa R. Civ. P."; "Iowa R. Crim. P."; "Iowa R. Evid."; "Iowa R. App. P."; "Iowa R. of Prof'l Conduct"; and "Iowa Code of Judicial Conduct" when citing those rules.

(2) "Iowa Ct. R." when citing all other rules.

c. Unpublished opinions or decisions. An unpublished opinion or decision of a court or agency may be cited in a brief if the opinion or decision can be readily accessed electronically. Unpublished opinions or decisions shall not constitute controlling legal authority. When citing an unpublished opinion or decision a party shall include an electronic citation indicating where the opinion may be readily accessed online.

E.g., No. _____, _____ WL _____, at *__ (____ 20__).

d. Other authorities. When citing other authorities, references shall be made as follows:

(1) Citations to codes shall include the section number and date.

(2) Citations to treatises, textbooks, and encyclopedias shall include the edition, section, and page.

(3) Citations to all other authorities shall include the page or pages.

e. Internal cross-references. Use of "supra" and "infra" is not permitted.

As noted in Chapter 2, for most Iowa authorities, the citation will look the same whether you are using the *Bluebook, ALWD Guide,* or Iowa court rules. Below are additional examples. The *Bluebook* and *ALWD* examples follow the format for court documents and legal memoranda.

B. Cases

Cases are most often still cited to print reporters. The citation includes the name of the case, the volume of the reporter, abbreviated reporter title, beginning page, page on which the information is found, and date. If the court that decided the case is not clear from the reporter, a court abbreviation is included in the parenthetical before the date.

Iowa Supreme Court:

McCarty v. Jeffers, 154 N.W.2d 718 (Iowa 1967).

Beebe v. Funkhouser, 2 Iowa 314 (1855).[11]

---

11. The official *Iowa Reports* must be cited if the case is not reported in the *North Western Reporter,* which began publication in 1879. The *North Western Reporter* became the official reporter in 1968 when *Iowa Reports* ceased publication.

Iowa Court of Appeals (since 1977):
State v. Elder, 868 N.W.2d 448 (Iowa Ct. App. 2015).

U.S. District Court for the Northern District of Iowa:
Turner v. Palmer, 84 F. Supp. 3d 880 (N.D. Iowa 2015).

U.S. Court of Appeals for the Eighth Circuit:
United States v. Hentges, 779 F.3d 820 (8th Cir. 2015).

U.S. Supreme Court
Iowa Court Rules (parallel citations):
Iowa v. Tovar, 541 U.S. 77, 124 S. Ct. 1379, 158 L. Ed. 2d 209 (2004).
Bluebook and *ALWD Guide* (no parallel citations):
Iowa v. Tovar, 541 U.S. 77 (2004).
Brumfield v. Cain, 135 S. Ct. 2269 (2015). [use S. Ct. if U.S. not available]

C. Statutes

A citation to a state statute includes the state code, section number, and year. Federal codes begin with title number.

Iowa Code § 232.111 (2015). [official version]
Iowa Code Ann. § 232.111 (West 2014 & Supp. 2015).
19 U.S.C. § 2411 (2012). [official *United States Code*]
19 U.S.C.A. § 2606 (West 2015). [*United States Code Annotated*]
15 U.S.C.S. § 13(a) (LexisNexis 2013). [*United States Code Service*]

D. Constitutions

Constitution citations include the abbreviated name followed by the pinpoint reference. Citations to current constitutions do not require a date.

Iowa Const. art. XII, § 1.
U.S. Const. amend I.

E. Administrative Regulations

Administrative codes typically are cited by title number, abbreviated name of code, pinpoint subdivision, and year. The *Code of Federal Regulations* begins with the title number, but most state administrative codes do not.

Iowa Admin. Code r. 17-13.3 (2016).
31 C.F.R. § 515.329 (2016). [*Code of Federal Regulations*]

F. Books and Periodicals

Books typically are cited by the book's author(s), title, and page or section where the information is found, and then parentheses enclose the edition (other than first) and copyright date.[12]

> Jerry L. Anderson & Daniel B. Bogart, *Property Law: Practice, Problems, and Perspectives* 234 (2014).

Periodical citations normally include the author(s), title, volume of the periodical, abbreviated periodical title, beginning page, page on which the information is found, and date.

> Anthony J. Gaughan, *The Case for Limiting Federal Jurisdiction over State and Local Campaign Contributions*, 65 Ark. L. Rev. 587, 602–04 (2012).

---

12. For more examples, see *Bluebook* Rule 15 and *ALWD* Rule 20.

About the Authors

John D. Edwards is Associate Dean for Information Resources and Technology and Professor of Law at Drake University Law School. He has directed Drake's Legal Research program since 1985 and served as Executive Director of Legal Research and Writing for more than two decades. He received his J.D. from the University of Missouri–Kansas City School of Law, his M.A.L.S. from the University of Missouri–Columbia, and his B.A. from Southeast Missouri State University. His most recent book is *Basic Legal Research Workbook* (5th ed., Wolters Kluwer), co-authored with Amy E. Sloan and Steven D. Schwinn.

Karen L. Wallace is Circulation/Reference Librarian and Professor of Law Librarianship at Drake University Law School, where she has worked since 2000. Prior to joining Drake, she worked in public libraries for over five years. She received both her M.A. and B.A. from the University of Iowa. She recently completed *Legal Research Supplement: Exercises on Lexis Advance* (4th eBook ed., LexisNexis) with co-author Melissa H. Weresh.

Melissa H. Weresh is a Professor of Law at Drake University Law School. She received her B.A. from Wake Forest University and her J.D. from the University of Iowa College of Law. She is past President of the Legal Writing Institute and an active member of the Association of Legal Writing Directors and the Association of American Law School's Section on Legal Writing, Reasoning, and Research. She has been teaching at Drake University Law School since 1997. Two of her other books include *Legal Writing: Ethical and Professional Considerations* (2d ed., LexisNexis) and *Professionalism in the Real World: Lessons for the Effective Advocate* (NITA), co-authored with Lisa Penland.

Index